Elgin Community College Library
Elgin, IL 60123

RUSSELL BANKS

RUSSELL BANKS

In Search of Freedom

KEVIN T. MCENEANEY

PRAEGER

AN IMPRINT OF ABC-CLIO, LLC
Santa Barbara, California • Denver, Colorado • Oxford, England

ELGIN COMMUNITY COLLEGE
LIBRARY

Copyright 2010 by Kevin T. McEneaney

All rights reserved. No part of this publication may be reproduced, stored in a retrieval system, or transmitted, in any form or by any means, electronic, mechanical, photocopying, recording, or otherwise, except for the inclusion of brief quotations in a review, without prior permission in writing from the publisher.

Library of Congress Cataloging-in-Publication Data

McEneaney, Kevin T.
  Russell Banks : in search of freedom / Kevin T. McEneaney.
    p. cm.
  Includes bibliographical references and index.
  ISBN 978–0–313–38165–2 (alk. paper) — ISBN 978–0–313–38166–9 (ebook)
1. Banks, Russell, 1940– —Criticism and interpretation.   I. Title.
PS3552.A49Z53   2010
813′.54—dc22   2010003008

ISBN: 978–0–313–38165–2
EISBN: 978–0–313–38166–9

14 13 12 11 10   1 2 3 4 5

This book is also available on the World Wide Web as an eBook.
Visit www.abc-clio.com for details.

Praeger
An Imprint of ABC-CLIO, LLC

ABC-CLIO, LLC
130 Cremona Drive, P.O. Box 1911
Santa Barbara, California 93116-1911

This book is printed on acid-free paper ∞

Manufactured in the United States of America

To Bob, Frank, and Joe
brothers in the light

Contents

Preface   ix

1. American Odyssey: Blue-Collar Intellectual   1
2. Finding a Voice: Early Stories   9
3. Parables of Inside-Out: Early Novellas   21
4. Ironic Conundrum: *Hamilton Stark*   33
5. The Limits of Liberalism: *The Book of Jamaica*   45
6. Homeric Grotesque: *Trailerpark*   57
7. Mainstream Realism and Zombies: *Continental Drift*   71
8. Naturalism as Postmodern Parable: *Affliction*   87
9. Oedipus in the Adirondacks: *The Sweet Hereafter*   101
10. Rambling Picaresque: *Rule of the Bone*   111
11. Hologram Pics: *Angel on the Roof*   131
12. Resurrection Dream: *Cloudsplitter*   141
13. Radical Irony: *The Darling*   161
14. Rural Noir: *The Reserve*   173
15. Postmodern Realism: Audience and the Writer   183

Notes   191
Select Bibliography   213
Index   219

Preface

Russell Banks finds himself revered, both in America and abroad, as one of the most prominent literary figures on the contemporary landscape. Yet, there exists a paucity of commentary on his remarkable output, even though his work has been translated into over 20 languages. While Banks has achieved wide name recognition in the public through two highly successful, award-winning films, *The Sweet Hereafter* (1996) and *Affliction* (1997), his work needs more commentary. Only one book in English on his work has appeared in the last decade. One reason for this may lay in the fact that Banks's individual works appear to be so seamless, often approaching the mystery and eloquence of a poem one would not wish to tamper with. On the other hand, reviewers, quick off the mark, have at times embarrassed themselves by underestimating the complexity of Banks's narrators, as well as Banks's intent or achievement.

Fundamental to Banks's liberal bias remains his critique of how freedom operates in America—psychologically, historically, and sociologically. As a writer, Banks has managed to adapt working-class realism to postmodernism, usually by employing narrators who project a limited understanding of American society. Characters (depending upon their self-knowledge) may have partial access to their unconscious or little access. Banks's critique of freedom and its limits falls as severely upon the left as the right, dramatizing illusions of freedom. Much of the perspective in this book attempts to underline ironies inherent in the lives of the diverse characters Banks has chronicled in his varied portraits of Americans. At the center of Banks's narrative strategy lies the conundrum of character: How well do we know ourselves or each other? What are our limits and the limits of the society we live in?

One of the goals in writing this book was to extend the context of debate around Banks's work—to broaden rather than narrow possible interpretation of his work. For this purpose, there is the presence of metatexts with which to compare and contrast Banks's narrative purpose at any given point. In many cases, these metatexts were consciously or unconsciously present to Banks's mind, but even if they were not, they remain diligent tools for highlighting parallels or contrasts. Since the basis of Banks's approach to writing remains poetic as Albert Camus advised, this approach illuminates both the architecture of his work, as well as important passages that might appear opaque to the general reader. While Banks has described his books as islands rather than a sequence, this is an attempt to chart a continuity of technique and philosophy in his approach, as well as a vision of the limits of freedom in his characters.

Banks's reading audience has continued to grow with each book and today perhaps it finds more resonance with the young than the old, a healthy sign of endurance. While much of Banks's work remains rooted in the landscape of the Eastern seaboard or Caribbean, his stories meditate upon the mythos of what makes us Americans, even as they raise questions about our hopes and illusions, our aspirations and problems as a society. In the final analysis, Banks writes about ordinary people in such an extraordinary way that he leverages our emotions and intellect to enter into the mystery of life's common challenges by creating debatable dialogue out of his primary technique, monologue.

I wish to thank my wife, Veronica Towers, for putting up with me during this blinkered process, my generous friend Martha L. Moffett for reading the manuscript, and my editor Daniel Harmon for his continued encouragement. My gratitude also extends to the librarians at Vassar College in Poughkeepsie, New York, Bobst Library at New York University, as well as the librarians of the Mid-Hudson Library System for their gracious assistance. And to my grandson Joshua whose patience was occasionally tested by my need to finish a sentence.

1

American Odyssey: Blue-Collar Intellectual

> Dean and I had the whole of Mexico before us. "Now, Sal. We're leaving everything behind us and entering a new and unknown phase of things."
> —Jack Kerouac, *On the Road*

There's no way of knowing when or where a great writer will be born. Such writers have displayed an ability to overcome tremendous odds or to recover resiliently when handed a seemingly thunderous defeat—for example, Homer. He lost his eyesight after writing the *Iliad*, had another epic stolen from him in his blindness, then bounced back to write the *Odyssey*, one of the most beloved, deeply subtle, yet entertaining and wise stories ever sung.[1]

On March 28, 1940, Russell Earl Banks, a first generation American (his father was Canadian), the eldest of four children, was born in Newton, Massachusetts, to Earl Banks and Florence Taylor. Like his father, Earl Banks was a plumber who followed his father's footsteps into the plumbing business during the Great Depression when he was only 16. Earl felt trapped by the confines of family and the economic tensions of work, frequently finding refuge in drink. It was a chaotic household where Banks grew up, amid the snows of Barnstead, New Hampshire (near Lake Winnipesaukee), with much yelling and winter claustrophobia, burdened with economic duress, "There was never enough money, and they were always packing up and moving out of an old place, where things had gone wrong, into a new [place] where everything would improve."[2] But nothing ever did. His background ran counter to the writer he would become:

> I come from a people who viewed success as a criticism of their life. Because if you're moving up, there's a kind of betrayal of the family. My father made a mockery of anybody who aspired to move up, unless you moved up as a wheeler dealer. That was a little different. If you could finagle a piece of real estate or a used car lot into something more lucrative, that would be all right. But to move up in the sense of moving into the world of ideas and trying to live your life through language—that was a betrayal.[3]

The illusory dream of moving out to imaginary better pastures haunts many of the characters in his stories.

From a young age, his eyesight in one eye was severely impaired—by whooping cough according to his mother, but Banks thinks a blow from his father might have created the affliction.[4] At the age of nine, knapsack bobbing on his back, Banks attempted a premature odyssey by bicycling to the airport at Concord, New Hampshire, with the intent of stowing away on an airplane, but was nabbed by police.[5] When he was 12, his father, accompanied by a girlfriend, fled to Florida. The subsequent divorce left Florence stranded without financial support. She quickly moved the family from New Hampshire to Wakefield, Massachusetts, finding steady work as a bookkeeper, but precarious economic conditions kept the family once more hopping from house to house, apartment to apartment.

Banks conscientiously became the substitute father in the family, helping to raise his younger siblings. A bright boy, he received high grades at Wakefield Memorial High School; he was even offered a scholarship to exclusive Phillips Academy in Andover for his senior year, but during the summer he accompanied a friend who pinched his father's car. They drove out to California where his friend, in an attack of guilt, confessed to a Catholic priest their theft and escapade. The priest turned the boys in to their parents, ending their little two-month odyssey.[6] The scholarship offer was abruptly withdrawn, yet in his senior year Banks, a popular jock with the nickname *Teacher*,[7] won a full scholarship to Colgate University in Hamilton, New York. In the autobiographical *Success Story*, Banks wrote:

> In this Ivy League school, however, among the elegant, brutal sons of the captains of industry, I was only that year's token poor kid, imported from a small New Hampshire mill town like an exotic herb, a dash of mace for the vichyssoise. It was a status that perplexed and intimidated and finally defeated me, so that, after nine weeks of it, I fled in the night.[8]

When lights were doused for the night, he carried his bulging duffel bag through into a whirling snowstorm. This tension between an intellectual gift and a desire to engage with the real world, conjured a prophetic dialectic in life and work.

Just after New Year's Day, Banks, under the influence of Jack Kerouac's *On the Road* (1957), hitchhiked to Florida with an impassioned desire to join the heroic rebel army of Fidel Castro because of Ernest Hemingway's endorsement of the photogenic-bearded Castro.[9] Once he arrived in Miami, Banks realized not being able to speak Spanish might be an impediment to becoming a revolutionary in Cuba. Hitchhiking to St. Petersburg, he worked at various menial jobs, including furniture mover. While working at a department store where he dressed mannequins and painted signs, Banks met 17-year-old salesgirl Darlene Bennett (the comic anecdote of how they met in the store appears in *Success Story*) and they impulsively married. Good at drawing, Banks fancied himself a burgeoning artist in paint, yet he also began dabbling with poetry and stories.[10]

Shortly thereafter, with Darlene six months pregnant, they moved to Boston's Back Bay neighborhood where Banks worked as a bookstore clerk and listened to regurgitated recitations of Allen Ginsberg's *Howl and Other Poems* (1956).[11] Banks became cool, snapping his fingers to jazz musicians like Miles Davis and Thelonious Monk.[12] At 20, Banks befriended an older unpublished writer, 27-year-old Leo Giroux, Jr., who acted as Banks's mentor in reading, encouraging him to read classics as well as avant-garde authors. Russell and Darlene had a daughter named Leona in May 1960, but their marriage, under the influence of bibulous bohemian bibliophilia, irretrievably broke down when they realized they had nothing in common.[13] Leona (Lea) rejoined the Banks household in early adolescence.[14]

Separated in 1961, Darlene and Russell returned to Florida. Distraught, Darlene moved into her parents' home, while Banks returned to Boston. That fall, Banks found the social life of the beatnik scene in Boston a distraction to his work—he deposited himself farther south in the Florida Keys. At Islamorada Key, he slouched for six months in a trailer park, working as a gas-pump attendant, as Nelson Algren once did, while scribbling. When he could no longer endure the stench of gasoline in the pages of the books he was reading, he pushed farther south to Key West where he found himself stranded at a cheap boarding house that was part bordello. He drank too many daiquiris at Sloppy Joe's Bar, Hemingway's old haunt, got fleeced at cards, and saw a man stabbed to death.[15] At the rooming house, he met an ex-convict and a rogue sailor who was AWOL (absent without leave), with whom he undertook to deliver a drive-away car to Los Angeles, but the three spent six weeks of rollicking good times in New Orleans. Dropping the sailor off at his Oklahoma home, they routed a diversionary detour into Mexico, delivering the car three months late.[16] That route roughly imitated the final drive depicted in Kerouac's *On the Road*, that leg being a tribute nod to Malcolm Lowry's *Under the Volcano* (1947). Banks traveled west to visit his mother (who has recently written an unpublished memoir) in San Diego, where she was working for the Raytheon Corporation. Banks stayed a few uncomfortable months, and then thumbed his way back to New Hampshire where he reconnected in Concord with his father who helped him acquire a union card and find work as a plumber's apprentice. He purchased a pickup truck.[17]

Darlene had quickly remarried, and at 21, Banks's tenuous relationship with Mary Gunst, an ebullient Emerson College theater major, appeared to be ending, especially when she transferred down to Virginia Commonwealth University for her senior year. Banks phoned her one last time to conclude the affair, but she surprised him by appearing on his doorstep the next day, dropping out of school to renew their relationship. They were married on October 29, 1962.[18] Banks continued to work with his father, achieving a rugged rapprochement with him.

In August 1963, Banks attended the Bread Loaf Writers' Conference, originally founded by Robert Frost. That summer, Algren, who had a reputation for being an erratic teacher, headlined the seminar, becoming the center of unpredictable, amusing events and entertaining gossip.[19] While Algren did not attend all classes, he scrupulously read his students' manuscripts, publicly singling out Banks's work, and referring him to his agent, Candida Donadio. Algren scandalized everyone by nailing a steak to the outside door of his room in protest at the lack of decent meat in the communal dining hall. Since Algren did not drive, Banks drove him into Middlebury bars, where over drinks, he encouraged Banks by telling him he was a real writer, giving the young man the validation an aspiring writer needs.[20] Toward the end of the conference, Algren carried on a flagrant affair with one of his students, Carolyn Gaiser, a young journalist from *Glamour* magazine posing as an apprentice poet.[21]

On July 7, 1964, Banks's daughter Caerthan, who has since become a screenwriter and director, was born. In the fall, Banks at 24, financed by his mother-in-law, attended the University of North Carolina at Chapel Hill.[22] It was here where "race became a meaningful part of my sense of self and sense of American history"[23] when an integrated party he attended was broken up by Ku Klux Klan gunfire.[24] Banks experienced a political awakening.

While at Chapel Hill, Banks had recruited Algren for a reading and lecture at the university. Algren disdained the elegant antebellum inn where the university planned to board him, so he bunked with Banks who had met him up at the airport. When the university refused to pay Banks's grocery and liquor store bill for the week (they would have gladly paid the much more expensive hotel bill), Algren undertook a public letter writing campaign in newspapers until the university paid up in order to shut him up. Algren quickly remitted the check to Banks.[25]

After failing to exert some influence on *The Carolina Quarterly*, Banks co-founded the journal and press *Lillabulero* with the poet William Matthews (1942–97), who was studying for a master's degree at Chapel Hill. *Lillabulero* evolved into a successful literary magazine which ran for nine years. In 1967, the magazine featured Banks's first published short story, "The Adjutant Bird," while the press published a chapbook featuring five of his poems in *15 Poems*, the other two poets being Matthews and Newton Smith. At Chapel Hill, Banks founded a chapter of Students for a Democratic Society (SDS) and participated in anti-war protests as well as civil rights protests.[26] Even today, Banks says, "I don't see American life, generally, across the board, without a racial or class dimension."[27]

In 1967, Banks hosted a party for Kerouac when he received a call from a local bar. Kerouac was in town, looking for a place to crash for the weekend. Since Banks was the only student renting a house, he became the host for Jack and the three Mi'kmaq Indians[28] driving him down to Florida. Kerouac had just been paid an advance for *The Vanity of Duluoz* (1968), which became the last published book in his lifetime. Banks described the bipolar behavior of Kerouac, careening from the wise and learned *Memory Babe* (his nickname) to a raging, bigoted drunk.[29] Kerouac was important to Banks not for the personal manner of his writing, but as a working class writer from his region who had received literary recognition.

Banks graduated Phi Beta Kappa within three years, receiving a Woodrow Wilson Fellowship in 1968. Shortly after his third daughter Maia (now a musician) was born on May 17, 1968, the family moved to Northwood Narrows, New Hampshire, where they purchased a rural Victorian house. Banks began teaching at Emerson College in autumn 1968, staying for two years and publishing his second chapbook, *Waiting to Freeze* (Lillabulero, 1969).

On January 13, 1970, his fourth daughter, Danis (now a college teacher) was born. That fall, Banks began teaching at the University of New Hampshire (Durham) while publishing stories in small magazines. His narrative poem *Snow: Meditations of a Cautious Man in Winter* (Granite Press, 1974) appeared. The following year he became Visiting Professor at New England College. He published his first collection of short stories, *Searching for Survivors* (Fiction Collective, 1975), and his first novel, *Family Life* (Avon, 1975). As for his early poetry, Banks dismisses most of his poems as juvenilia, "I cringe a little over some of the early poems."[30]

Banks became Writer in Residence at Princeton University and Sarah Lawrence College in 1976. Later that year, he was awarded a Guggenheim Fellowship from the John Simon Guggenheim Memorial Foundation which allowed him to put aside teaching and spend 18 months with his family in Jamaica from May 1976 to September 1977, but the protracted working vacation resulted in divorce. Banks returned to teach at University of New England from 1977 to 1982, but while in Jamaica, he completed his second novel, *Hamilton Stark* (1978), an existential novel about identity, and a second book of short stories. He also gathered material that would become *The Book of Jamaica* (1980), a novel about a deluded academic that established him as an important writer, the novel winning the American Book Award from the Before Columbus Foundation. He had also completed the mordantly witty novella *The Relation of My Imprisonment* (1983), which he had trouble placing with publishers. Banks's father passed away in 1979 at the age of 63 due to liver failure.

Looking back, Banks considers travel beneficial for young writers:

> because you have no real sense of who you are until you get outside your own backyard and look at it from the other side of the fence. It's like when you think you don't speak with an accent until you go someplace where everybody speaks with a different accent.... When I traveled into the South, it was the first time I heard a New England accent.... Because everyone around me had this southern accent.... It's something that young writers used to do as a matter of course. It was like, I've got to work on a Merchant Marine boat; or I've got to go to France and hang around Paris; or I've got to visit India or Mexico or, like in my case, the Caribbean.[31]

Through developing an ear for accents, rhythms, and local idiom, writers eventually arrive at creating authentic dialogue; they also can arrive at a larger cultural assessment of their own background through contrasting experiences and examining alternative historical points of view.

Trailerpark (1981) presented 13 stories of working-class characters interlinked as a novel. In 1982, Banks married Kathy Wilton, the director of the Associated Writing Program. Wilton persuaded Banks to experience urban life and they settled in Brooklyn, New York. Banks landed jobs teaching creative writing at Columbia University graduate school and Princeton University, while Wilton found work as an editor at Harper & Row,[32] which from 1985 on would become Banks's publisher. Banks also taught briefly at New York University and the University of Alabama. With the publication of his breakthrough novel *Continental Drift*, which garnered the John Dos Passos Prize for fiction and was voted one of the best books of the year by *Library Journal*, Banks was recognized as not only an important American writer but a writer of international stature.

In 1988, Banks and Wilton divorced. That same year Banks married the poet Chase Twichell, author of *Northern Spy: Poems* (1981), *The Odds* (1986), and subsequently *Perdido* (1992), *The Ghost of Eden* (1998), *The Snow Watcher* (1998), and *Dog Language* (2005). They purchased a summer home in Keene, New York, and she taught with Banks at Princeton when he was offered a professorship in 1982. With Robin Behn, she co-edited *The Practice of Poetry* (1992), a handbook on teaching poetry that remains widely employed in college classrooms.

Banks published another collection of short stories, *Success Stories* (1986), many of which in a humorous vein feature a semi-autobiographical character by the name of Earl Painter, as well as social parables displaying the influence of Jorge Luis Borges. Both new and selected stories, *The Angel on the Roof*, appeared to great acclaim in 2000.

The gritty novel *Affliction* (1989) about the mental breakdown of a police officer received mixed reviews, yet was translated into a successful 1997 movie directed by Paul Schrader. Actor James Coburn won an Oscar for Best Actor in a supporting role as Glen Whitehouse, while Nick Nolte received an Academy Award nomination for best actor in a leading role of Wade Whitehouse, landing the award for best performance at the Golden Globe Awards. The film also picked up numerous awards at other festivals.

Banks's novel *The Sweet Hereafter* (1991) received international critical and popular acclaim. The film version was directed by Canadian Atom Egoyan who transferred the Adirondack setting to British Columbia. At the Cannes Film Festival, *The Sweet Hereafter*, starring Ian Holm, won three awards, including the Grand Prize of the Jury. In America, Egoyan received Academy Award nominations for Best Adapted Screenplay and Best Director. In Australia, the film won Best Foreign Film and many other awards at various festivals. Banks played a cameo role in the film; he can be seen discussing the film on the DVD release.

Rule of the Bone (1995), set in the Adirondacks and Jamaica, presented the wild picaresque adventures of a 14-year-old boy in his own racy idiom.

It has been called a modern classic that resembles Mark Twain's *Adventures of Huckleberry Finn* (1884), and the novel has been found to be not only a pleasurable read but an engaging tool for students. Often cited as Banks's culminating masterpiece, *Cloudsplitter* (1998), a Pulitzer Prize finalist, recounts the story of the abolitionist John Brown from his son Owen Brown's point of view, yet Owen remains a fictional character, not the historical Owen. The novel examines problems of race, the difficulties of being the son of a legend, and the tragedy of repressed sexuality. A novel about class structures and the relevance of art, *The Reserve* (2006) occurs during the Great Depression.

Banks has penned a meditation on the history of America and its favorite myths in *Dreaming Up America* (2008), which was prompted by his appearance in a French documentary by Jean-Michel Maurice. His French publisher at Actes Sud was so excited by the oral transcript of the interview, that she had it published in 2006 as *Amérique notre histoire*. Subsequently, the book appeared in Spanish and Italian, and Banks decided to bring out an American edition in 2008 with a small press.

For most of his life, Banks has been a successful teacher as well as productive writer. He enjoyed the Howard G. B. Clarke Professorship at Princeton from 1982 to 1997 when he retired, yet he has continued to teach at other schools, particularly the University of Maryland and the University of Nevada at Las Vegas.

Although one of America's most accomplished short story writers, winner of the St. Lawrence Award for Short Fiction, the O. Henry Award, and Best American Short Story Award, Banks remains best known, both critically and popularly, for his novels, which employ the monologue format (exceptions being *Continental Drift* and *The Reserve*). Narrative voice, its timbres and nuances, constitute an essential aspect of his stories as they are colored by irony. Banks often shuffles chronology around in the memory of his narrator. Two of Banks's most distinguishing hallmarks lay, on the one hand, in an avant-garde experimentalism and, on the other, an earthy realism grounded in working-class sensibilities. This dialectic has yoked both characters and methods that were hitherto thought to be separate or unrelated. While nearly all of his antecedent literary models are American realists, a deep, inward psychology, more common in French or Russian novels, appears in his characters. As a former poet, his cadenced prose sometimes exhibits a natural poetic polish unusual in American letters. Unlike many authors who discover a successful formula and repeat themselves, each novel by Banks provides a completely new voyage for writer and reader.

Recently, Banks has been more active in screenwriting. He has written a screenplay of Kerouac's *On the Road* for Francis Ford Coppola to be directed by Gus Van Sant, director of *Good Will Hunting* (1997) and *Milk* (2008). Banks has penned screenplays for *Rule of the Bone, Cloudsplitter*, and *The Darling*.[33] Martin Scorsese will direct a film on the latter, based upon Banks's screenplay. Banks himself is producing *The Book of Jamaica*; he wrote the screenplay for *Trailerpark*, which is scheduled for release in 2010.

As for how Banks's working routine operates, he says, "I work in the mornings. I have a little studio about 200 yards from the house. It's a renovated old sugar shack once used to water down maple sap into maple syrup, and usually I'm here in the mornings and I work until early afternoon."[34] Banks's working habits validate Kerouac's observation that, "sketching language is undisturbed flow from the mind."[35] Banks usually employs a computer when composing:

> anything that will speed up that initial composition helps me deceive that internal censor and editor that tends to judge and to close me down and restrain me. And the closer that speed gets to conversation, the more spontaneous I can be, the more surprising I can be to myself, and the more easily I can tap my own unconscious, to be honest.[36]

Yet unlike Kerouac or other writers like Thomas Pynchon or Don DeLillo who shun the press, Banks likes to circulate when not writing, "I'm a gregarious and sociable person. I grew up in a big family. Writing is a solitary process. I like coming out of the cave and seeing if anyone is there."[37] Banks continues to be accessible to readers through his numerous public readings, recorded radio conversations, and the many interviews he has given, especially to small literary magazines that may have difficulty sustaining circulation. When young, Banks cultivated an older audience, but as time went on, younger people discovered his writings, becoming his predominant audience.

Banks now lives in Miami Beach, Florida, and Saratoga Springs, New York. He has had the honor of being named a New York State Author and is a member of the American Academy of Arts and Letters as well as PEN International which awarded him its Hemingway Award in 2004. Banks has been a past president of the International Parliament of Writers (which offers safe haven to writers under threat) as well as the founding President of the North American Network Cities of Asylum. His papers have been placed at the Harry Ransom Center, the University of Texas at Austin, whose collections include papers of Virginia Woolf, James Joyce, and D. H. Lawrence, as well as many notable American writers. Close writer friends include William Kennedy, Toni Morrison, Paul Auster, Jim Harrison, Richard Ford, Salman Rushdie, J. M. Coetzee, Caryl Phillips, and Madison Smartt Bell, who was once a student of Banks.

Like the young roustabout Japhy[38] from Kerouac's *The Dharma Bums* (1957), at the age of 64 and sporting a bad knee, Banks in the company of novelist Phillips, the Caribbean-born author of *Crossing the River* (1993) and *A Distant Shore* (2003), climbed the more difficult route to the summit of Mount Kilimanjaro (Hemingway's favorite peak) in Africa.[39] In his spare time, Banks still paints watercolors and pastels.[40] Two of Banks's later novels, *Rule of the Bone* and *The Darling* exhibit a deep appreciation for the music of Charles Ives, but in his CD player you might just as well find Tin Hat Trio, Clifford Brown, Bill Jackson, Jimmy Rodgers, or Duke Ellington.[41]

2

Finding a Voice: Early Stories

> But the doctor would not laugh with his friend. There were three things which he hated in this world, he said often and angrily: death, venereal disease, and organized religion.
> "In that order," the doctor always amended. "And the story, clean or otherwise, that can make me laugh at one of these has never been thought up."
> —Grace Metalious, *Peyton Place*

Searching for Survivors

The literary ambitions of Russell Banks began with poetry, yet swerved toward fiction; he wanted to be a poet, "but had not the gift"[1] as he modestly notes. His first book, *Snow: Meditations of a Cautious Man in Winter* (1974), presents an excursion into narrative introspection. While the poetry displays competence, it's not remarkable—thought indulges in discourse more than lyricism. For nine years, he co-edited a small poetry publication he co-founded with the poet William Matthews, *Lillabulero*, penning four poetry chapbooks between 1967 and 1974, before publishing his first novel, *Family Life* in 1975. Robert Niemi offered an astute discussion of Banks's poems[2] which employ metaphor as background and ambiance for the foregrounding of personal narrative, a general weakness in the methodology of those who practiced the technique called *projective verse* (sometimes *objective verse*), which was one of the avant-garde American fads of the sixties and seventies (epitomized by poets Charles Olson and Ed Dorn) that has not worn well over time. When Banks began to pen short stories, they exhibited a relaxed and unselfconscious lyricism he never quite achieved in his poetry. He became especially adept at employing one of the most common and effective poetic techniques: Eloquent lists conjuring up mood and atmosphere, a painterly quality of evocation that would mark him as distinguished stylist:

> He listened to the beer in his mouth and throat, and to the rain, the footsteps overhead, a muffled radio somewhere down the hall, to the cars on the street

below hurriedly splashing past the building, a bus sloshing to a stop at the corner. He got up again and went to the window, pulled back the heavy, red velvet drape with one hand and looked intently out.[3]

The publication of *Searching for Survivors* (1975) the year after his meandering poem launched Banks's career as a young writer to be watched. Banks's early story "Searching for Survivors" exhibits an obsession with linking the historical past to the present through the history of the Hudson River, the explorer Henry Hudson, the automobile named the Hudson, and the narrator's dog named Hudson. While the narrator fails to reconnect with a childhood friend, he conjures the past to inhabit a fantasy future: A land-bound New Hampshire resident familiar with Hudson's adventures imagines discovering Hudson's lost journal and wonders whether or not he would have joined the mutiny against Hudson or departed in the small boat with Hudson when he was set adrift in Hudson Bay. He imagines Hudson survived into old age, telling the stories of his adventures. The preposterous fantasy offers an obvious displacement for the narrator's undisclosed problems, left as mysterious as the death of heroic Henry Hudson. While not a notable story, it signals in embryonic fashion Banks's future obsession with a haunted monologue set in a historical framework, both real and imagined. The theme of survivors bracketing the book's 14 tales foregrounds history in the first survivor tale and it will foreground the personal in the book's closing story. The inset about the childhood friendship that does not survive into adulthood in this story adumbrates the greater personal tragedy revealed in the book's last story.[4]

The longest piece in the book, "Survivors II," presents an extended meditation on family grief. Inspired by the death of Banks's younger brother, the work is more of an exercise in collage, yet its narrative moves in the mode of realism. The younger brother decides to take a train from Los Angles to Boston, arguing that trains are safer than planes, yet he's killed in a train accident (like Banks's younger brother Steve). Photos provide theme and structure: All eleven sections post like verbal photos from different points in time; readers are invited to put the photos in any order they choose.[5] The effect of the framing highlights a circular meditative pathos: Photos were placed around the casket of the departed brother at a wake, the last section being the one that precedes the opening section. (Banks will once more use an eleven-part circular structure in his novel *Hamilton Stark*.) The story explores mutual grief amid the difficulty of communicating sincerely when family members have not seen each other for long periods. The family shows signs of self-conscious repression; this creates an awkward pathos among them, yet there is a flicker of happier moments that serve to deepen the poignancy rather than deflecting it. While the combination of realism and experimentalism works in harmony, the story reads more like autobiographical documentary than fiction.

Employing contemporary history for background, "With Ché in New Hampshire" signals Banks's interest in radical politics. This story supplies a variation on James Thurber's seminal story, "The Secret Life of Walter Mitty."[6]

Finding a Voice: Early Stories

The narrator provides a blustery monologue of his imagined radical friends and leftist activities on a global stage as the most trusted secret agent of Ché Guevara. This fantasy of James Bond derring-do occurs as the narrator has his beard removed in a barber shop located in small-town New Hampshire. While Thurber's mild-mannered Mitty possesses a humorous, vengeful edge, Banks furnishes satire on those leftists who are all talk and no action. This whimsical story becomes an accusation against small-town isolation and indifference to the world at large, and a send-up of those who think revolution a glamour affair divorced from grim realities—an illusion that receives routine servicing in American movies and television, perhaps even more so today. A less successful companion piece, "With Ché at the Plaza," depicts a narrator meeting an elegantly dressed man at The Plaza Hotel in New York City, imagining him to be Ché Guevara. The narrator entertains fantasy dreams of gambling with Frank Sinatra. This impish satire on celebrity worship indirectly illustrates how damaging an obsession with media stardom corrupts the consciousness of ordinary people, permitting them to lead deluded, wasteful lives.

With both stories, the winsome enthusiasm of the narrator seduces the reader, yet it is precisely this charm that becomes the target of an irony that perceives the world to be an extension of adolescent narcissism. Such delusional enthusiasm can also be found in the war vignettes of Ambrose Bierce as illustrated by his most famous story, "An Occurrence at Owl Creek Bridge," where the Confederate estate gentlemen finds himself seduced by the charm of the Union soldier provocateur dressed in a Confederate uniform. While Bierce employs the techniques of romantic storytelling within the deluded mind of the rebel as he frames the story's beginning and end with the cold technique of reportorial realism, Banks remains content to let his narrators be not so much unreliable in a modernist manner as delusional in the postmodernist manner; the connection between delusional narcissism and perception remains common to both Bierce and Banks. Banks's subjects would like to escape the smallness of their lives, they have hidden problems, yet the brevity of the stories forbids further exploration; Banks hints at a larger cultural malaise within New England and the country at large. Banks would like to liberate Americans from the facile, "I'm okay, you're okay" psychology Americans shower in, because the world remains more complex and perilous than Americans are usually willing to acknowledge. At this stage, Banks is not yet able to articulate the complexity that he implies, yet his agenda contains a subtle political edge, marking him as unique among contemporary American writers.

"With Ché at Kitty Hawk," the third Ché story (later slightly revised and renamed "Theory of Flight"), provides slices of life as they focus on the pathos of folly and the way a divorce with children imprisons the wife rather than the husband (men can fly free of the Earth, while women are bound to Earth by children). Set on the Outer Banks near Kitty Hawk before the area became crowded with luxury rentals, tourist flip-flops, and Jacuzzis, "Theory of Flight" displays considerable success depicting the consciousness of a woman victimized by patriarchy and the biological imperative, something most male writers are not able to do in a convincing manner. This feminist story stands out in a collection that often appears to dwell, even if in slyly satiric manner, on the rampaging rants and narcissism of the male ego.

"The Neighbor" tenders a satiric sketch of the counterculture injunction *back to the land* as it depicts a black husband in his fifties and his white wife with four teenage children, two daughters from the current marriage and two stepsons, who decide to remake their lives as rural farmers by living off the land. Since they know nothing about farming and animals, the neighbor has contempt for their incompetence and perhaps an unwelcome attitude toward the racially mixed marriage. The self-indulgent and excited children ride a newly bought horse to death when the parents are away; bringing the neighbors to view the family as normal human beings, wayward children being something a neighbor easily comprehends. The neighbor displays sympathy amid the family's ignorance concerning farm life, helping them with his tractor to bury the dead horse. In the end, the old rural values of New England rise above racism, yet the future of such inexperienced city folk in the country portends the kind of tragic pathos that Robert Frost penned in such poems as "Out, Out" where the young boy loses hand and life to a chain saw.

"The Neighbor" paints a darker picture of New England, as if the two stories comprise a dual portrait. In a more blatant postmodern technique that relies on summary instead of linear narration, "The Lie" offers an explanation for evil: New England guilt going back generations, the theme and explanation that Hawthorne chose to explain his liberal social leanings, although he was a political conservative. Banks's explanation for inherited evil in New England presents a psychological pattern of generational lies rather than some mythical pact with the devil as in Nathaniel Hawthorne's "Young Goodman Brown." There's no midsummer *Walpurgisnicht*, merely an accidental murder by a boy and his father's pinning the murder on a local homosexual who's innocent. Hawthorne and Banks derive their liberalism from anxiety focused upon generational guilt and the public confession of it admits the quest for justice and liberty as part of the process of discovering freedom. In both Hawthorne's (descended from one of the judges of the infamous Salem witch trials) and Banks's sociology, inherited evil lingers as a haunting aspect of New England identity and as an explanation for the surviving family lines of New Englanders.

Both pathos and mild irony find evocation amid nostalgia in "Defenseman." The troubling aspects of a son's insecure identity come to the fore when he tries to imitate his father by becoming a hockey player, falsely believing that by doing so he will free himself. Later in life, he recognizes both the joy he has found in recalling his father's pleasure in teaching him to skate and the quiet pleasure mere skating now affords him when free of youthful competitive games and oedipal rivalry. He describes his skating as a dreamlike glide through a matrix of pleasant memories. (The matrix metaphor will acquire more sinister ambiance in *Hamilton Stark*.)

"Investiture" conjures a fable about a secret assignation of a country's leader when he sets out to mingle with the populace. The assassin deals a death blow with a blackjack to the back of the leader's head, claims the leader was hit by a hit-and-run Japanese truck. Despite not being a Catholic in an apparently Catholic country, he succeeds in becoming the new leader, vowing never to mingle with the populace. This boasting monologue has a conspiratorial tone and that intent creates an archetypal ambiance evocative of some of the timeless fables of Jorge Luis Borges. Although not particularly effective, it prefigures the fable format of Banks's novella *Family Life*.

The shortest and most enigmatic entry in the book, "The Nap," comprises a single anecdotal paragraph offering a prose-poem meditation on the nature of stories. A reader lying in bed grows bored by the book he's reading and puts the open book down on his stomach, then takes a catnap, "a private tradition." When he awakens, he expects to understand differently what he's reading, and that this time there's nothing different. He's reading a contemporary spy thriller. The gnomic meditation on reading presumes the reader has a passing acquaintance with Aristotle's concept of *catharsis*, whereby the audience (or reader when transferred to the closet drama of a novel) discovers something different that they've never seen or understood before. Aristotle in his *Poetics* defines what distinguishes great transcendent drama from mediocre drama that evokes sympathy for the characters. Although the spy story that the reader follows appears to be sufficiently complex to be considered art, it remains ineffective art. The spy thriller genre, even at its peak, cannot change the consciousness of an attentive reader. The reader's occasional catnaps while reading paradoxically inculcate a discipline that on the surface appears to be laziness, but in fact offers the greater discipline of a fully attentive reader.

"Impasse" introduces the character Ham, the father of a young baby, who works at a bookstore; he begins an affair with a woman named Rosa, rationalizing the affair as natural since he doesn't love his wife. Leaving the bookstore on a rainy day when business slows, he *innocently* visits Rosa; they make love in her apartment. Ham's complacent in accepting Rosa's sexual advance yet it has been made clear he's been actively pursuing her with an affair in mind. The poignant irony, after their sexual climax, of the story's last line echoes tragically, "And oh, the clarity that would follow." Divorce initiates a muddle rather than anything resembling clarity and the enthused exclamation calls attention to the character's delusional self-indulgence. The use of time displacement within the story and the joking use of the character's third-person reference to himself signals the prelude for much more intricate and experimental ways to investigate a character named Ham in Banks first full-length novel, *Hamilton Stark*.

"The Drive Home" presents a rambling satire on a dedicated narcissist. A man has an argument with his wife, and then he leaves his wife and daughter. He takes a bus from Boston home to his parent's house; on the bus there is a folk singer whose guitar the main character breaks to display anger and physical superiority. He arrives in New Hampshire finding his parents moving out of their house. The alienated narrator resembles the narrator of "Blizzard," about a man who leaves his wife during a snowstorm. Neither of these two stories with autobiographical roots has been transformed into art and the book would have benefited from their omission.

As a first collection, *Search for Survivors* displays varied influences and the voice of a writer testing different masks. The more intellectual and experimental stories in the collection appear slightly self-indulgent and arrogantly whimsical in their presentation of off-beat satire. The slight fables and parables were early leads to *Family Life* and *The Relation of My Imprisonment*, but modes subsequently dropped by a more mature Banks. Time often appears as thematic rather than linear. The more enduring stories selected from this collection by the author for reprint in *The Angel on the Roof*—"The Neighbor," "The Lie," "Searching for Survivors," "With Ché in New Hampshire," and "Theory of Flight"—adopt a minimalist neo-realism, developing character and interiority with atmospheric ambiance. These stories marked him as a promising writer and advanced his career.

THE NEW WORLD

Published the same year as *Hamilton Stark* (1978), the 10 stories of *The New World* find arrangement in two parts: five tales of "Renunciation" and five stories of "Transformation." These headings become integral to understanding the works. The epigraph for "Renunciation" by the poet James Tate reads, in part, "so that my eyes will not become blinded from the new world." Read these pieces as warnings, each tale proposing to target something to be renounced. All are set in New England, the first four being satiric tales, the fifth a self-satirizing autobiographical fiction about young manhood in an attempt to write a contemporary coming-of-age novel like Herman Melville's *Redburn* (1849). Most of these pieces for this collection were composed on the island of Jamaica while Banks worked on *Hamilton Stark*.[7]

"The Custodian" imparts a fable about a family so proud of its New England heritage that its last member so fears disgracing such a sterling tradition that he concludes life without an heir. Only after his father dies when he's 43 does he briefly consider marriage. He discusses this with several women, most of them already married, who become intensely sexually excited, thereby disturbing him and driving him away. The bemused tone of the fable appears appropriate. The sterile family portraits project their Gothic gaze. Like Robert Frost, Banks denounces the New England heritage of sexual repression.

"The Perfect Couple" presents an allegory about small-town gossip, ignorance, and repressed secrets. Two bachelor outsiders buy farmland nearly adjacent. After some years they disappear, returning with two adopted children, a boy and a girl the same age. The town keeps gossiping and speculating about their life and each conjecture becomes more ridiculous than the next. What the town and the children are not told is that they are brother and sister. They grow up kept apart from the town, but their fathers let them see much of each other: They announce their wish to marry: One father has a stroke on the spot, the other goes nearly mad. The young teenage lovers run away; unable to feed themselves, they eventually commit suicide by unplugging a hole in a rowboat. A counterpoint subplot features a happy folksinger who's too carefree to live in the repressed, fishbowl town. The New England heritage of close-lipped family secrets and embroidered gossip is satirized. The isolated cultivation of ignorance destroys the next promising generation. These first two stories examine the pathology of social castration endemic to small-towns.

"A Sentimental Education" tells the story of a rich girl slumming. When her parents depart for vacation to Mexico City, well-to-do Veronica decides it's time to lose her virginity and have some adventures amid the lower class where life is more real and gritty. Her consciousness exhibits a dreamy schizophrenia. She goes to a bar, picking up an auto mechanic. He earthily makes love to her and she's disorientated by her repeated orgasms. Next Sunday morning he again takes her in the open field on the back of his pick-up truck, then an hour later in the grease pit under a car he's working on. Certain she's now pregnant with a daughter she calls Pearl, she departs, happy as a lark, cured by her rub with all that is gross, resolved to bring up her Pearl as she was brought up. She hasn't the slightest notion in her head of the nature of Hawthorne's ironic style of writing, his feminist point of view, or his social satires on the hypocritical mentality of the upper class. The auto mechanic, Vic, is a brutal jerk and Veronica does her best to ensure that the genetic stock of her family will be physically fit but mentally slow. Since this archetype of rich girl slumming is nearly timeless, the working-class cynicism with which Banks grinds out the story conveys a bitter satisfaction. As the story appropriates its title from a Gustave Flaubert novel about two wealthy friends who meet later in life to recount their life stories, it's also an attack on the kind of upper-class realistic Romanticism practiced by Flaubert in his decadent writings. This slut-for-a-day story functions as a female counterpart to the virgin idiot painted in "The Custodian." What's renounced is the temptation for the writer to dwell upon upper-class satire.

"About the Late Zimma (Penny) Cate" offers excerpts from a rambling sentimental memoir concerning a log cutter's wife. The devoted log cutter praises his now dead supportive wife who brings him tea and sandwiches while he works cutting cord after cord of wood; she encourages him to defy the court when he's falsely (he says) arrested, and supports his vague ministerial studies later on in life. What's renounced by the writer is any temptation to romanticize the life of hard peasant work and the temptation to be hypocritical on the subject of women. Below the surface of the text lurks an idle man who has exploited his good wife all his life; his false charm freighting ironic shock.

"The Conversion" has the dubious distinction of being the longest piece in the collection. Divided into two parts, it reads like two chapters of a failed coming-of-age novel based upon the author's agonizing adolescence. The main character's name is Alvin Stock, the same character name that appears in the failed, unpublished novel by Rochelle in *Hamilton Stark*. Alvin, a 16-year-old high-school student, suffers from self-hatred and repression, frustrated by the inability to acquire respect from his father or sexual satisfaction from girls. He sees himself as the dreamer and the dreamed, "Wherever he ran, he would have to bear both his selves along."[8] Alternately subservient and violently rebellious, he angrily masturbates and daydreams of escaping to places like New Orleans when not contemplating suicide. He despises himself for suppressing an inner violence and disdain for friends and family. He has great ambition, a powerful physique, but low social status; insecure, he desperately desires validation. On the brink of fulfilling his sexual fantasies when a fast girl invites him to her house to party after a school dance, he has a vision, seeing the angel Raphael the healer—he returns home, announcing that he wants to become a minister.

In the second chapter, set the following summer, he's still hanging out with his friend Feeney from Rochelle's manuscript in *Hamilton Stark* where he accompanies Stock in a well-related incident of high-school bar brawling. They have a double date and Alvin finally loses his virginity to the older sister of Feeney's girlfriend. It turns out that the girl will be working at the summer camp where he's trying to land a job. He goes for the interview and lands the job; he's enthused about the new job, but in a fit of ambivalence, calls up the man who hired him to tell him he doesn't want the job. Stock contemplates the list of ironic motivations adults have conjectured about the job, especially how it will lead to associating "with a better class of people than his parents."[9] Once again he changes his mind, resolving to call up and ask to start early the next morning. It's a portrait of volatile ambivalence, effectively depicting the confusing mood swings of male adolescence. The accumulation of concluding ironies achieves resonance. The theme of renunciation relates to the religious calling, but also the author who has renounced the completion of his coming-of-age novel, although a few accomplished fragments appear recycled into *Hamilton Stark*.

The completion of that long-labored novel will result in the transformation of Banks as he appropriates a largely autobiographical novel, transforming it into art. The five stories of the second section under the heading "Transformation" offers historical meditations on the theme of transformation.

"The Rise of the Middle Class" features the heroic revolutionary Simón Bolívar (1783–1830) who liberated the present-day countries of Venezuela, Colombia, Ecuador, Peru, Panama, and Bolivia. Banks sites Bolívar in an awkward moment when he was in Kingston, Jamaica, seeking protection from the English. An assassin attempted to kill him, but has mistakenly murdered his host instead. Banks takes liberties with the story to tell his own shadowy Borges-like fable. Bolívar begins to write a letter to a friend he wants to visit when the assassin strikes. He's able to fend the knife-wielder off, his bodyguards killing him. For a brief moment Bolívar indulges in self-pity after the failed assassination, envying the life of a mutilated slave not immanently haunted by death. He realizes the absurdity of such self-pity, noting that slaves and the lower classes don't care about his revolutionary ambition because it will not change their lives; he returns to letter writing, but a letter obsequiously accepting an offer of protection from the English Protestant king. Bolívar steps out onto his balcony to display his profile in the dark: A shot rings out, confirming

Finding a Voice: Early Stories 17

he's in the crosshairs of history. Readers witness his transformation from an ordinary man into a statesman. As a seeker of freedom, Bolívar discovers himself caught imprisoned by his struggle—he no longer has time to be a private man with friends he likes, but must mingle with those who can aide his cause. This short fable about the perils of freedom functions as a reminder that the freedom of the middle class in the New World was created by revolution despite the European resistance. A deeper irony appears: The prosperity of the middle class was founded on the institution of New World slavery; the role of the slave Three-Fingered Jack illustrates this epiphany. Economical and thoughtful, this story paints a memorable historical meditation.

"Indisposed" presents a fictional version of the eighteenth-century painter and illustrator William Hogarth's marriage. Well-written in a Hogarthian manner, Banks's feminist story contravenes what little is known about the marriage. In the story, Hogarth marries the strapping young woman whom he casually and indulgently uses in the manner of his comic illustrations. She wakes up one morning, tired of her household drudgery, healthy but immobilized by rebellion. She spends the day in bed, refusing to rise. As the day takes its course, William carouses and seduces his wayward niece. Tall Jane has had enough—she rises from her bed to throttle and beat up short William. As a historical feminist parable, it amuses but does not convince.

"The Caul" presents transformation as paralysis, leading to obsession and death. Literary commentary on Edgar Allan Poe remains a mosquito-filled swamp when it comes to psychological speculation about Poe, much of it being unsupported armchair analysis. Poe was haunted by the early deaths of both his mother and especially his wife, his young first cousin. Banks goes to great pains in making his setting accurate, the last known public reading of Eddy, as he was known to his relations. Eddy was courting a widow of substantial wealth, perhaps hoping to find a permanent patron. Elmira Shelton lived directly across from the cemetery where his mother Eliza was buried, yet Banks has Poe making the pilgrimage to her stone "hundreds of times, as a young boy, as an adolescent, and as a man, even in military uniform, even while drunk."[10] Those *hundreds* of pilgrimages, especially as a boy, are hard to imagine because Eddy lived in London from age 5 to 13 at the feet of expensive tutors.

Banks conflates the widow, Poe's mother, and his poem "The Raven" into a haunting evil eye that ironically precipitates his death. My problem with this fiction is that Eddy went out of his way to satirize the ridiculousness of the Mediterranean evil eye superstition in "The Tell-Tale Heart" where the conjured paranoia of the evil eye incites a random murder—a story with legs that inspired Fyodor Dostoevsky to write *Crime and Punishment* with its different cultural and philosophic context in reply to Ivan Turgenev's Bazarov character in *Fathers and Sons*. This evil eye wraps Edgar in silence, perhaps giving him writer's block. The caul (an amniotic cap) is the memory of his mother's death haunting him all his life, thus explaining Eddy's interest in the Gothic genre. Banks's story insinuates irony in that Poe recites the poem "The Raven" which concludes with the word *Nevermore*, implying that either he or the widow have rejected a second marriage. It's true that after the death of his sweetheart Jane Stannard (of insanity, perhaps inherited syphilis) in 1823 when he was 14 and the later death of his first cousin and wife Virginia Clemm in 1847, Eddy grew cynical about love, yet the poem was published in January 1845.

Edgar was known to go on despairing drinking binges and if he went on his last binge in Baltimore because he thought he could no longer write or thought the wealthy widow resembling his mother had rejected him, then it might be an explanation for his demise. But Edgar was a life-long alcoholic and such a drinking binge need not have any rational explanation from a writer who admired rationality in fiction because there was so little rationality in his rebellious life. When Banks wrote the story, it was not known exactly why Poe died and doctors were repeatedly suing the government without success to open his grave, but the puzzle has recently been solved by Peter Ackroyd's jaunty biography *Poe: A Life Cut Short*. Eddy was touted from bar to bar in a typically corrupt Baltimore election in the fourth ward, being bribed with drink for every time he voted. Apparently, his patriotic enthusiasm caused him to vote too many times—his friends carried his comatose body to the hospital where he died a few days later.[11] Banks's story contains an authentic Poe-like ambiance, but having read a great deal of Poe, it is hard to agree with the story's psychology.[12] While some presume that a mother-fixation complex illuminates Poe, I regard it as a biographical canard because his psychological problems revolved around his overbearing stepfather, as is often the case with orphans. Likewise, I interpret Poe's use of the Gothic as a literary convention and not a personal obsession. Few biographers agree about Poe's psychological problems because Eddy was such a compulsive and colorful liar in life as well as in his letters, yet many of his lies grew from cynical jokes derived from humiliating poverty. Some think he grubbed "The Raven" for the pittance of his next meal.[13] The year before Poe died, James Russell Lowell in *A Fable for Critics* (1848) cited the origin of the poem in a scene about the raven Grip from Charles Dickens's novel *Barnaby Rudge* (1841): "There comes Poe, with his raven, like Barnaby Rudge, / Three fifths of him genius and two fifths sheer fudge." Lowell appears to have had the last word on the poem.

"The Adjutant Bird," first published in *Lillabulero* in 1967, centers upon personal transformation as a mystical universal while it employs historical themes around New England ice and Henry David Thoreau. The narrator waxes ebullient, discovering that ice as a form of water has a mystical significance, that New England ice has been marketed and transported as far away as the India Thoreau had Hinduistically conjured to be in New England. He quotes Thoreau, happy to be mystically united with Thoreau's global transcendentalism. Yet such a revelatory transformation in nature becomes ironically personal, as he cannot translate the epiphany to his beloved: Transformation appears ecstatic but limited, even some can conceive of the local as global and *vice versa*. It's a cheerful and charming intellectual romp.

"The New World," the title essay, offers academic musings on the possibilities of transformation. Banks is not really interested in cataloguing the folkloric

Finding a Voice: Early Stories

variations of the two stories he tells, any more than he's interested in giving any specific interpretation. He charts larger cultural parameters and an indirect explanation of his own art. The focus of his fascination with the baroque Spanish poet Bernardo de Balbuena (1561–1620) and his Jewish goldsmith remains cultural: The different reactions of the Puritan English to the experiences of the New World as compared to the Catholic Spanish or Jewish. Cultural differences emerge: Spanish Catholics and Jews perceive art as the natural activity of humankind, accepting the influence of the New World in terms of images, geography, and inspiration for art that acceptingly grafts elements of the New World onto the tree of European culture, despite the ruthless conquest of its native inhabitants. The Puritan intolerance for artistic images and secular literature (as pagan practice, lies, or blasphemy) leaves artists of Puritan extraction with an obsession to shatter the Puritan heritage "with the possibility of rebirth, of conversion, of utter transformation."[14] This accounts for much in the history of English and American literature from Emily Dickinson's inner light nonconformity to Walt Whitman's pagan embrace of sexuality, to D. H. Lawrence's and Robert Frost's Puritan hostility, to the religious conversions of Evelyn Waugh and Graham Greene. Unlike the Spanish approach to transformation which resembles grafting, writers from the English and American heritage inherit the burden of attempting a *radical* transformation.

Although aspiring to the first rank of poets, Balbuena wrote imitatively with baroque wordplay in the shadow of Jacopo Sannazaro's pastoral lyricism in *Arcadia* (1504) and Ludovico Ariosto's wittily digressive epic *Orlando Furioso* (1516), the end result being more curiosity than achievement. Banks doesn't mention it, but the excessively fanciful imagination that preoccupied Balbuena was destroyed by Cervantes's amusing satire on the pastoral and epic modes Balbuena favored. The utter transformation *Don Quixote* effected was to sweep away that baroque style of writing as idle and mannered dreaming.

Banks remains fascinated that Balbuena saw no contradiction between being poet, priest (an abbot in Jamaica and eventually bishop in Puerto Rico),[15] and businessman in the same way that his Jewish goldsmith saw no contradiction in being a pious Jew, successful artisan, and businessman catering to non-Jews. Balbuena, who grew up from the age of two in the New World and was educated in Mexico City, saw no split between the Old and the New World, while American Puritans see themselves as a tribe nearly alien to Europeans.

An important aspect of this dense essay consists in Banks's fascination with Balbuena's baroque technique in his epic poem, which Banks describes as "maze-like in structure, in which the object is not so much to find one's way out as it is to find one's way in."[16] This offers a good description on the structure of *Hamilton Stark*. Banks delightedly reposes in the enchantment that the fictional hero of Balbuena's epic presents a virtual portrait of the author—the identical situation with *Hamilton Stark* where the antihero becomes a baroque fragment of the self. Banks's discovery of Balbuena through his Jamaican residence provided the technical key, perhaps even more than Laurence Sterne's *Tristram Shandy* (1776), for the unusual conceptual structure of *Hamilton Stark*.

Just as Balbuena employed the text of Ariosto's *Orlando Furioso* as a background metatext for his epic, Banks would chose the best-known novel from his own background as his metatext—*Peyton Place*.

Yet unlike Balbuena's imitation of Ariosto, which subsequently led to the mediocre status of Balbuena's work, Banks understood the lesson of Cervantes and used the metatext of *Peyton Place* as a subject for parody and ridicule. This difficult essay on the culture of the baroque and an accomplished poet, who remains so little known to the English-speaking world, provides the key for understanding how the postmodern masterpiece *Hamilton Stark* evolved. The final, fifth transformation synthesizes the various transformations of the Old World and the New World with Banks's invention of a transformative authorial self—in exploiting his unresolved contradictions, he creates a radical transformation of himself into an author whose hero inhabits a baroque shadow of himself.

3

Parables of Inside-Out: Early Novellas

> The village was burnished by the descending sun. The chatter of girls collecting offal from a buffalo herd cut into the hush. Doves rose and dotted the saffron sky above the muri paddies. A child wailed somewhere amid the congestion of mud huts. Then the silence returned.
> —Leo Giroux, *The Rishi**

Family Life

When Russell Banks turned toward fiction, he wrote metafiction in the self-conscious conceit of Laurence Sterne, concluding with the bleak, despairing wit of Samuel Beckett. *Family Life*, a prose-poem novella, presents an assembly of slides divided into 12 chapters (like the 12 books of Virgil's *Aeneid*) with 12 subheadings. The first chapter begins with three prologues: The opening salvo announces a classical epic tragedy in the vein of Virgil and Homer's Trojans as imagined by Hector Berlioz's opera *Les Troyens*. The second prologue identifies the genre at play, the literary mock-fairy tale, the announcement of which arrives like a thunderous *deus ex machina* after a list of nearly 70 writers not known for fairy tales, unless one dourly considers John Milton's *Paradise Lost* to be in that genre, yet Charles Dickens's *A Christmas Carol* may fit the bill, but neither of these exhibit the playful mischief of the literary mock-fairy tale as invented by Giambattista Basile (1566 or 1575–1632), the imaginative creator of the ogre, whose mischievous humor was updated in popular culture by the film *Shrek*.[1] The third prologue indicates the novella's supercilious technique,

---

*The novels of Leo Giroux, Jr., although not badly written, may be characterized as belonging to the craft of historical pulp thrillers rather than art. In a clear reference to Russell Banks, the dedication of Giroux's 1985 novel *The Rishi*, about a resurgence of the ancient Hindu Thugee cult of stranglers in Boston, reads: "To Laura, my wife, who, in her generosity of spirit, never demanded that I be a plumber, carpenter, electrician...."

the form of surreal fable, labeled in a didactic manner as paradigm. Then it moves to the action *in medias res*.

Before plunging into the playful landscape of wit that Banks offers, it should be noted that the literary fairy tale in America was revived by Donald Barthelme whose postmodern experiments catapulted the rather obscure short story writer into celebrity prominence when *The New Yorker* published his novella *Snow White* (1967). In *Transformations* (1971), the poet Anne Sexton adapted the genre to her sardonic confessional style of poetry, the most successful of these poems being the much-anthologized "Cinderella." Perhaps Banks was hoping for the same success that Barthelme enjoyed, yet like Sexton, he offered more satire than ingratiating wit.[2]

Despite the literary bravado of the book's three prologues, the writing remains Rabelaisian rather than academic. The immediate action concerns sexual orientation within the royal family. King Egress hears of a suitor for one of his three sons, informing Queen Naomi Ruth; she's disturbed by the King's breezy acquiescence, asking him whether he's ever had a male lover. The King confesses he once caught and screwed a loon—it turns out that the suitor is called The Loon (one of many aliases). The chapter concludes in a litany of alliterating *L*s, much as Vladimir Nabokov's opening paragraph of *Lolita* trills with *L*s as Nabokov imitated the lilting *L*s of Francesco Petrarch's 11th, 12th, and 13th sonnets describing the beauty of his beloved Laura. But Banks conjures as much low culture Looney-tune camp affectation with "Lone, Lon, Lonnie, l'Ange, Lawn, Lune."[3] The narration has been third-person imbued with a manic tinge.

The Queen begins an affair with the wine steward who explains that sexual practices depend upon their P-factor, the amount of pain accumulated within their family. (The punning P-factor alludes to the Princess and the Pea as well as alcoholic urination.) But the Queen finds little of interest in the wine steward's wise observations, discovering relief in epic rutting. Immersed in guilt for not feeling guilt, she takes up a torture implement, penitentially breaking her thumbs. She boldly confronts her husband, asking him whether he has ever had sex with a man or boy. After the answer, she contemplates writing a novel based upon *Cinderella* or *The Song of Solomon*. Her life is reduced to writing before her mirror, dreaming, and ringing for the wine steward. The Queen's narration has been first person.

The third chapter opens with first person narration from King Egress the Hearty as he squats on the toilet, the next slide providing a mock-heraldic poem (common in the Irish literary tradition) on his ancestors going all the way back to *the word*. The rest of the novella proceeds to hopscotch back and forth between multitudes of perspective in concise cornucopia-like medleys that, surprisingly in an authorial *tour de force*, can be easily followed even by a nearly inattentive reader. After a parody of Robert Frost, the King notices the wine steward slinking from the Queen's apartment; he suffers a flashback about his father beating him to harden him for kingship. Ruling with rigid brutality will continue the time-honored family tradition; he orders the wine steward killed, and his sergeant summarily dispatches him with a grenade. The chapter

Parables of Inside-Out: Early Novellas

concludes with the King's rationalizations ascending into abstractions; he resolves to *pen* his memoirs with the assistance of his submissive female secretary.

Three sons appear: Orgone, the champion athlete with Gargantuan organ, a braggart bisexual narcissist; the hunter Dread, obsessed with psychology, guns, and death; and young coke-head Egress, a pop-culture prankster who derides the obsessive violence of his brothers, finding recreation in writing rock-band lyrics. Two black rooks fly ominously from the tower of King Egress, recalling the two morning ravens of Odin that make him omniscient; a black cat crosses Orgone's path.

In the following three chapters, Dread, young Egress, and Orgone, accidentally and unconsciously, commit suicide: Dread from a gun accident while thrilled to be hunting cougar; Egress, depicted as a Hamlet-like figure haunted by the Green Man (the personification of death), from drunkenly eating his drinking glass while celebrating his latest socially hostile lyric; Orgone dies from blood poisoning after cutting his foot on a bottle of cologne in the shower. The state grand inquisitor extracts a confession of murder and treason from the Green Man who's then promptly condemned to execution.

Distraught, King Egress falls further into the arms of the gym janitor Loon, his only consoler, who lives in a tree house in Central Park (designed by Christopher Wren at one point and then by Michael Graves at another) where the King shows up wearing sackcloth, ready for a guilt-ridden medieval pilgrimage to the Empire State Building, the devotional fetish destination of all who worship empire. A tribe of Abenaki Indians thread in and out of the novel as symbols of honesty, contrasting with the ruthless and violent nature of Western institutions and family behavior. Traversing a playfully nonsensical geography, the King and the Loon approach Manhattan, but when the King's guilt vanishes, they cease and party as if the pilgrimage has been completed.

Chapter 10 excerpts Naomi Ruth Sunder's novel, *Remember Me to Camelot*, yet the *novel* reads as heartfelt autobiography concerning the difficulties of family life in the military where the husband appears as absent warrior, first as a pilot in the Korean War and then in the Vietnam War. She provides a sentimental and nostalgic snapshot of small town high-school romance that appears, apart from her pride in her children, to be the romanticized point of her circumscribed life. Disillusioned by the rigors of an absentee husband, she takes a lover. She receives notice her husband has been shot down over North Vietnam and is now a prisoner of war. She begins to put her life together by getting the high school diploma she abandoned when she became pregnant at 15. She gets a driver's license, takes up yoga and hobbies, keeps her lover Ben, and remains determined to be her new independent self should her husband one day show up on her doorstep—and if he doesn't like it they will divorce.

Naomi's *novel* reveals the pedestrian coda—the previous nine chapters were the looking glass effusions and dreams of a woman writer who began equating the all-male world of military violence with abusive homosexual regression, satirizing the male culture's valorization of sports, hunting, and recreational drugs.

As a counterculture satire clothed in mock fairy tale, the novel exhibits wit and comic bitterness toward the monstrous patriarchal thumb which represses both domestic common sense and family sanity in the name of witless empire-building. The perspective remains trenchantly feminist, exposing the bizarre megalomania of men determined to cling to power in spite of the absurd evidence of its self-destructive cost, even descending to sackcloth fantasies of martyrdom abetted by absurd rationalizations in order to preserve extended adolescence. The fact that men dress this sensibility as wisdom makes the analysis a more chilling critique.

The 11th chapter re-enters the mock fairy tale world as the King returns home after seven years to find, like Agamemnon returning home from Troy, that there's a new regime in town, although the Queen raises no plot against the King—she merely asserts that she is now in charge and that's the way it is. The King briefly goes underground to plot the counterrevolution to destroy the new feminist state. The Loon deserts him but the King recruits the Green Man who yet he lives because the Queen had pardoned him. Being by nature a traitor, the Green Man helps the King organize an army. The Sons of the Pioneers rock band, whose lyrics had been written by young Egress, eagerly join the coming revolution with their motorcycles, but are relegated to public relations work. The King assembles a mighty army, leading the counter-revolution against pacifism, feminism, and mercy. Rapine and slaughter ravage the countryside. The climactic battle in the capitol produces a stunning Pyrrhic victory:

> The city was deserted, empty, and all major buildings had been destroyed. The streets were filled with rubble, concrete, wrecked automobiles, buses, trains, mattresses, broken cases of food, furniture, clothing, and glass, as if there had been an earthquake and it had occurred at the one moment when everybody was out of town. Egress was at first astonished, and then, when he had begun to piece together what had happened, a process in which he was aided by the Green Man, he was deeply depressed. One might say broken.[4]

Ironically, the Green Man (like the medieval Green Knight), the personification of death and chaos, has triumphed in the end. Male leadership has been duped by exploitative narcissism and a delusional belief in the infallibility of men as the rightful governors of the world—militarism has reached its logical conclusion of consuming destruction as it does in Berlioz's opera *Les Troyens* whose concluding chorus sings:

> Undying hatred for the race of Aeneas!
> May our sons be hurled against theirs
> In relentless war for all time!
> May our ships attack theirs
> And send them shattered to the bottom
> Of the sea! By land and water
> May our last descendents, armed against them to the end,
> One day astonish the world with their total destruction.[5]

Such unremitting anger marshals the satiric conclusion to Naomi's protest novel. The early seventies were a time when women's social anger and discontent peaked—it was unusual for a male novelist to articulate and validate that anger.

The final 12th chapter, an epilogue, describes after their spilt a series of chance encounters between Naomi Ruth and Egress Sunder with a Beckett-like fatality immersed in ambient pathos. The device may be inspired by the Biblical *Book of Ruth*, yet its spare technique arrives via Samuel Beckett; unlike *The Book of Ruth* the conclusion is tragic. The divorced couple casually bumps into each other around the globe: Paris, London, and New York. When they meet, Naomi can't resist a dig at Egress's affair with The Loon. On the beach, Egress blames Naomi for the devastation and destruction of other people involved in their lives. Naomi grimly replies, "It's Greek, and that means everything's interlocked. When the house of Atreus finally collapses, the entire city has to collapse around it. I had nothing to do with all that destruction at the end."[6]

At a museum, Egress discovers Naomi's current lover to be the contemporary painter he most admires. At a party, Egress remains in denial about his regret. The bleak episodic scenes of this chapter arrive as objective narration in the third person. The chaotic and absurd mock fairy tale world of epic exaggeration has vanished into the ordinary landscape of the banal, just as the ribald humor of the early chapters has been replaced by the somber post-partum tone of elegy. Naomi, who has changed greatly, appears considerably happier than Egress who can't quite get over the great love of his life. As they age, they both become slightly nostalgic for each other and their youth, yet they cannot communicate in any way. The book concludes with a resounding agreement—"No!"

While the plethora of Banks's cut-up slides gluts the glib surface with fragmentation, the book remains tightly organized. Surface fragmentation conjures the predicament of an elementary postmodern puzzle for the reader to assemble, albeit in reverse through a mirror. Even though the puzzle is not difficult to decode, reviewers and commentators remained obtuse to the novella's reverse *looking glass* structure and upside-down surreal humor. As in Homer's *Iliad* or Virgil's *Aeneid*, war and destruction accomplishes nothing.[7] One reason readers may have difficulty decoding the novel resides in the weak verisimilitude of the feminist looking glass novel-within-a-novel—it sounds as if it may have been penned by a man rather than a woman. Others have complained that Banks's comic high jinks don't come across as really funny,[8] although this perception may be prompted by the mixing of genres and consequent loss of focus—as comedy turns to tragedy, the tragedy overshadows the previous comedy, casting a self-indulgent light on it, yet that is exactly what Banks intended and achieved. The influence of Donald Barthelme resonates throughout the novella. Banks lacks the excessively high-spirited flippancy of Barthelme's knowing faddishness and lacks the complete descent into cynical frivolity that attracts Barthelme's sarcastically appreciative audience. This neglected first novel (novella, actually) retains its relevance more today than when it was first published in 1974, yet upon publication empathetic comprehension failed to appear.

The novella's core story remains the melodrama of a young marriage gone sour. The highly artificial cast of the narrative functions to disguise autobiographical elements of Banks's failed first marriage to 17-year-old Darlene Bennett. The elaborate artifice of *Family Life* scaffolds a confession of failure and the guilt of abandoning a daughter. The Loon character probably presents a transfigured cartoon of Banks's first literary mentor, Leo Giroux, Jr., about seven years older than Banks, whom he met while working at a Boston bookstore. Leo, later the author of three novels, *The Rishi* (1985), its sequel, *Dark Ashram* (1990), and *The Black Madonna* (1991),[9] informally tutored Banks before his early death of a heart attack in 1990 at the age of 55. Their friendship, conducted in bars with a habitual womanizer (Leo), must have been disruptive to a young woman from the South, who, insecure in the North, would have demanded more than the normal attention younger clinging teenage girls bring to a marriage. After Banks left her, they never communicated with each other.[10]

THE RELATION OF MY IMPRISONMENT

If *Family Life* displayed the high artifice of exuberant wit, then *The Relation of My Imprisonment* (1983) plumbed the depths of Banks's mordant, mischievous wit with a dry humor. Although *Hamilton Stark* (1978) was published before *Relation*, the slim novella was finished before it; both were written during Banks's sabbatical in Jamaica from 1976 to 1977, but Banks couldn't find a publisher for *Relation*, even though excerpts from it had been published by United Artists Press (1980–81). When belatedly published in book form in 1983 with a small press in California (Sun and Moon Press), reviewers presumed that it was his latest book[11] when in terms of writing chronology, it was his second, and not fourth novel.

On the one hand, the narrative provides a comic parody of the Puritan genre of confessions, appropriating title and style from John Bunyan's testimony (mostly dialogue) penned in 1660, yet not published until 1672, when added to a later addition of *Grace Abounding to the Chief of Sinners*. On the other hand, *Relation* presents the tragedy and martyrdom of non-conformist belief if it persists in nonconformity. It is another peculiar fable cast in the somewhat deceptive garb of history, presenting the illusion of both period verisimilitude as well as virtual absurdity which is as drolly comic as it is nearly probable in the solemnity of its historical narrative tone. Deirdre Bair's review, published on April Fool's Day, concluded, "The narrator satirizes charitable organizations and liberal guilt. He speaks of engineers and administrators, of boards of directors, accountants and appropriate publicity.... This is a marvelously written little book, fascinatingly intricate, yet deceptively simple. Well worth reading more than once."[12]

While such Puritan testimonies and confessions do, in honesty, include the confessions of sin, the over-the-top admissions in Banks's narrative provide comic excess. A Puritan might confess to having taken a second wife or

Parables of Inside-Out: Early Novellas

having seduced a serving girl, but they don't admit to orgies, threesomes and foursomes, the narrative briefly becoming salacious yet stopping short of pornography. Moreover, the temptation of sexual degradation appears in the narrative as less a struggle than the gross temptation of nostalgia evoked by idle confinement. The citation of phantom devotional writings (*Book of Discipline*) and enigmatic pseudo-scriptural references (like *Vis.* or *II Carol*) parody the scrupulous convention of Puritan narratives that brim with documented citations from Judeo-Christian scriptures like the Book of Ezekiel or 2 Corinthians. Such an odd combination of absurd comedy and serious social critique recounted in a rational tone display the ingenuous influence of Jonathan Swift's satiric essays.

The flippant and vengeful behavior of the stern and moral judges with their choleric bursts of anger and vehement irrationality, evoke the precedent of Laputa's (Whoredom) academic scholars in the third book of *Gulliver's Travels*; these judges belong to the province of farce, yet convey the kind of intractable rigidity and ridiculous "reasoning" now often associated with Puritans. Americans cannot help but recall that one of the primary resentments of American colonists was imprisonment without trial or the holding of secret trials. The manner in which the coffin maker is treated, in terms of the repeated psychological demand for orthodox recantation from heresy, actually contains more parallels to the theme of pseudo-political correctness within Joseph Stalin's Great Terror as limned in Eugenia Ginzburg's great classic *Journey into the Whirlwind* (1967) than it does to American history, with the possible exception of the notorious Salem Witch Trials.[13] Indeed, the experience of being at the mercy of local despotic authorities combined with the mystical experience of self-purification during solitary confinement during extended incarceration, more closely resembles the experiences Ginzburg underwent in her confinement than those of wayward Puritans.

The kind of Puritan parody Banks indulges in was first developed by Herman Melville in *Moby-Dick* (1851), one of Banks's favorite novels, where Puritan sermons are satirized at some length. Gregory Peck has a memorable scene with this material in John Huston's uneven 1956 movie based upon Ray Bradbury's script. While Ishmael's testimony resembles that of a survivor like the Biblical figure Job, the testimony of the coffin maker continues almost to the moment of his happy death. Like Melville's short story "Benito Cereno" from *The Piazza Tales* (1856), the parable of the coffin maker exposes social hypocrisy and a materialistic society. "Benito Cereno" tells the story of a sea captain who comes to the assistance of another captain who has experienced a slave revolt; the anti-hero rescues the captain, helping him to restore slavery, and execute the ringleaders as Melville delicately satirizes the "innocent" mentality of the racist captain. The story becomes a bitter prophecy of the coming Civil War between the United States.[14]

A more topical counterculture influence on Banks's peculiar narrative may have been music, specifically the acid rock band the Grateful Dead as well as the ancestry motif contained in some Rastafarian music (Ethiopian poetry emphasizes distant genealogy) which he would have heard while revising the novella in Jamaica. The folkloric motif of the Grateful Dead (Banks may be obliquely poking fun at the legion of fans ["Deadheads"] that unthinkingly follow the band), from which the band receives its name, appears on the third page of the narrative:

> My friend persisted and pleaded with me none the less, until I begged leave finally to closet myself briefly for prayer and guidance in this question and proceeded to close myself into the coffin that my father had employed his brother, the revered master to my apprenticeship many years ago, to build one for me. And as so often has occurred in times of woe or quandary, the face of a beloved ancestor, in this case the wise face of my mother's great aunt, passed before me and gave me these words. Your guide in life can proceed from no other source than the mercy you tender the dead. To suffer for such tenderness is to receive mercy back from the dead when no others will show it to you.[15]

Folkloric themes concerning the Grateful Dead constitute a nearly universal belief throughout global culture. Simply put, it means that if you do a favor for a dead ancestor or help out a relative or friend in this life, the relative or friend in the afterlife will intercede among the gods for your benefit. This folkloric belief is deeply embedded in Christianity by way of belief in the Resurrection whereby Jesus, Mary, the Holy Spirit, or some saint may intercede on behalf of one who prays to or through them. Luther and the Protestant Reformation in general attempted to remove or suppress this aspect of Christianity as patently pagan by rejecting the idea of intercession in favor of direct communion with divinity.

In the passage quoted above, the nature of the controversial heresy is clarified: Followers of the Grateful Dead cult receive their commissioned "sacramental" coffins to pray while confined inside them, the near-imprisonment inside the coffin becoming a strict aide to meditation, yet the pious pray to and commune with their ancestors, not the Christian God. The court ban on coffins attempts to prevent the spread of this pagan heresy, allowing for deaths from disease to be transported in coffins under a rubric for public health. Banks may have appropriated the idea for his imaginary heretical sect from the life of the poet and divine John Donne, who donned a shroud for his memorial portrait, and when advised by a physician to drink cordials and milk for 20 days to restore his health, said to his doctor after ten days of yielding, "He had drunk it more to satisfie him, than to recover his health; and that he would not drink it ten days longer, upon the best moral assurance of having twenty years added to his life: for he loved it not; and was so far from fearing death, which to others is the King of Terrors, that he long'd for the day of dissolution."[16]

Amid our hedonistic age of continual gratifications, many tend to forget the seventeenth-century Puritan dispensation that underlies Banks's narrative. The attitude of Banks's coffin maker toward his death and martyrdom for his beliefs accurately depicts the era despite the delicious hint of comic exaggeration. In his commentary on the era of the poet and divine John Donne, who was rumored to have occasionally slept in his coffin "for practice," his biographer comments:

> Life, men thought then, was a preparation for death, and it behooved each one to be ready to meet it. The surest way to meet such a moment was to have been through it often in the mind, to have endured it all in anticipation, and so to be able to meet it with the confidence of becoming a Christian who trusted in the saving grace of Christ's sacrifice. There were many manuals instructing men how to die; the scholar kept a skull on his desk or carried some other *memento mori* on his person; the great man who fell from high place was judged by the propriety of his behavior on the scaffold.[17]

Although Banks's narrative admits a subtle mockery of the Puritan dispensation, it affirms the stubborn dignity and heroism of such heroic self-discipline and commitment to a nonconformist ideal. Just as much as the coffin maker wears the comic halo of a saintly Socratic gadfly, he wears the dignified shroud of Job offering an exemplary manual on how to die with an ecstatic, mystical joy.

The paradox of such commitment and devotion is that in facing death squarely one discovers a resurrected exaltation in the moments of life one has left to live. The practice of meditating upon death remains a fundamental method in traditional Buddhism while both the Greeks and Romans "slept in tombs to dream of, question, and receive inspiration from the dead."[18] Contemporary American culture has forgotten its traditional religious roots.

While the specific locale of the coffin maker's community is never disclosed (it appears peculiarly devoid of specific landscape other than that the land provides wood and stone), since the Puritans invented this testifying *Relation* genre, the reader begins to assume that the narrative takes place in historical England. Yet it is not exactly the historical England known because some wittily planted anachronisms stumbled upon later do not square with that time period: international currencies, barbells and the culture of body building, prison cuisine, gourmet fantasies, gang protection, pin-stripe suits, and the most troubling of all—that the Society of Prisoners (the comically abbreviated SOP) which administers prison relief, has a membership in the *millions*[19] and is one of the most powerful political organizations in the unnamed country. In contrast, J. M. Coetzee's political fable *Waiting for the Barbarians* (1980) places its testimonial-like narration in an archetypical colonial power, yet its desert geography (rather than narrative style) clearly identifies Dutch South Africa.[20] Any reader cannot help but be reminded that the country with the highest ratio of incarceration remains the United States. According to the U.S. Department of Justice midyear 2007 estimate, the number of prisoners in American jails reached 1,595,037 prisoners.[21] America enjoys the distinction of have the highest per capita incarceration rate in the world. Yet the problem of America's swelling prison population was well under way in the late 1970s (when it was nearly half a million) as a result of the prohibition on marijuana as well as the social disintegration of traditional morality. If not for the peculiar style of seventeenth-century diction, Banks's novella might have been classified as science fiction not only because of the narration's devotion to time distortion but because of its political critique: It turns out that the majority of prisoners there have been convicted of bisexual or same-sex orientation, regarded as a serious political offense against the state.[22]

The custom of summer solstice (Midsummer's Eve, about June 24) pardons for criminals practiced by the seemingly Christian court presents a highly ironic custom since that calendrical festival has historically been a pagan event associated with either fire or fertility rites. Such a peculiar custom recalls Shirley Jackson's "The Lottery," wherein the celebration of the annual scapegoat, a stoning lottery that ambiguously resembles the American Fourth of July holiday or perhaps Memorial Day. As in Jackson's close-knit Puritan town, the community of Banks's coffin maker demands unthinking obedience and the observance of blind tradition. While both narratives attack blind tradition, Banks adds the comic perspective of Christians unconsciously observing pagan feasts, which has always been true of how Christianity tried to absorb pagan feasts like Roman Christmas (Saturnalia), Easter (the Great Goddess or Mithra), Celtic New Year (All Saints' Day), and the March 17 feast of Liber Pater (trying to convert the drunken revelry of the day's celebration for the opening of the new spring wine to a sober observance of that famous abstainer of drink, the Roman citizen St. Patrick). The coffin maker remains well aware of such holidays and takes a stern Puritan view, at first refusing to join the Mayday masquerade party:

> the celebration of the first day of the month of May was a deliberate carry over from the days when it had not yet been thought of to worship the dead and men and women went around year after year making holidays out of seasonal and celestial cycles and changes which they foolishly associated with patterns and needs of their own mortal lives. The amnesty associated with the solstice and applied every year to the short-term prisoners and the tried and convicted political and religious offenders willing to sue out a pardon, as they called it, was a celebration of this type.[23]

The interpretation of dreams to correct errant ways also runs counter to the Puritan tradition, which rejects dreams in all their manifestations as merely tempting delusions of the devil. The appearance of fathers and uncles in dreams played tremendous significance in American Indian culture and tribal leadership depended upon a chief being able to correctly analyze and interpret important dreams. For the coffin maker, his dreams help him to re-convert from his pagan ways and once more embrace the truth of worshiping the wisdom of the dead.

Prisoner resistance, a motif which constitutes a traditional aspect of political incarceration, receives an elaborate comic twist based upon the Judeo-Christian principle of proselytizing. The subterfuge of smuggling a single coffin into prison blossoms into a conspiracy that not only enables the prisoner's wife to support their children and relatives, but makes his jailer Jacob a wealthy and powerful politician when he subsequently becomes the director of the Society of Prisoners. Yet, when Jacob leaves the prison for his new post conceived and engineered by the coffin maker, the narrator confesses that he was more destitute and isolated than ever.[24]

The chronicle of the coffin maker concludes with a litany of disgusting diseases inspired by perhaps The Book of Job; like Job, the coffin maker bears all with saintly refinement and ascetic endurance. Amid a multitude of communicable diseases, he discovers a hallowed ecstasy when placed in a coffin of his own, secure in his complete renunciation of the follies of the world and time's illusions. After 20 years of incarceration without a public trial, he finally achieves the happy death of a pious man, providing a public confession for his sins, displaying the path of his sect's belief in the enlightened liberation from the sinful world of time. Meditation upon death has a long devotional history in Christianity,[25] yet today the practice has virtually disappeared from our hedonistic society. The novella remains a parody on traditional ascetics, despite such ambiguous hagiography. After events on 9/11, the theme of incarceration without charges or trial once more surfaced as a subject of debate.

Banks's early novellas revealed a talented writer with a satiric streak, yet the oblique nature of his refined wit and intricate ironies did not capture an audience to support the writer. His second novella, a considerable advance over his quirky first novella, displayed an interest in the nuances of voice and style, and disclosed a writer interested in examining the present through the lens of history. Banks's talent for unusual narrative strategies marked him as promising writer, yet the lack of memorable conversational dialogue in his work left open the question of how he would proceed as a fiction writer. Banks continued to follow his strength by experimenting with new narrative forms as he explored the short story format and a new novel, *Hamilton Stark* (1978), which invoked such an excess of strategies that the novel has become a classic metafictional landmark.

4

Ironic Conundrum: *Hamilton Stark*

> Hitherto the nature of this narrative, besides rendering the intricacies in the beginning unavoidable, has more or less required that many things, instead of being set down in the order of occurrence, should be retrospectively or irregularly given.
>
> —Herman Melville, "Benito Cereno"

In the patronizingly vague review published by *The New York Times, Hamilton Stark* (1978) appears to occur in a self-created vacuum:

> This is a one-man show, or, rather, a kaleidoscope with Hamilton as the brightest piece in a constantly shifting pattern.... Sometimes all this works, and sometimes it doesn't. The use of the daughter's novel is hilarious, and so are the tapes by the wives. The little essays are often ponderous and distracting, the digressions often witty.[1]

The context or metatext for Banks's novel is the one novel that everyone in the area of New Hampshire where Banks grew up whispered about. It changed the cultural discourse of America in the 1950s: *Peyton Place* (1956), which in its first month sold more than 100,000 copies, spent 59 weeks on the best-seller list, eventually reaching sales of more than 12 million; it became an Academy Award winning movie, and instigated the first prime-time television soap opera series in 1964, introducing the young actors Mia Farrow and Ryan O'Neal. The show ran for over five years comprising 524 episodes with not a penny going to author Grace Metalious because she failed to sign all the legal documents to the movie and television deal that her lawyer had prepared.[2]

Banks's novel explicitly refers to *Peyton Place*,[3] and many of the novel's plot elements have glancing parallels or reverse parallels to the novel by Metalious, although there are many autobiographical shards from Banks's own life intertwined in his novel. If *Family Life* had been conceived of as a reverse looking glass, *Hamilton Stark* was conceived of as a shattered mirror of both the history of New Hampshire and of Banks's own autobiography fictionalized into a postmodern puzzle that sought to probe the origins and manifestations of domestic violence and abuse in the cold impoverished New Hampshire valleys. Banks applies geographical, anthropological, historical, psychological, and sociological tools to the banality of the detective genre.

The novel's academic methodology creates meditative distance from the passionate subject matter; this approach constitutes the opposite of Metalious's visceral bone-popping prose. What is obvious in a detective novel—a whodunit—remains ambiguous enough in Banks's parody of the genre so that readers would have to think about the author's imagined murder and the reasons for his imagination arriving at that fantasy rather than have a fictional murder literally spelled out for them. The reader must become the detective, yet one's enjoyment of the novel depends upon cerebrally putting all the clues together and then standing back to admire the completed puzzle because the reasons for the author imagining the murder are far from clear. Unless one re-reads the first chapter over again after finishing the novel which has 11 chapters—re-reading the first chapter again makes 12 chapters, the magical number of a shadowy Virgilian epic; the number 11 also denotes infinity or infinite repetition. The double singulars one may also represent the double portrait that the novel paints, a portrait of the fictional character Hamilton Stark and the self-portrait of the author, although the two appear as so intricately intertwined that they are, practically speaking knitted into a Gordian knot. To tack one's sail to such a different breeze that blew Metalious to the top of the best-seller list, was to doom a much better novel about an obscure solitary character to the niche of little-known classic. Well-written conundrums are not transformed into Hollywood movies or successful soaps.

The narrator, who appears to be a college teacher fond of reading classical authors like Livy, returns in spring (probably mid-May after turning in grades) of 1974 to his summer house in New Hampshire, stopping by his friend A.'s house (the house of the fictional character Hamilton Stark) first. When he arrives at A.'s house, A. is not there; he notices three bullet holes through the driver's side window of A.'s Chrysler and then he imagines three events around which he could construct a first novel. Event one, the murder of Hamilton Stark's fifth wife Dora and Stark's arrest for murder. Event two, meeting down the road Stark's distraught daughter with a gun—she's out to kill him after just slightly wounding him. Event three, some years later, he reads an oddball newspaper article about an eccentric man who lives in Northern Canada inside his own tomb—this character named Ham, who resembles the coffin maker of *Relation*, is clearly his fictional character Hamilton Stark and offers a possible conclusion to the novel. The opening of the novel presents three different possibilities; a device first employed by Flann O'Brien in his postmodern comic masterpiece *At Swim-Two-Birds* (1937).

The mystery the reader must solve is how the eventual novel could have at one time be constructed from these three events or why they were considered at all because what follows is not any of the proposed novels based upon this first inspiration, but another novel altogether embroiled with the self-conscious description of how it came to be constructed, yet it remains relevant why the first three possibilities were imagined. The novel might follow in the footsteps of Metalious (event one or two) or provide a more personal and oblique narration like Herman Melville's "Bartleby, the Scrivener"[4] which culminates with a symbolic ending (event three). The reader must try to figure out why the author might want to construct such a novel with these possibilities in order to understand the novel that the narrator will eventually write. Eventually, the writer chooses something approximate to event three that is more personally symbolic to himself and the novel he has composed than the literary, Melville-like option. Yet it remains important why he would consider event one or event two as the basis for his yet to be written novel, which will eventually be completed by midwinter of 1975 when the novel ends with a dramatic climax that resolves the personal and aesthetic situation of both the author and reader. Event three with Ham living as a recluse in his own tomb, turns out to be a fantasy that provides a psychological solace for his eventually missing friend.

Banks employs allusions to *Peyton Place* in a variety of ways: counterpoint and foil, and a critique to be confirmed as well as parodied because his novel presents different perspectives and methodologies as well as his own conclusions about small-town New Hampshire written from a postmodern male perspective, although the testimonies of several women provide important documentation about Hamilton Stark. The plot of *Peyton Place* itself appears in relation to the skimpy insert on Hamilton Stark's fourth wife, 18-year-old Maureen Blade:

> A psychiatrist might suggest that, in marrying him, she was working out, through identification with his well-known acts against *his* parent, her own desires to behave similarly toward *her* parent, a drunken lout, Arthur Blade, a chronically unemployed lout who had mistreated his eldest daughter for years, beating her and, it was rumored, even making sexual advances against her. One might, if one were that same psychiatrist, also suggest that in marrying Hamilton she was seeking a replacement for her father, for, not more than a month before the marriage, Arthur Blade had been committed to the New Hampshire State Mental Hospital in Concord, where his extreme alcoholism could be treated, at least temporarily.[5]

Much of the sensational plot of *Peyton Place*, banned in Canada and many other countries, came from the journalist Laurose Wilkens who told Metalious the story of Barbara Roberts, a local girl of 20; she had been sexually abused by her father who at times had chained her to her bed for days while he raped her. While threatening to kill her and her brother one night, he chased them around in the kitchen; she took her father's gun out of a drawer and killed him. Roberts received a 30-years-to-life sentence but was eventually freed by the exposé crusade of a young cub reporter by the name of Ben Bradlee. Metalious's editor, Kitty Messenger, changed the father in the novel to a stepfather in order to remove incest from the novel, due to marketing considerations.[6] Metalious, after a few more novels that did not achieve such notoriety, died of cirrhosis in a Boston hospital at the age of 39.

Alcoholism runs as background leitmotif through Banks's novel. The narrator's hero drinks a fifth of Canadian Club and a case of Molson ale religiously every weekend, usually Saturday. Employing the novel-within-a-novel technique as in *Family Life*, Hamilton's daughter Rochelle recounts the story of her father's drunken bar brawling in his high-school years. The narrator who assembles his narrative in such an unconventional way (although it coheres in its complexity) might be accused by the reader (unjustly) as exhibiting the fragmented workings of an unorganized alcoholic. Those persons who do not drink in the novel often appear to be more psychologically unbalanced than those who do drink. As in some passages in William Faulkner's novel *The Hamlet* (1940) and in some of his short stories like "A Rose for Emily" one may question the sanity of a whole community, and the reader may be even surprised that the whole of the Suncook valley itself is not described as an extended mental asylum populated by those who drink excessively and those who Puritanically abstain at a psychological price. Later in the novel, there are some drinking anecdotes concerning a former drinking side-kick of Hamilton's, a certain Feeney, a booming laugher, recalling the character from "The Conversion" or the Loon character from *Family Life*, except the mentor figure becomes reduced to sidekick status as a machine operator.

Peyton Place's plot receives reverse parody: Rochelle, the daughter of the narrator's hero and friend A., called Hamilton, has a platonically incestuous crush on her father. Aware of this problem, Hamilton coldly ignores it, his manner of treating any serious problem in relationships, as interviews in the novel with former wives reveal. Instead of the murder of a man, the writer considers the murder of a middle-aged woman and having the hero wrongly arrested by his brother-in-law because of the family feud between them. One of the reasons the narrator considers Stark a hero, is that he doesn't act out his anger on others—he employs passive resistance, internalizing his anger into obsessive rituals of work.

The central focus of the novel itself revolves around plumbing as an expression of quintessential Americana and the effort of Americans to contribute to culture by building a better life through plumbing. Although the narrator of the novel is a Christian Socialist, he takes as his hero a truculent right-winger who embodies the stodgy, conservative ideas and morals of the early 1950s. No theoretician, Stark nonetheless has moments of introspective wisdom and social commentary: Chapter eight lists 100 ordinary (some revel in the banal) yet quirky anecdotes about the character's unconventional behavior for the reader to ponder. Everything contains a double perspective whereby the wit and wisdom of Hamilton may appear to be either off-beat genius or the ravings of a recalcitrant and obtuse curmudgeon. The line between wisdom and foolishness as well as sanity and insanity in the novel remains, as it sometimes does in Faulkner, consistently blurred while the narrative undermines any *normal* reader's response in judging such matters—this is the novel's peculiar humor as ironies accumulate like layers of snowflakes drifting to the ground during a New Hampshire snowstorm.

The novelist has an insomniac, somewhat overweight, and pompous psychiatric friend, C., who often supplies the author with advice on his main character and novel, much of it relevant and sometimes even wonderfully observant. As a commentator, the psychiatrist's analysis remains perceptive, but he's eventually revealed as a paranoid lunatic overcome by public opinion in chapter ten when he wakes the writer up in the middle of the night with a ridiculous monologue that exposes him as being in the process of a breakdown due to his preoccupation with narcissistic ideas about the fine line between genius and insanity. His obsessing about Friedrich Nietzsche's will-to-power appears to put him over the edge as it did Nietzsche. Like Nietzsche, the psychiatrist arrives at a nervous breakdown; his advice and analysis construct an indirect attempt to recruit the author as his lover—psychiatric transference has been comically reversed!

C., an important minor character who could be considered to function as a one-man Greek chorus in the novel, causes and personifies the dramatic reversal in chapter ten when the author and analyst switch roles—this reversal of the chorus (or sidekick oracle) works well in defiance of traditional narration. The avant-garde techniques assembled by Banks in this labyrinthine novel present innovations as daring as those of Laurence Sterne, O'Brien, or *nouveau roman* writers who abandoned traditional plot, authors like Nathalie Sarraute, Alain Robbe-Grillet, Claude Simon, Marguerite Duras, or even Italo Calvino, especially his contemporaneously written novel *If on a Winter's Night a Traveler* (1979), which exhibits parallel postmodern devices inspired by Sterne.

Although the novel appears to have proceeded through the factory assembly line of fashionable postmodern prescriptions, it manages to transcend those rubrics with Virgilian shading that makes every part of the novel refer to other parts as in an uroborus, the dominant image of chapter nine. It appears as if a conscientious master plumber was given all the possible blueprints to build an upper-class academic structure in the wilderness, then in a fit of plodding persistence he penned a novel about a working-class man who grew up in squalor and who may or may not be a hero—how can a working-class man be a hero, at least certainly not like Aeneas, Odysseus, or Rinaldo? Any consideration of the many strategies for producing a proletarian novel developed by the Soviets (as, for example, the proletarian laborers in Vasily Shukshin's stories) finds rejection as irrelevant because the book features American characters and landscape.

Each chapter is a verbal portrait of Hamilton highlighting the evil effect he has had on the people around him—just as in Oscar Wilde's *The Picture of Dorian Gray* (1890)—while he keeps his good looks and sanity, and the last slide or "canvas" chapter visually depicts a few footsteps in the snow and then just white snow as if we are viewing an abstract white painting. The indeterminate conclusion challenges the reader to discover just where sanity or insanity lies through the use of the reader's imagination to complete the novel as the reader wishes.

In a detective novel, the conclusion reveals whodunit, thereby assuring all readers that society will identify and remove from society agents of evil. In the early days of its origins in early-eighteenth-century English journalism, the genre expressed the hope that society would be changed and that rampant crime would be suppressed.[7] Today, the genre in America exists primarily as an expression of status quo: Criminals will be caught and prosecuted, society will not change, and prosperity will not be threatened. To produce a detective novel in which crime exists as the wayward fantasy of an author tempted by tabloid success (as in *Peyton Place*), and is replaced with the theme of the difficulty of human relations and the psychological games each sex engages in amid a battle of the sexes reduces the meditation on evil to the most basic stratum of ordinary life. Moreover, in any novel, it is expected to identify with the hero, but instead this novel charts the steps by which the narrator disabuses himself of the hero he has created, creating a character who is both hero and anti-hero, much in the way that Virgil had built a shadowy ambiguity into his hero Aeneas and the building of an empire that would be synonymous with violence and repression.[8]

The demythologizing of the narrator's hero presents three different analyses: Hamilton's daughter Rochelle in her novel depicts the character Alvin Stark (that is, A., whom the narrator calls Hamilton Stark) as being at times possessed by the demon Asmodeus. Originally a Persian demon, Asmodeus has appeared as a trickster demon in Hebrew and Christian writings on magic, a demon associated with lust and anger. Rochelle portrays the character based upon her father as being periodically possessed by the demon. The narrator and the psychoanalyst C. agree that such a presentation based upon primitive magical superstition represents mere wish fulfillment on the part of the daughter and is not in any case an effective way to write a contemporary novel. The narrator clings to his conception of Hamilton as a secretive and naïve holy man, a concept that the psychoanalyst successfully argues against. C. thinks Hamilton embodies the principle of a spiral uroborus, a character who is self-devouring but leaps forward in unpredictable directions, moving ever forward to some catastrophe that will be projected in anger against society. Although the narrator agrees to scrap his own analysis of a holy man, he rejects correctly the psychoanalyst's view as the psychoanalyst's own absurd projection during a momentary breakdown.

Resolving to clarify his interpretation of both A. and his character Hamilton, the narrator drives to A.'s house, only to discover that Stark has vanished, perhaps because Stark can't be placed into any of the categories people want to place him in. Perhaps the nonconformist Stark remains merely the fantasy projection of the narrator. In any case, the narrator has lost his real-life friend A. while the character of his novel on which A. is based (Stark) has disappeared. Has Stark completed the cycle of self-devouring and merely vanished like some mythological creature? Has he committed suicide? Has he died of an accidental fall from Blue Job Mountain during the snowstorm? Has he been assumed up into heaven or nirvana? Has he just moved on to begin a new life somewhere else? Did the narrator murder Stark? Or has the author deliberately involved the reader in a snowstorm of ambiguity? Readers or critics must justify their own interpretation, but in many ways the plot has become irrelevant because its possibilities might be the product of the gossiping neurosis of New Hampshire's residents, including the Barnstead librarian,[9] to fictionalize and sensationalize the ordinary like Metalious.

For the narrator, the process of writing the novel has been self-devouring. In the process of writing the novel he has lost two friends, A. and C., who became characters in the novel. Furthermore, the fundamental foundation of the novel (about a third of the novel) consists of anecdotal stories penned by Rochelle in the vein of realism from her uncompleted novel *The Plumbers' Apprentice* (as if she were the sorcerer's apprentice), as well as the transcripts of tapes by Rochelle who has conducted interviews with some of her father's past wives. Rochelle compares her father's laugh to that of a loon.[10] Once Rochelle and the narrator became lovers, she gave him her novel and all its research material as a gift because she could never publish the novel about her father for fear of hurting him, yet the bestowal and the selections, editing, and modifications the narrator has made from the novel lead to argument and bitter recriminations, destroying the affair between the two lovers. The reader had been previously warned about thinking about a lover in terms of fiction:

> Oh, reader, dear reader, remember this, never permit yourself to invent a woman or a man who is capable of bewildering you while he or she seduces you. You will lose the thread of your argument, you will find your story line impossibly tangled, your plot utterly overthrown, and your faith in your powers of observation and analysis sliced to limp ribbons of insecurity. Call it love, call it whatever you will, but know the risk. If you must, as I must, think of your life as a novel and of the creatures therein as "characters," then unless you keep yourself from falling in love with one of those creatures, you will have to give up the idea of control. You will have to become not an inspired author, but one who is simply not in control of his own novel. It happens, it happens frequently.[11]

The theme of control and independence from others remains the central obsession of the narrator as well as of his hero, Hamilton Stark, whom he admires for his control over his life amid his chaotic difficulties in his relations with others, especially with women and patently crazy-extended family, although Stark cannot remember *anything* when he's drinking or enraged. He idolizes Stark for being self-transcendent in a secular age. While the narrator has rejected the psychoanalyst's interpretation of the spiraling uroboros to diagnose Stark's psychosis, the narrator accepts that image as the very structure upon which the novel is based—he merely rejects the violent interpretation of the image but like so much of what he rejects, he puts to good use in constructing his novel around a novel within an autobiography that is ultimately more social commentary about the gulf between self and society than most novels provide.

The tortured explanation of the failed affair between Rochelle and the narrator comprises a ten-page footnote in chapter nine. Such preposterously long footnotes were pioneered by O'Brien in his posthumous *The Third Policeman* (1967) where the footnotes threaten to overtake the novel. While O'Brien's footnotes mock historical pedantry and scientific research, Banks employs them to run an important psychological subplot. Chapter nine chronicles how the narrator fell in love with Rochelle, the excess of their ecstatic and intimate progress (the narrator, who declares he's an emotional rather than romantic man, finds himself afflicted with a demonic lust, driven crazy by her red hair and sexy low voice), and then the painful epilogue of their aggrieved dissolution in stubborn anger. Entitled "Ausable Chasm," the chapter title appears to be a landscape metaphor for the beauty and mystery of Rochelle's sexuality, but it concludes by becoming symbolic of a sexual and geologic wound in the landscape itself. Since readers receive only the narrator's version of Rochelle and their failed love affair, it is assumed a bias in the explanation, yet the narrator feels threatened by Rochelle's intellect, which shines considerably brighter than his own; fearing her intellect and body will devour and control him, the narrator devours *her* by accepting the gift of her novel and using it in ways she strenuously disapproves. The narrator sounds as honest as he can be, but readers must be aware that veracity—like many aspects of the novel— breathes an ambiguous and indeterminate air. The only aspect of the novel without ambiguity remains the realistically written inserts about the character based upon her father penned by Rochelle, who was raised in Florida and doesn't understand the mystical nature of real estate in New England.[12] Curiously enough, the only criticism that her father Ham offers Rochelle on her novel about him is that it lacks humor,[13] thus providing a parody of the *The New York Times'* criticism of *Family Life*. While the novel has not destroyed the guarded author, the casualties lie all about him as on a battlefield; this operates in startling contrast to the effect of Metalious's novel where all the people on whom she based her characters conspired in helping to destroy *her* life.[14]

Banks depicts his own guilt about how the writing process draws from the life of those around the writer and how such activity wreaks havoc and destruction in the writer's relationships with others, yet to dwell upon the literal reality of such autobiographical elements as they relate to Banks's novel provides no illumination about the novel, resulting only in idle speculation and fruitless gossip removed from the wisdom of the novel. Banks has transformed his own autobiographical elements into something far more interesting and complicated than mere autobiography: Art that echoes and shadows personal difficulties, especially the quandary of quagmires possible in sexual relations offers a thorny theme often transformed into comedy by writers like John Updike or John Irving, but few will present such problems as tragicomedy. The most obvious autobiographical event retails the story of Hamilton Stark who thought he killed his father with a frying pan and fled to Florida.

Another metaphor central to the book's organization presents the matrix, the title of chapter two, which includes a long excursus on the geology, fauna, and flora of the Suncook Valley, as well as a short history of the Abenaki Indians and their leader Horse (from *Family Life*). This chapter presents the environmental and historical parameters that bear a vague relationship to the sociological mentality of the people who later inhabit the Suncook valley, implying

Ironic Conundrum: *Hamilton Stark*

a geographical determinism about the harsh valley. The valley itself offers a matrix whose climate predisposes people to an odd combination of *deeply instinctual* violence, compulsive conformity, and rebellion against such conformity by innovative heroes like Horse, but also by implicated extension people like Metalious and the narrator's friend A. (Hamilton Stark) and presumably the author himself who by the end of the novel has flown beyond the confines of the Suncook valley, something that Metalious never really accomplished. While this chapter remains the most lyrical chapter in the book as it romps through landscape and history, it presses difficulty on the reader because (like chapter one) the purpose of the chapter becomes clear only when retrospectively considered within the framework of the novel. Banks never mentions that there may be an environmental or hereditary determinism present yet such an implication hangs in the air like a menacing bank of cloudy weather on the horizon, providing some a damp bone-chill atmosphere. Although no murder takes place in Banks's novel, nearly all the characters in it appear to be entertaining fantasies of murder or at least the narrator thinks that is what is going on in most people's minds.

While Banks employs realism as occasional insets (the narratives of Rochelle), the novel's repertory remains eclectically postmodern, which makes the novel difficult to discuss, especially because of its circular organization. To walk a reader through any linear organization creates discursive disorder. Such an organization had been pioneered by James Joyce in his novel *Finnegans Wake*, a multicultural mythological encyclopedia written as a multilingual thesaurus prose poem that celebrates a Virgilian relativity of language in a bewildering array of languages, patois, and songs from around the globe. The complex question of structure in Banks's novel was not easily resolved and required reorganization and rewriting of the novel numerous times.[15] The end result produced a novel that foregrounds the narrator and reduces the need for dialogue, except in the vivid realistic insets written by A.'s daughter Rochelle. The narrator appears overly anxious to defend his appropriation of Rochelle's novel (he even appropriates a postcard sent to her from her father) and at times comically stumbles in getting his plot and various aliases straight, as when he cites Betsy Cooper of Rochelle's novel as his Nancy Steele in his novel, although no such character ever appears. In that same passage the narrator also states that in Rochelle's novel the state capital of Concord goes under the name Loudon, "called that both in my novel and in A.'s life."[16] When *he* never calls the state capitol by that name in the novel—but how can a fictional alias be in A.'s life, unless it was the satiric name that Hamilton gave to New Hampshire's capitol.[17]

In the preface to Banks's collected stories, *The Angel on the Roof* (2000), Banks traces his interest in storytelling to his mother, whose gossipy stories were outright autobiographical fantasies, including the one about characters from Metalious's novel *Peyton Place* coming to his mother's house for a Christmas party (Barnstead being 25 miles from Gilmanton). Banks concludes that "in the middle of the 1940s people did not drive 25 miles over snow-covered back roads on a winter night to go to a party given by strangers."[18] Banks sardonically mentions that when visiting his mother in San Diego (which would have been in 1962),[19] she had said that from all of his varied experiences of travel and upbringing he should be able to write another *Peyton Place*.[20] Banks's adroit displacement of *Peyton Place* remains both obsessive and convoluted.

At the conclusion of imagined event three from chapter one, the recluse who lives in his own tomb declares he's luckier than most, "I got what I wanted, not what I deserved,"[21] thus riffing on the deathbed quip of Metalious who said, "If I had to do it over again it would be easier to be poor. Before I was successful, I was as happy as anyone gets."[22] Banks remained, for a while poor, and retained his sanity with a novel that was a literary success and thus evaded the terrors and pitfalls of the celebrity world. In the Biblical story of Noah, it wasn't Ham who was cursed but his offspring.

By the end of the novel, the novel's narrator has ironically come to resemble, oddly enough, the novel's opening definition of an ideal hero: An anti-hero projects someone above the throes of love and above its need, a man who may or may not be sane, like Hamilton[23] or the narrator. On a second reading, readers may question whether the whole novel merely enacts the narcissistic ravings of a madman who, at times acts out the self-aggrandizing comedy of a twit and refuses not only the prospect of love, family, community, and society, but rejects, in his extreme misanthropy, all of human nature and culture. He pontificates over his own Nietzschean will-to-power republic of the ideal self for the sake of his own sanity. At least the narrator's friend A. (Hamilton Stark), attempted reconciliation between self and society, something the opportunistic narrator apparently never seriously attempts.

One might argue that book concerns a narrator-persona of Banks and the hall of shattered mirrors he has constructed, through an oblique and baroque confessional memoir. The hall of mirrors motif, perhaps inspired by the effective use of the imagery near the conclusion of Orson Welles's 1947 cult masterpiece *The Lady from Shanghai*,[24] was decidedly popular in the late sixties, appearing in Robert Stone's *A Hall of Mirrors* (1967) and John Fowles's *The Magus* (1966), which bears a glancing resemblance to Banks's novel. Both anti-heroes have a failed romance, both have an older mysterious spiritual mentor who proffer paradoxes and psychological games, and the reality of both novels appear to vanish like smoke at the indeterminate conclusions. While Fowles's novel enjoys an exotic setting on a Greek island, Banks's novel endures an equally remote but less romantic setting amid the crusty snow of New Hampshire. One might even interpret Banks's novel as a parody of Fowles's religious mysticism, as well as Fowles's popular middle-class appeal. Anecdotes, witness testimony, phone calls, tape monologues, and notebook excerpts function in *Hamilton Stark* much the same way as the fantastic masques in Fowles's novel. Bristling backwoods blue-collar common sense displaces the European pageant of history and phantasmagoric philosophy.

In the end, the hero of Banks's novel becomes the reader who must identify with the writer's conception of the novel in order to enter the labyrinthine maze of the plot and examine the plot's false leads, those maze-like dead ends. While both author and reader provide the prototype of the hero, the novel contains no hero, since a projection of heroism can be only Nietzschean fantasy born of narcissism or criminal solipsism. One possible interpretation may be that the narrator has murdered Hamilton Stark and become his own hero (in reality a Dostoevsky-like anti-hero) by seducing the daughter of the man he admires, murdering her father, and intimidating her. Yet, no hypothesis offers real satisfaction. On a more cheerful note, one may see the vanishing of Stark as a mystical ascension to the heavens (or parody thereof), or the mysterious disappearance of an unusual man like the famous disappearance of the American writer Ambrose Bierce.

Indeterminacy as an element in Western narrative first appeared the *Decameron* (1349–53) by Giovanni Boccaccio where during a plague, a group of seven young men and three women friends retreat to an estate, telling stories to each other for ten days. Either a narrator's preface or the stories themselves provide glancing allegories or criticism of other behavior, especially on the topics of romance, sex, ethics, and religion, but ultimately it is not possible for the reader to draw up a complete scenario of who had nighttime affairs as the women bitterly compete for the privileged men's attention and admiration, although some conjectures remain plausible. The reader (the audience was women who would debate and judge the characters) becomes a teased but delighted victim to the varied ingenious flirtations and their coy subtleties. The stories include material with humanistic themes as well as implied philosophic ambiguities encased in accomplished oral narrative.

Banks's novel without a hero imitates the circular stasis of the uroborous that can be shattered only if the reader discovers a way *into* the labyrinth of repetition. The reader may then *rewrite* the novel from its splintered shards, assembling pieces at will. By discovering a way out of traditional plot, Banks somewhat recapitulates what Gabriele d'Annunzio did before him in novels like *The Flame of Life* (1900), which eliminated plot in favor of erotic lyricism, although Banks's subject consists of the project of self-actualization with ironic echoes.

By providing an open conclusion, Banks slyly parodies the mystery genre as well as psychological conventions in biography, arguing that we cannot really know anyone, since life remains a mysterious process and that mysterious flux lies behind our feeble attempts to interpret what in the end cannot be reduced to our unstable projective illusions.

Banks's masterpiece questions the very presumptions of narrative literature itself while challenging the achievement of its great masterworks by outperforming in the postmodern techniques that emerged from the Second World War (especially the narrative monologues of Samuel Beckett and Robbe-Grillet), becoming so dominant in South American fiction during the 1960s. Yet in raising such questions, the book deprives itself of both an upper-class audience and general readership. What elite connoisseur would read a novel about the enlightenment of a misanthropic, cursing New Hampshire plumber, even if he speaks several European languages and Inuit when drunk, and whom the author compares to a Sufi mystic, Zen master, and Jesus Christ (and himself to disciple Peter)[25] before turning on the reader with accusations of cultural prejudice for underestimating the virtues and mystical abilities of his character? Where is the sanity of that? Few educated readers might be aware of the dynamic connection between plumbing and literature pioneered by Sir John Harington (1561–1612) when he invented the first flush toilet (about 1563).[26] In his 1591 translation of Ludovico Ariosto's *Orlando Furioso* (1516), Harington jokingly transformed the sculpted stone statues of famous Italian ladies (Canto 42) into a digression on the serpentine aesthetic of pipes and the eugenic wonders of proper English plumbing, one of England's greatest contributions to civilization.

A general reader might be interested in Banks's tabloid melodrama of event one or two which the author has neither exploited nor erased, yet such a reader is not likely to be fascinated by the novel's considerations of Søren Kierkegaard's ideas concerning repetition which demands a reader read the novel more than once to discover the depth of its baroque humor. Like Hamilton himself, any reader might be more likely to be interested in the actor Errol Flynn, who was at the epicenter of the Cuban Revolution, writing articles about Fidel Castro for the *New York Journal American*; Flynn described gun battles over five days spent with rebels and how he took a bullet in the leg. Although Flynn's last movie *Cuban Rebel Girls* (1959) was panned by critics, his neglected documentary *Cuban Story* has garnered renewed respect.[27] Banks will employ the legend of Flynn in his next novel.

5

THE LIMITS OF LIBERALISM:
The Book of Jamaica

> Then I fired four more times at the motionless body where the bullets lodged without leaving a trace. And it was like knocking four quick times on the door of unhappiness.
> —Albert Camus, *The Stranger*, translated by Mathew Ward

A 1976 Guggenheim Fellowship allowed Russell Banks to live in Jamaica for 18 months. He brought his wife, Mary Gunst, and their three children with him and rented a small house. By the time he left, his marriage had disintegrated, but along with some indulgence in drink and marijuana, his freedom from the routine of teaching permitted him to complete his long labors over *Hamilton Stark*, place the publication of a new collection of short stories, *The New World* (1978), with the University of Illinois Press, and begin the draft of a new novel about a character in Jamaica.

While there are some parallel themes linking the new novel with the completed novel, Banks set off in a new direction that employs more realism while retaining a simplified postmodern relativity immersed in irony. *The Book of Jamaica* (1980) reads more engagingly, its density enlivened by a more relaxed and immediately meditative prose, while once more investigating the theme of identity within the framework of a quest novel. *Hamilton Stark* had concluded with an ironic ambiguity that appeared to be a self-devouring liberation while depicting the gossipy paranoia of New Hampshire culture. *The Book of Jamaica* will arrive at conclusions about the nature of race and culture in society. While it follows the quest of the narrator, the larger picture painted reveals a social context far more arresting, extroverted, and ultimately more shocking than the cold valleys of New Hampshire.

The narrator of *The Book of Jamaica*, as in *Hamilton Stark*, presents a college anthropology teacher on sabbatical. The novel is divided into four parts, the first part being "Captain Blood," a reference to the swashbuckling movie made from Rafael Sabatini's novel that made Errol Flynn, a Tasmanian who identified with his Irish father's roots, a much-celebrated movie star in his very first Hollywood appearance. Having rented a house, the professor becomes fascinated by rumors surrounding the island's most famous settler who attempted to revive Jamaican tourism and whose last wife, the actress Patrice Wymore, still lived and farmed on Jamaica.

Flynn was a legend during his lifetime and he continues to be one today. He starred in many movies, wrote several books, had strange and wild friends, and it's debatable whether he was more famous for his wit or his drinking. Having died young and still handsome of a massive heart attack at the age of 49, he still remains something of an enigma, the subject of numerous biographies, memoirs, and unauthenticated rumors, even the subject of fiction.[1] The narrator becomes fascinated by the story of the brutal murder of a young woman and tries to unravel the mystery—was Flynn or his personal doctor involved in the murder, and if so, to what extant? In the Sabatini novel and in the movie, Flynn plays an Irish doctor who becomes the whimsical victim of English injustice. He's sold into slavery, escapes, and becomes a good and just pirate. The anthropologist appears fixated on the sensationalism of blood as a literal reality. In the novel and film, the surname Blood contrasts ironically with the reputed noble blood of English aristocracy—Peter Blood, the good doctor of humble Irish birth incarnates the only real nobleman in the epic, a thought that never occurs to the professor.

While trying to solve the murder through an alternate reality scenario, it is as if the anthropologist attempts to construct a complicated murder story by penning a baroque script akin to Orson Welles's *The Lady from Shanghai* (1948), for which Flynn leant Welles his sailing yacht for the sultry Caribbean boat scenes featuring Rita Hayworth in a modest but strikingly stylish bathing suit.

In his effort to unravel the mystery he conjures, the professor researches Maroon society, befriends a number of working-class Jamaicans, and descends into an underworld of secret late-night bars and domino players. Terron Musgrave, a friendly Maroon Rastafarian with leonine dreadlocks in his mid-thirties (the professor's age), often stays at the professor's house. The professor becomes fascinated by Musgrave's poetic patois and cultural orientation. While Terron has an apocalyptic belief in the end of Western civilization which deepens his belief in good deeds, the narrator's awareness of evil merely confirms his passive skeptical pessimism.

Like a contemporary Don Quixote, the professor sets out to confirm his belief in bookish Western rationality and causal thinking, only to be befuddled by realities that don't correspond to his cultural preconceptions. The earnest would-be sleuth uncovers contradictory but firmly held beliefs about the murder of the young wife. Terron sees Flynn as a guilty mythic *prince of darkness* who arrogantly laughs in the face of goodness and who practices the dark arts of magic, a literal Captain Blood. Evan Smith, a friend of the convicted murderer DeVries, thinks Flynn was a bad man, irrational, a decadent sybarite, but that the local butcher DeVries did indeed commit the murder, giving a sociological portrait of DeVries which makes sense to the professor when he converts the social interpretation into a psychological portrait. Others think

The Limits of Liberalism: *The Book of Jamaica* 47

that Flynn or his doctor committed the murder and that Flynn participated in or coerced a cover-up.

An elderly cook in a restaurant who knew DeVries, insists DeVries was evil and Errol Flynn had nothing whatever to do with the case, except that the murder happened on property he owned. Perplexed by varied views and the lack of evidence he uncovers from visits to various sites associated with the murder, his skepticism plunges him into a hellish depression—the solution to the murder vanishes into an unsolvable puzzle about evil. This "Captain Blood" section of the novel ends with a symbolic but real contemplation of the cliff hole through which the dismembered victim's body was stuffed before plunging into the surf below. He idly yearns for a Dantean vision whereby he could speak to the ghost of Flynn and discover the medieval certainties that governed Dante's vision of good and evil, but that, of course, is not to be. He is left with the void of ambiguity and the mute landscape of crashing waves. His attempt to verify gossip achieves nothing, as in *Hamilton Stark*.

Also as in *Hamilton Stark*, there is a society corrupted by Hollywood and legends from the celebrity world, as well as the plot of a murder mystery that comes to nothing, yet the crime in this novel is real, not imagined. While the portrait of the narrator in *Hamilton Stark* offers a satire on rural New England society, the portrait of the narrator here raises questions about how Westerners perceive Jamaican society. It creates a suspenseful drama of mystery about that society, even more fascinating than the quixotic investigator, since the people he meets exude a self-confident aura beyond the habit of the skeptical scholar who recedes into the background while the peopled landscape of Jamaica presents a more vivid and exciting foreground. The narrator's a blind tourist in a culture he doesn't understand.

The novel's opening epigraph from Octavio Paz's "Laughter and Penitence" suggests that while Western cultural discourse is causal and linear, its counterpoint in Meso-American culture proceeds by way of analogy and correspondence, metamorphosis and masks, by way of changing images that evolve into their opposites, completing a circle through the agency of changing rhythms. The epigraph that opens the book's next section, "Nyamkopong," the name of Terron's Maroon town and the town where a white Jamaican friend of the professor asks him to look up a Colonel Phelps, cites the European Marxist theoretician Walter Benjamin: "Only he who has made his dialectical peace with the world can grasp the concrete." That is, only a man who accepts the process of change around him can understand what is actually happening in the world. The professor decides that in order to understand Jamaican society, he must attempt to enter into it, and the irony is, that although he thinks he understands what's happening, he obviously doesn't have a clue.

The questing and seeking consciousness of the narrator now adopts a sardonic tone and he becomes self-righteously politically correct in orientation. It is as if the novel were to begin all over again with a different perspective. The first book now appears like a discarded draft, false start, or confessional nightmare related to the baleful cultural influence of Hollywood, but its purpose and irony at this point is withheld from the reader. It functions asa rubric to ignore tourism and white Jamaicans like Flynn (and the upper strata of society he moved in) in order to focus more closely on the Maroons, the African descendents of the Ashanti tribe that successfully resisted both the Spanish and British colonials on Jamaica. The professor recounts settling his wife and children into the house he's rented, telling them "we will not be tourists,"[2] and that they will see only natives. He resolves to behave strictly as a social scientist doing research.

Turmoil and anxiety grip Jamaica during this period because the first non-white Jamaican President Michael Manley has socialist leanings and the island suffers from capital flight amid the exodus of many fearful whites. Despite the anthropologist's resolve to begin with an open mind, he can't escape his academic and religious background, imagining himself in "an episode of *The Pilgrim's Progress* and everyone I met there and every place I went to had a strictly allegorical function and no real life of its own—except for me, who, alone among the characters, was also the reader of this book."[3] But an allegorical consciousness (as in John Bunyan or Dante) is European, neither Meso-American nor African. While the narrator does not quest for his own identity, he does have a quest to discover a new understanding of history through comprehending the identity of the Maroons, yet he remains bounded, limited, and haunted by his background.

The writer finds himself admiring the impeccable taste of Jamaicans in their appreciation of music, comparing it to the cultural taste of late-nineteenth-century architecture in New Orleans or eighteenth-century New England, how they "could instantly distinguish the phony from the authentic, the derivative from the original, the merely sentimental from the genuinely romantic."[4] The professor also enjoys the many small family shops that are combination bars and grocery stores without an awareness that such establishments can still be found today, for example, in County Monaghan in Ireland.

Arriving in Nyamkopong, he has his first meeting with Terron whom he at first dismisses as a hustler but will later befriend. He then confers with Colonel Phelps, a pompous Maroon with English manners who invites his guest to the celebration of Cudjoe's birthday, Cudjoe being the renowned and legendary Maroon freedom-fighter. Terron introduces the narrator to his spiritual father, Wendell O. Mann, the Maroon secretary of state, who gives a long rambling talk about the history of the Maroons and the English Queen which contains more comic myth than anything resembling history, yet prefatory to that the narrator fumbles—disorientated, bewildered, and so insecure that he denies being an educated man and if to prove it, he keeps pace with the secretary's rum drinking. The absurd myth contains a glancing folk wisdom that gives the anthropologist some insight about how the Maroons perceive white society, yet that realization does not come to him until the next week during the festivities of Cudjoe, when he begins to understand the circling dances the celebrants perform in order to enter the truth of mythic time (as with the Uroborus of *Hamilton Stark*).

But first he returns home to attend an upper-class white party, finding himself an outsider to the blatant racism at the party. After the party, he reflects on how people put labels on others and can see no farther than their noses. Suddenly, he realizes how alone he is, adrift without any friends he can identify with, guilty for being aloof, never taking sides in the battles for love or moral justice, but merely approving or disapproving of people in a casual way. He decides to despise those who hate others because of race or class and now attempts common cause with those whom he approves of—the Maroons—but doesn't understand, even if in doing so, it will sunder him from his family who dreams of returning to the familiarity of New Hampshire. The narrator begins a quest for self-renewal, repudiating the diary tourist travelogue of "Captain Blood," the first section of the book. From this vantage point, one can retrospectively realize the depth of his deluded *conversion*. Although he told his family they were not to be tourists, he and they had lived as tourists, until his conscience revolted at the ugly party. On January 6th, he invites Terron to live with his family and he often stays there.

He commits himself to acting for the Maroon cause of greater independence, favoring the secretary over Phelps, whose faction supports assimilation with the central government. The novel begins to read like a Puritan testimonial of his ministry and possible martyrdom. Mr. Mann, smiling, mysteriously tells the anthropologist that when he returns from his visit to New England, "You will see what you want to see." Perhaps this is echoing the mysterious line (but comic, about a smell machine) from the sergeant in Flann O'Brien's *The Third Policeman*, "The next time you come here," MacCruiskeen promised, "you will see surprising things."[5] By now the anthropologist and Musgrave have become close friends and the anthropologist has adopted Mann, who calls him son, as his mentor for Maroon culture. Before returning back to Jamaica alone on April 1st, April Fool's Day, the professor drives down on weekends from New Hampshire to Boston in order to conduct more research on the history of the Maroons, providing the reader with a summary of his research.

On his return to Jamaica, the professor has become a Robinson Crusoe with his man Friday, Terron, on a New World island, except the island is not deserted but populated by displaced descendants of the Ashanti tribe and a ruling colonial class with two tiers, the upper-class white colonials and those native Maroons who desire assimilation. Furthermore, there is another cultural split among all natives concerning Rastafarians—some believing them to be righteous brothers; others dismissing them as dope addicts and thieves. Mann resents the unpredictable but secretly arranged police raids and arrests for growing marijuana as a violation of the 1738 treaty, which gives the Maroons legal jurisdiction over all matters except capital murder. Correctly blaming Phelps, the town's mayor, for these illegal incursions, Mann engages in a bitter feud with Phelps, who takes bribes from the government, rationalizing his position as necessary for an inevitable growth toward island unity and market prosperity.

Real trouble begins when Phelps demands that Mann hand over the treaty to the government so that a copy of it can be made.[6] Fearing that a copy instead of the original will be returned, Mann angrily refuses. Having spent so much time listlessly drinking rum in Nyamkopong, the tourist begins to suffer from a status crisis, fearing that he is slowly becoming an ordinary man with little purpose and not the social intellectual distinguished from other ordinary people.[7] After informing the narrator that he will soon show him the sacred Peace Cave where Cudjoe signed the historic treaty with the English, Musgrave agrees to accompany the now doubting and somewhat paranoid anthropologist back to his rented house in Port Antonio (on the northeastern end of the island), first stopping for a visit at Musgrave's aunt's house in Kingston where he discovers some temporary relief in Jamaican communal life. With the car's motor running, Mann puts his hand through the driver's window, resting it on the narrator's shoulder, telling the anthropologist that while he doesn't know he will return once more, he knows he will.[8]

For the third subsection, the narrative shifts from first person discourse to the second person in order to dramatize demonic possession. Now known to the natives as *Johnny*, the anthropologist participates like a puppet in the intrigue; he is under the control of an *obi*, a shaman, Mann who says, "You return to the ground against which you can see your otherness, and so you go on seeing yourself as if for the first time.... You are becoming your own stranger."[9] It is a clear allusion to Albert Camus's novel *The Stranger* (1942), a study of cultural alienation based upon the Cain and Abel story, where on the spur of the moment the anti-hero, overcome by emotion (symbolized by a blinding sun), commits a murder in the context of a dispute; he cannot explain, nor understand, nor show remorse for the murder, since he neither believes in the social community nor God. Vague unconscious fears of racism may have prompted the murder since the man he shot was an Arab who drew his knife. In contrast to the anti-death-penalty Biblical story where Cain after murdering Abel, finds himself exiled as an outcast. The French government executes Meursault by guillotine.

A central irony in Camus's novel is that the Cain and Abel story is a fundamental story revered in both the Judeo-Christian world and the Islamic Arab world. Meursault's act of murder is absurd enough because Meursault himself doesn't understand exactly why it happened, but additional irony accumulates when the civilized world does not honor its religious traditions. In the end, Meursault absurdly appears to be executed primarily because he's an atheist, thus further highlighting the civilized world's prejudice and intolerance. The plot illustrated Camus's philosophy of the absurd, which reflected a world that lacked clarity and meaning—the novel was prompted by the haphazard horrors, racism, and holocausts of World War II that left so many people senselessly dead. While the world lacked meaning and purpose, as history so often illustrates, that does not excuse humankind from morality or the need to search for hope, which Camus often saw in the hope that rebellion incarnates.[10]

The rest of Banks's novel will illustrate Camus's theme as it relates to race in Jamaica, except that the psychology of the alienated character in Camus's novel will be reversed: As the trial of the insensitive Meursault proceeds, he will become more aware of his humanity and responsibility as his prosecutors become less, while in Banks's novel the tourist will become less aware of his humanity the more he becomes involved in the trials of the Maroon community, and in the end the anthropologist's upper-class white tourist status will ironically exempt him completely from common justice as if the institution of slavery still flourished. Camus is adept at probing the confusion and bitterness of Meursault's mentality, just as Nelson Algren had penetrated the mind of a criminal in *Never Come Morning* (1942), published the same year as Camus's novel and translated that same year into French by Jean-Paul Sartre.[11]

Employment of the second person perspective creates an alienated strangeness in the narrative, born out of guilt and the desire of the narrator to distance his actions from responsibility, denying his ultimate actions. The theme that a shaman has possessed the narrator freights much irony because it's a magical explanation for a crime committed by a Western rationalist, a college teacher of causal history and the lessons learned from history, a self-professed liberal who loathes violence and racism—and as it turns out, in theory rather than practice. One other possible reason for the shift to the second person narrative may be that it is a devilish parody of Terron's manner of talking. Musgrave often talks of "I and I," referring to his better spiritual self and his more faulty self, a version of the *Ka* and *Ba* of Egyptian spirituality, the soul and the body. The narrator's address to "You" may be an address to the strange demon in him since he believes he's become possessed: "You" represents the demonic other whom he denies to be a part of his self.

On the level of metafiction, the use of the second person may been seen as an accusation against the reader because by now the reader is a little more than halfway through the narrative and it's natural for the reader to identify with the anthropologist's liberal and considerate analysis of what he sees, so that the narrative switches from the traditional device of employing a hero to the presentation of an objectified anti-hero. Unless the reader catches the purpose of this shift, the reader is in danger of reading the narrative unconsciously in a racist manner, but if the reader understands the shift the reader will see that the narrative offers a confession of how even well-meaning liberals— because of their race-isolated backgrounds, which provide a breeding ground for distrust and paranoia—can spontaneously commit heinous racist crimes that are irrational and absurd. Banks had used confession with ironic context in *Relation*—here the irony is more broadly contextual than prismatic. Like the *innocent* Captain Amasa Delano of Herman Melville's "Benito Cereno" who finds himself symbolized by an albatross, a somnambulistic white noddy,[12] the tourist becomes another New England insensitive sleepwalker trolling through the events of his own cruelty. Like Delano, the visitor also victimizes members of the Ashanti tribe.[13]

The use of such an unusual and startling hinge in the novel, to switch the narrator from hero to anti-hero in mid-book, brings with it a high degree of risk, yet the switch remains so dramatic and thought-provoking that the artistic device can be judged successful as it provokes a reversal of perspective in the mind of a reader. Since the ironies are so oblique and contain an unexpected vantage point, a puzzled reader might need to read the book twice to understand the novel fully, as is the case with *Hamilton Stark*. Reviewers who labeled the book as merely *travelogue* missed the boat by failing to realize that the narrator is a fictional character, not Banks, the author, although parallels between the character and the authorial voice bespeak guilty hubris, as in *Hamilton Stark*.

Everything the narrator sees or experiences shines with a shimmering irony—from the Disney world billboards amid muddy slums in Kingston to the liberal anthropologist's wild prophecies of the decay of London and Paris, while Kingston, Caracas, and Mexico City rise as futuristic beacons of cleanliness.[14] Banks poignantly satirizes the lunatic rant-raps that radical liberals are sometimes prone to utter as well as the futility of becoming patronizingly involved in events that do not concern outsiders.

After his trip to Kingston, the anthropologist visits varied locales associated with Flynn, of the initiatory "Captain Blood" section; now the reader can retrospectively understand the ironic significance of the narrator's fanciful meditation on *obi* possession concerning Flynn. The anthropologist concludes that, "Tourism, more than any other single industry, corrupts and corrodes a people's integrity and independence."[15] This white writer would be unlikely to say this of Greek, Chinese, or Egyptian tourism, but he self-righteously parades this nonsense to satisfy his politically correct interpretation of life in Jamaica. Flynn did much to help attract tourism to Jamaica and by doing so improved the Jamaican economy, which needed all the help it could get, although Flynn's venture in white-water bamboo rafting never turned a profit. The narrator thinks that because he travels about the island with Terron as his guide, he's not a tourist, he's a part of Jamaican society—in short, and he's a delusional narcissist.

Amid mounting intrigue, the anthropologist agrees to visit Colonel Bowra at Gordon Hall where Ashanti customs and secret passwords are more strictly authentic; he's disorientated by the African rituals, and despite his library research on the Ashanti, the incompetent anthropologist, in a scene of comic ridiculousness, doesn't know the name of even a single Ashanti god. Since he has a working Japanese van, he agrees to act as messenger between the rugged, remote cockpit country (jungle countryside riddled with meteor impact depressions) of Nyamkopong and the more populous town of Gordon Hall, so that the two Maroon communities will be united in closer contact to resist what appears to them as a government grab at their semiautonomous legal status. The anthropologist enjoys driving over the tortuous and sometimes dangerous terrain, picking up hitchhikers, and stopping in small bars, thus getting a wider sociological picture of Jamaica.

He attends a Policeman's Ball as the only white person there, yet he has nothing in common with the people—he's performing proletarian research, mingling with the natives to satisfy his quixotic ego. He cannot have any meaningful conversation with anyone, so he gets drunk like an alienated clown and passes out. Pleased with himself, the anthropologist thinks this was a wonderful *experience* as he now appears to collect experiences as if they were trophies for his liberal display of humanitarian self-satisfaction.

The third part of the novel, "Obi," begins with third-person narration, the anthropologist referring to himself as the American. In a brief scene, the American writer agrees to try to arrange and pay for a mercy murder of the sick mother (dying of cancer) belonging to an acquaintance of Terron Musgrave. The matter-of-fact tone makes the scene shocking, but as events turn out, he forgets either to arrange for the murder or even to ask Mann to pray for her. The Rasta's mother miraculously gets better and the Rasta feels indebted to *Johnny* for his help.

The American anthropologist is now called Johnny, the moniker by which Maroons refer to good white men. Johnny drives a noisy group of men from Gordon Hall to Nyamkopong. Johnny doesn't understand the real purpose of the trip—to murder Phelps for treason, something accomplished the first night they spend in Nyamkopong, Phelps being shot twice at close range, once in each eye. Johnny appears to have become an accessory to murder yet that never occurs to him.

The fourth and final part of the novel, "Dread," opens with an epigraph from Hugo Ball, the Dada anarchist who cofounded the famous Cabaret Voltaire in Zürich patronized by Vladimir Lenin, James Joyce, and Tristan Tzara among others,[16] meditating on the difficulty of the Socratic maxim, "Know thyself." This functions as a choral reminder that Johnny does not know himself. Even the professor's estranged wife, who spends her time in a different white social circle, now calls him Johnny as if he's become a stranger.

Terron walks to Johnny's house in Port Antonio, informing him the police have killed Benjie, his young ganga-growing partner, shooting him five times. This happened after they raided the House of Dread where the Rastas in Nyamkopong were sleeping. Terron believes Benjie to be innocent. While it's not clear at this point who actually murdered Phelps, the murder was performed with Benjie's stolen gun, found under his pillow in the morning raid. The other brethren were beaten with billyclubs. Terron warns Johnny he may be deported because he's a foreigner who's been associating with the brethren.

Johnny flirts with Yvonne, a barmaid prostitute, and admits losing track of his life; he keeps late hours playing dominoes and drinking, perhaps having an affair with Yvonne. The professor had experienced a night of infidelity last April with a woman named Dorothy. The police stop by his house a couple of times and politely check his visa and the grounds. The professor's wife scolds that he's got a big head and that he can't tell the difference between the country's economics and his personal experiences.[17] The owners of the house suddenly appear, pitching their house at a bargain price; they attempt blackmail when the renters express no interest in buying the house.

The owners come to cart away their furniture, effects, and appliances piecemeal as they are cheaply sold. The professor's wife informs him she and the children are leaving the next morning. He agrees it's best for the children to return to New Hampshire, but declares he's staying on until August. He's now a squatter; when the electric company terminates the power, he uses candles. When evicted, he departs with his typewriter and effects, boarding a bus (the van has died) to Nyamkopong where Mann is not pleased at his sudden arrival, telling him that Phelps's widow at first blamed him and Colonel Bowra for murdering Benjie. Mann tells the professor that it was indeed Benjie who committed the murder: Mrs. Phelps had hired him to kill her husband because she wanted to marry a wealthier man. The police had shot Benjie when he panicked and pulled out the gun to shoot a policeman. There was no mystery. Mann will assume Phelps's post and rent his house from the widow for a pittance.

The professor argues with Terron as he becomes fearful for his life, rejecting Terron's reasoning that since he's white, his life is protected. Terron continues to be worried about his marijuana crop amid the complex intrigue surrounding its harvest. The professor takes a bus to Kingston and proceeds to hitchhike to Gordon Hall where people celebrate election day. He wants to tell Bowra the news about Phelps. Amid the dancing and drinking festivities, a large muscular youth becomes angry at the white professor's presence, pushing him against a building. The professor's kit bundle breaks open, the kettle rolling downhill. His machete falls between them. The youth reaches down for it, the writer kicks his hand away, picks up the machete, and severs the young man's right hand at the wrist in a scene reminiscent of the sudden murder in Camus's novel *The Stranger*. In both novels, racial paranoia ignites violence.

The enigmatic refrain, "You will see what you want to see," spoken hauntingly by Mann and Bowra, functions as leitmotif prophecy in the novel. In the end, the professor will indeed see himself as a violent racist like Camus's Meursalt, a real and not fictional Captain Blood. The Errol Flynn theme has become ironic. While the professor was not vouchsafed an interview with Flynn in hell, the story the professor recounts to the reader is a monologue by one of the damned confessing sin while displaying elements of denial, much like the narrators in some of Edgar Allan Poe's short stories such as "The Tell-Tale Heart" and "The Cask of Amontillado."

Although the professor has not killed anyone, he has committed a violent crime. A prominent politician at the party reluctantly agrees to bundle the professor off to the airport in the back of a pickup truck. Johnny's white skin has exempted him from justice. Ironically, the messages the professor wanted to impart to Bowra are already known. Not only has the professor's attempted identification with the Maroon community been a failure, he has harmed a member of it and reinforced the most egregious stereotype of violent white colonialism and privilege in a manner reminiscent of slavery. Banks wrote to Robert Niemi that in the context of a radicalized society like Jamaica he, "couldn't avoid being implicated by race and that's one of the themes"[18] in the novel.

Like Zora Neale Hurston, the anthropologist character had a grant to write in Jamaica. Hurston had a 1936 Guggenheim Fellowship to study magical practices in the Caribbean[19] and Banks had a 1976 Guggenheim Fellowship to write a novel. Like Banks, Hurston was intensely productive during the Guggenheim, writing *Their Eyes Were Watching God* (1937), within seven weeks at the end of her grant.[20] The white anthropologist in Banks's novel

The Limits of Liberalism: *The Book of Jamaica*

appropriates a similar approach to field work that Hurston adopted—that of a participant in the culture, the kind of anthropological approach that Margaret Mead later popularized. Most critics assert Hurston couldn't satisfactorily resolve the dilemma of simultaneous researcher-participant in her memoir *Tell My Horse* (1938).[21] Hurston had spent only three months in Jamaica before moving on to Haiti where she was more interested in researching Voodoo, yet like Banks's anthropologist she mingled in the Jamaican mountains with the Accompong Maroons.[22] Having read Hurston, Banks went to Accompong and realized that a white participant-observer would be thoroughly excluded; he heightened the situation by having his fictional anthropologist deluded with drink and ganga as he mingled nearly exclusively with men. Hurston thought Jamaican culture heartily misogynist, paying much attention to surviving African customs (as does Banks) and status variations in skin coloring.[23] In vivid contrast to Hurston, the white anthropologist lumbers in gross ignorance as an academic hack; his world remains conditioned by his absurdity, lending a shocking, political humor. Camus urged people to recognize the absurd, but not to acquiesce to it, and to maintain probity in the face of moral uncertainty.[24] Banks critiques the limits of white Western anthropology as a hubristic, delusional, and corrupt enterprise.

Both *Hamilton Stark* and *The Book of Jamaica* present narrators immersed in their own victimization, as in the early novels of Algren, like *Never Come Morning* and *A Walk on the Wild Side* (1956), for which Banks penned an introduction in its 1998 reprint. Both of Banks's early novels reflect and refract shards of Banks's autobiography with a transmuted and transforming artistic irony. While the violence of *Hamilton Stark* remains imaginary, the violence in *The Book of Jamaica* is presented as real. In both novels, Banks depicts how gossip, narcissism, and intrigue corrupt society as he provides meditations on the cultural signatures that afflict each respective society, as well as the persona relating the stories. Both books satirize presumptions while offering a trenchant critique on the limitations of traditional thinking. Freedom itself appears beyond the grasp of people caught in the web of their history, culture, and individual delusions. Although both novels are masterful in their peculiar ironies, understanding the role that innovative technique plays in the novels remains essential to understanding how Banks creates oblique perspectives on self and society. While these novels offer complex and compelling intellectual puzzles, Banks was not able to establish a popular readership.

6

Homeric Grotesque: *Trailerpark*

> Alis, alas, she broke the glass! Liddell lokker through the leafery, ours is mistery of pain.*
>
> —James Joyce, *Finnegans Wake*

Trailerpark (1981) contains 13 linked short stories, the first and last bracketing stories relating more intimately to the other stories, but since all the stories focus on the residents of this small trailer park of ten rentals (two trailers are unoccupied), characters interact with each other. The stories are not organized chronologically; they become like concentric rings in a pond when a stone is tossed, each story reverberating in irony or pathos to each other as they rebound off each other. Russell Banks says, "I structured it as I would structure a novel, with an arc of the narrative but it's more fragmented than that. It was an attempt to write a novel with stories or in stories."[1] Both time and character impinge and echo through other stories, recollecting the past, displaying how the past informs the future. Like *Hamilton Stark* and *The Book of Jamaica*, the reader must read the book twice to comprehend its intricacies.

Set in imaginary Catamount, the geographical center of New Hampshire, where in real life there is nothing—no town, no houses, just woods, a road, and a mill—the same mythical place in central New Hampshire where Banks's two-chapter story "The Conversion" was located. *Trailerpark* remains the most complex collection of stories that Banks has published. The opening story provides character revelation through short statements by members of the trailer park community. While the narration for the most part remains

---

*Liddell refers to Lewis Carroll's friend Alice Liddell with reference to *Through the Looking Glass*, but Liddell, given the context of Greek and Roman references on the page, also refers to Liddell-Scott, the editor of the landmark Greek-English dictionary, a theme which connects immediately to "lokker through the leafery" and the "mistery" of language, arching to the larger theme of doubleness sketched in the passage as a whole.

realistic, the writer sometimes breaks the frame of the realistic narrative in various ways.

Linked or intertwined stories are nearly universal. More notable examples are the many inset stories in Homer's *Odyssey,* some stories from *One Thousand and One Nights,* the medieval Germanic epics *Parzival* and *Tristan and Isolde,* the Renaissance epics *Orlando Innamorato* and *Orlando Furioso.* More recently, stories linked by sociological theme had prominence, especially James Joyce's *Dubliners* (1914) and Sherwood Anderson's *Winesburg, Ohio* (1919). Both Joyce and Anderson attempted to explode romantic notions of middle-class propriety as well as expose pathology, stagnation, and backwardness within the received moral tradition; both employed irony within a symbolic but gritty realism centered upon a sophisticated psychological examination of characters.[2]

Banks's stories address the working class people who think they are middle class (a notion nearly all Americans who make less than $50,000 subscribe to). The middle class,[3] including the lower middle class, of homeowners struggling to make mortgage payments on their houses, tends to disdain trailer parks as hillbilly ghettos where the "culture" of guns, misanthropic outsiders, and dysfunctional families proliferate like toxic weeds. When a young drifter searching for material to write about, Banks had once dwelt in a Florida trailer park; his stories humanize the plight of such inhabitants while re-enforcing the popular stereotype of trailer parks as a refuge of desperate outsiders. The collection of stories belongs to the Gothic genre and its themes include abortion, arson, drug dealing, insanity, murder, racial and religious prejudice, and suicide.

The Gothic genre began with Horace Walpole's *The Castle of Otranto* (1765). Although Walpole was not viciously anti-Catholic,[4] it was the dramatic anti-Catholic bias of the Puritan Gothic novel that justified the very existence of the secular novel as Puritan devotional testimony in its more popular and sensational novels like Ann Radcliffe's *The Italian* (1797) and "Monk" Lewis's *The Monk* (1798). Once the Gothic was an established genre, it moved in other directions: Mary Shelley's *Frankenstein* (1818) condemns capital punishment and questions the social relevancy of atheism, while Bram Stoker's *Dracula* (1897) offers a political satire on idle bloodsucking landlords. When Banks reviewed Joyce Carol Oates's Gothic novel *Bellefleur* (1980), her first bestseller, he wrote:

> It is certainly possible to read and enjoy a novel with characters and incidents like these: [William] Faulkner, Garcia Márquez, Flannery O'Connor, and many other modern writers have asked us to face grotesque forms of violence, and by so doing have explored basic themes of character and destiny. But when there is no dramatic logic to those events and characters, when what happens is not inevitable but merely gratuitous, the book fails to move or inform us. Particularly disturbing in this case, however, is not that *Bellefleur* fails to move or inform us, but that it seems to function as a means of expressing the author's fantasies, for that is what one is forced to conclude from the sheer gratuitousness of the violence and nightmare.[5]

Homeric Grotesque: *Trailerpark* 59

    While Banks, recently publishing his own Gothic stories in magazines, pointed out in the review that there's an element of hypocrisy when the grotesque finds acclamation by Americans in South American fiction but remains often disdained in American contemporary fiction, he finds the traditional social connection and critique of the Gothic genre missing in Oates's novel, demurring that while well-written, the novel appears to be pointlessly solipsistic. He's disturbed that there appears to be no social message.[6]

    In the preface to *Winesburg, Ohio*, Anderson informs the reader of his theory of the grotesque[7] to help the reader understand his stories:

> It was the truths that made the people grotesques. The old man had quite an elaborate theory concerning the matter. It was his notion that the moment one of the people took one of the truths to himself, called it his truth, and tried to live his life by it, he became a grotesque and the truth he embraced became a falsehood.[8]

    Those who find an abiding certainty to guide them immerse themselves in living a life of lies. This remains as true of Anderson's characters as it is true of the troubled characters in Banks's Gothic narratives.

    The stories in *Trailerpark* demonstrate an intricate relationship but their puzzling lack of chronological order (as with Banks's story "Survivors II") demands that a reader construct a timeline. Just as in any epic, one begins *in media res* and the story about Flora Pease plunges us into the middle of the trailer park's activities. For the sake of clarity, one may divide the stories into two camps: Eight background stories, which include "The Right Way," "Principles," "The Child Screams and Looks Back at You," "Politics," "Cleaving, and Other Needs," "Burden," "Comfort," and "God's Country"; and five contemporary events in the following order: "Black Man and White Woman in Dark-Green Rowboat," "The Guinea-Pig Lady," "Fisherman," "What Noni Hubner Did Not Tell the Police About Jesus," and "Dis Bwoy, Him Gwan." These contemporary events run from late summer of 1978 when Terry Constant rows Noni Hubner on the lake to mid-October 1979 when Bruce Severance is murdered by Boston drug dealers. It's important to note that while the book's mood ends with hilarious irony, the collection inhabits the terrain of black comedy leading up to murder. Tears should be added to the laughter, the peculiar effect elicited by Anton Chekhov's great play *Uncle Vanya* (1897). Since arranging the correct sequence casts a slightly different light on the stories, lets discuss the stories not in the sequence of the collection, which is a dramatic and thematic arrangement, but as they have occurred chronologically.

    The collection displays a doubling typology in the cast of characters: Two heroes, Carol Constant and Merle Ring; two villains, the Boston drug dealers; two pathetic characters, Flora Pease and Noni Hubner; two narcissists, Captain Dewey Knox and Leon La Roche; two spineless opportunists, Terry Constant and Bruce Severance (one might also add the minor character Buddy Smith to this category); two ineffective daydreamers who want to do good yet don't,

Nancy Hubner and Marcelle Chagnon; and two bitter characters, Doreen Tiede and Tom Smith.

THE BACKGROUND STORIES

"Cleaving, and Other Needs" paints the picture of a couple, Doreen and Buck Tiede, who have only one successful coupling after a husband attempts to murder his wife for infidelity. When he pulls the trigger of his shotgun, they discover it was not loaded; they made sudden and ecstatic love of the floor, but are unable to reproduce their explosive collision. Doreen has been quite unwise and desperate in her infidelities, choosing the trailer park drug dealer Bruce for her first infidelity (apparently successful), then the gay bank teller Leon for disappointing oral sex, then the plumber braggart Howie Leeke who broadcasts their affair in the local bar and hotel, the amusingly named Hawthorne House where drunken degradation reigns. Ashamed of sex, Buck turns Doreen cold and unresponsive. Buck's neurosis and Doreen's naïve acceptance of the situation have prolonged their marriage beyond endurance. *Other needs* refer to the simple satisfaction of communication lacking in their relationship. "Cleaving" refers both to the long-delayed dissolution of their marriage as well as their one magic night of Gothic reprieve. The momentary ecstasy of their near-death sex prolongs the marriage of a couple not suited for each other, the story becoming a critique of young couples naively rushing into early marriage for sex and a sociological reminder of the inhibiting Puritan heritage.

"God's Country" describes the recruitment of Carol from Boston into the backwater New Hampshire town of Catamount, despite her racial color. As her Dickensian name indicates, she's the most trustworthy, conscientious, and sane member of the trailer park, although her brother Terry continually takes advantage of her. Ironically, she and Merle typify the only two who embody all of the old New England values of hard work and responsibility. There are subtle hints of slightly veiled racism in the story. Little does Carol know that when she moves into the romantically described "God's Country," she's moving into New Hampshire's peculiar version of a claustrophobic Nordic hell.

Perhaps the realism of Maxim Gorky's play *The Lower Depths*[9] about a community of outcasts provides a precedent for these interlinked stories as much as Anderson's *Winesburg, Ohio*. Yet Banks's neorealism often breaks the frame of its spell through the use of second-person narrative (especially in "The Child Screams and Looks Back at You") or authorial third-person commentary, as in the concluding monologue of "What Noni Hubner Did Not Tell the Police About Jesus," comparing Noni to a flower, the lady slipper, which begins with self-conscious apology to the reader for an outdated convention that becomes surprisingly effective. In a realistic narrative which embeds the comparison within the story, as in John Steinbeck's "The Chrysanthemums," the metaphor finds gradual exfoliation and parallel discovery. When Banks intrudes in this authorial fashion, the metaphor functions in a Janus mode, asking the reader to reflect back on what is known about Noni, especially the story about the rowboat on the lake and her submission to her mother's insistence on an abortion, as well as forward to what will happen to her amid her religious conversion—her hallucinatory visions of Merle as Jesus, her abduction of her mother, and tying her up at the cemetery. Noni, like many people at the trailer park, becomes a grotesque in the manner of Anderson's characters because she blindly follows her mother. Her one attempt at freeing both her mother and herself ends with the police arresting her.

The theme of police investigating the trailer park offers irony. The police respond to the mother-daughter conflict between Nancy and Noni, while they haven't a clue about the more egregious crimes of arson and drug dealing, although one may presume that they will be around more after the murder of Bruce, but the chronology of the narrative suddenly concludes with his death.

Marcelle's well-meaning but lax guardianship as manager of the trailer park has produced the very soap-opera horrors that Nancy Hubner, earlier, in terms of chronology, fears and rejects in "Politics" but later finds herself immersed in. Marcelle has become a grotesque who is a behind-the-scenes enabler of the fishbowl sex, drugs, and insanity that plague the trailer camp. Authority in New Hampshire appears to operate as local anarchy under the guise of loose laissez-faire liberalism. Marcelle's story, "The Child Screams and Looks Back at You," explains the psychic wound that transformed Marcelle into a grotesque who allows the empathetic truth of liberal sympathy to blind her to the wider reality.

Nancy's middle-class quest for liberation leads to the formation of a more rigid personality under the banner of radical politics. While she's too privileged and bound into middle-class lifestyle to seize the freedom she wants, the truths she embraces create a fearful rigidity and self-righteousness in herself that do little to help her when she's freed by her husband's death. She relocates to a trailer park where she embraces the delusional truth that she had loved her husband. Attempting to live that fantasy lie puts her on the brink of madness, goading her unbalanced daughter (who has just had an abortion) to attempt an exhumation of her dead husband in order to dispel her mother's grotesque delusion that she once loved him.

"Principles" provides an etiological story illustrating how a grotesque evolves. Claudel Bing grew up with working-class values on responsibility and morality but the Vietnam War convinces him that luck is the explanation of who lives or who dies, especially among the unlucky Vietnamese victims of the war. Being an American assures him that he's lucky by virtue of American exceptionalism. When he and his new wife depart for their honeymoon, his wife Ginnie forgets to turn the gas stove off, and their just-purchased trailer goes up in smoke before they can insure it. He experiences unlucky despair, turning to drink for solace. When Ginnie begins running around with the randy plumber Leeke, the braggart plumber who leaks indiscretions, Claudel descends to alcoholism, losing his job, living at Hawthorne House as the house drunk, begging for drinks. He believes that he's been cursed with bad luck like the Vietnamese peasants he saw dying randomly. Listening to a young man tell his story of how and why he was arrested for speeding, Claudel experiences a revelation: Joy in living depends on "the way you pay attention to things."[10] He realizes he had never held a real philosophy of life and this enables him to find a menial job stacking tannery hides, allowing him to move out to the trailer park. Claudel's glum incomprehension of Merle when he visits him in the ice-fishing house provides some of the more hilarious lines in the concluding amusing story, "The Fisherman." While Claudel operates as vaguely functional, his grotesque *philosophy* simplistically concludes that some people have good luck, some bad.

"Burden" discloses the anguish behind Tom Smith's suicide. Tom can't forgive himself for turning his son out of his trailer after Buddy has stolen items to sell in Boston, stealing also from neighbors, but also lifting personal mementoes of no commercial value as well as home appliances. Buddy remains a compulsive liar (lying is his grotesque truth) and we learn that he tells Leon that he has a metal plate in his head, a red-herring anecdote that the writer and musician Richard Farina routinely incorporated into his party-act bluster.[11]

"The Right Way," about Dewey's 14th birthday, presents an illustration of how youthful experience that is colorfully dramatic creates in an impressionable personality the rigid structure of a grotesque. In Dewey's case, he takes to heart his father's injunction that *the right way* to do things sometimes includes dissembling to those closest to you, in this case his mother:

> There was a right way to do everything, even something as simple and unimportant as shoveling a path though snow to the kitchen door. The boy's father believed that, he said it, too, and now the boy believed it. The pleasure you got from looking at a job done the right way proved that there was such a thing as the right way. Not just the best way, not the easiest way, not even the logical way. You did things in life the right way, and then, afterward, you got to admire what you had done.[12]

He lies to his mother about the speakeasy he and his father had visited, operating in a solipsistic manner through *the right way* principle the rest of his life without questioning its authenticity. The story also contains a digression on the prevalence and persistence of anti-Catholic bigotry in rural New Hampshire, a theme that appears in *Peyton Place*.[13] The young teenager's experience in being initiated into the adult world of truth's double standard explains the rigidity of the Captain's approach to problem solving, as well as the Captain's blunt insensitivity in the story "Comfort" when he offers no comfort to the distressed homosexual seeking solace. Instead of offering some sympathy, the Captain reacts *the right way* with distant and cold neutrality, triggering the paranoia and shame of the hypersensitive youth.

THE CONTEMPORARY STORIES

"Black Man and White Woman in Dark Green Rowboat" is menacingly Gothic insofar as it's about abortion. Robert Niemi elaborates on its literary lineage, citing parallels with Ernest Hemingway's "Hills Like White Elephants"[14] and Theodore Dreiser's lake scene in *An American Tragedy*,[15] while Ross Leckie discusses aspects of romantic and fetishistic racism, as well as several startling innovative techniques in Banks's narration.[16] Terry and Noni go boating on the lake and discuss her upcoming abortion. Noni becomes a grotesque when she submissively agrees with her mother Nancy's "truth" that miscegenation is not socially acceptable in a New Hampshire family, yet Nancy doesn't object to seeing black men as sex objects, since she felt a lack of romance compounded by boredom in her marriage. Also, her daughter's affair with a black man validates her recently acquired liberal politics as outlined in the related story of her life in "Politics," as well as her own casual affair with the younger man Bruce. Yet Terry, who doesn't approve of abortion, merely feebly objects with glum resignation and appears to be more upset about realizing that the abortion will end their affair—he doesn't put much attempt or any eloquence into arguing against the abortion, merely being content to register his resentment.

A Gothic leitmotif that runs through several stories, the presence of the American Indian stone fishing weirs on the lake, "used for centuries until the arrival of the Europeans,"[17] receives its most complete development here amid the backdrop of abortion. The Indians were considered savages by the settlers, but the settlers brought institutionalized race-based slavery, and that problematic legacy still echoes through American society. The presence of the stone weirs reminds the reader Indians never practiced abortion, but the Indians have been exterminated, forgotten by the local inhabitants who think of them only when visitors appear. Then they suddenly give, "the place a history and a certain significance, when outsiders were present, that it did not otherwise seem to have."[18] Just as Terry and Noni seem to be oblivious to the natural beauty of the lake as they casually discuss death, all the lakeside denizens except for Flora and Merle appear to be alienated from *nature* itself. The stone fishing weirs haunt the lake as a reminder that a civilization that valued its ecology was exterminated and replaced by a society that casually practices abominations that would never have occurred to the Indians.

Noni's fetish attraction for the exotic black man receives its real life complement in Bruce's romantic naitivité and his murder by the drug dealers while Terry's passivity and reluctance to be involved in any messy relationships remains true to character when Terry plays the passive partner in Bruce Severance's drug dealing in the intimately linked "Dis Bwoy, Him Gwan." Terry's just a drifter sponging off his sister—it's almost as if he doesn't have an identity outside of his alienation which provides the sole pathetic "truth" of his life, making him as much of a grotesque as Bruce, who like Noni, judges Terry to be cool merely on the basis of skin color, both of them refusing to see the lack of responsibility or grit in Terry's character. The pathology of this kind of patronizing racism toward people of color remains a problem in New Hampshire where there not many people of color; such blind patronization is, of course, a peculiar extension of racism in rural New England. It's a subject rarely brought up and Banks's dramatization becomes doubly effective as it remains the sinister sub-plot in two stories about death—abortion and murder. Banks's adroit handling of the narrative heightens the shocking aspects of both background and foreground.

"The Guinea-Pig Lady," the first story in the collection, introduces the whole cast of characters at the trailer park, which is why it's the longest story in the book. Briefly, it's the story of a middle-aged woman who has retired from the U.S. Air Force where she worked as a maid and steward for officers. She moves into the trailer park at a time when the manager is desperate to rent out a unit. Despite the ban on pets, she secretively keeps guinea pigs which begin to multiply dramatically. Gossip about this gets around the park and eventually the manager visits but agrees not to interfere unless it becomes a problem, which happens over the winter. Flora calls them her babies, eliciting the sympathy of the manager who had to deal with her own child's death. The guinea pigs, grown for food in the Meso-American culture, multiply to the hundreds. As the crisis peaks, Banks provides an anthology *précis* on how each of the trailer park members would handle the situation while the manager decides what to do, an opportunity for both comedy and summary character revelation.

The methodology of pervasive irony in the collection recalls Banks's citation of Homer's *Odyssey*, "the mother of all stories,"[19] the first on his list of the top five important world books. The epic requires multiple readings (or hearings) to savor the panorama of accumulated ironies, broad and subtle. Both *The Odyssey* and *Trailerpark* display the convoluted circularity of an oral epic designed for performance.

Doreen (a single mother with a child), not surprisingly once readers come to know more about her in "Cleaving and Other Needs," argues the most severe solution for the proliferating guinea pigs. The reader hears Nancy advocating "Christian charity"[20] when a couple of months ago she insisted that her teenage daughter have an abortion because the child would not be all white. When one first reads Flora's story, readers cannot notice the irony because it has not yet encountered the abortion issue, due to the shuffled chronology. Dewey sounds quite reasonable in his first declaration, but when readers come to know him better, one can't take him seriously. Leon's statement that "If the *Suncook Valley Sun* learned that we had this kind of thing going on here, that we had this type of village eccentric living here among us at the trailerpark, we would suffer deep embarrassment"[21] appears amusingly ironic in the light of Noni's later arrest and the conclusion of what happens at the end of eccentric Merle's story, "The Fisherman," but horrifically ironic if one considers the concluding murder of Bruce. A second reading reveals a layered *frisson* one does not expect to discover in short stories.

In late September Flora sickens with a high fever; the manager calls an ambulance to take her to the hospital, and she, realizing that someone will dispose of her pets, escapes from the hospital to burn down her trailer with the pets. The mystery of arson is not solved. Flora builds an impromptu hovel on the border of the state park and land owned by the corporation that owns the trailer park. She squats as a filthy untouchable. She was abused as a child and later by officers in the Air Force which had provided a structure to cling to, but retired and set adrift, she cannot cope on her own, going mad. Her delusion that by caring for guinea pigs she could find an identity that would function as a refuge from her memories of abuse turned her into a grotesque.

Marcelle, the park manager, wells up in sympathy for Flora, believing that someone else (probably another renter) had burned the trailer down; she believes this because she thinks of life as a tragic parade of the innocent dying. At that moment, one cannot understand the depth of her emotion until reading "The Child Screams and Looks Back at You." Her belief in life as the solemn tragedy of the innocent is the truth she lives by and this truth has blinded her to reality, making her a grotesque, isolated in her own tragic fantasies.

The central story in the collection, "The Fisherman," appears as the last story. The sensible reason for such "dislocated" architecture is that the finale presents a comic send-up of the Gothic genre. The story functions like a keystone in an arch without which the novelistic structure would collapse. In the story's opening paragraph, the reader is encouraged to think abstractly; the narrator casually tosses in a reference to the sun moving to the pampas, which conjures for the literate reader a sly reference to one of Jorge Luis Borges's more famous stories, "The Lottery in Babylon," a parable about the tyranny of egalitarianism.[22] But the well-read American reader will more correctly conjure up Shirley Jackson's famous short story "The Lottery" as the background metatext. The offhand parallels are both enticing and revealing.

Jackson's Gothic parable centers upon the ritual of selecting a sacrificial scapegoat through a small town lottery as a human sacrifice. This annual ritual appears as an inherited local tradition, a sinister black box containing one slip of paper with a black spot tags the victim. The parable evokes comparison to compulsory military service, mocking New England traditions of unthinking conformity, and contains a feminist social critique, as the victim's execution proceeds by stoning, a traditional method reserved for adultery in the Middle East. The story concludes with neighborhood friends and the mother's children cheerfully casting stones at scapegoat Tessie.[23] The grim, shocking power of Jackson's story resides in her genial matter-of-fact tone.

Banks's satiric "Fisherman" is part parable but also part fable, since it contains the fabulously unlikely event of a double lottery winner. But it's also a farce, a climactic, witty send-up of the trailer park community, as well as of the Gothic genre itself. At this point like a juggler, Banks floats many balls in the air. Confirmed contrarian Merle, a *cousin* of the coffin maker from *The Relation of My Imprisonment* and related to Herman Melville's Bartleby, who "endured summer to get to winter,"[24] stands in the circus spotlight. Merle was the unnamed lakeside character in "Black Man and White Woman in Dark Green Rowboat" scraping the bottom of a rowboat; his unobtrusive presence in the story, combined with his laconic comment that Terry and Noni are not in touch with nature since you can't expect to catch fish on a hot summer day, provides a subtle accusation to which Terry and Noni remain completely oblivious. Merle functions as a contemplative moral foil for the sins of the community as well as scapegoat. While Flora attempts to get in touch with nature through her guinea pigs but fails, Merle has successfully integrated old Puritan traditions with the intimate appreciation of nature that guided the American Indians.

All of Merle's first lottery winnings were generously and secretly given to the inhabitants of the trailer park. When he's entered into the grand prize drawing later that year everyone begins to imagine they are all collectively participating in the dream drawing, which appears to be during Christmas shopping season. Merle, retired and not interested in material acquisition, squats five months of the year around-the-clock in his bobhouse (his fishing shed named from bobbing a line through ice), storing his previous winnings in a cigar box. All the denizens of the trailer park, including Buddy Smith and Claudel Bing, come to advise him on what to do with his winnings before he has won. These hilarious conversations remain the funniest set pieces Banks has ever penned. When Merle wins the fabulous grand prize, the money goes right into the cigar box. At that point, the small community becomes infected with rabid communal greed.

Maureen, a five-year-old literary descendant of Nathaniel Hawthorne's innocent Pearl, is bundled up to trudge across the frozen lake amid icy winds by her cynical mother Doreen. She's supposed to talk to Merle about the money but the child is, of course, not interested in the subject and remains fascinated by the wonders of nature, gazing down into the waving strands of weeds that the ice holes reveal as enchanting colors shimmer in reflection on the shed's walls. Merle's conversation with the young girl achieves a natural purity that contrasts vividly with the Gothic story lines that have enveloped the trailer park community. The delirious peasants are driven into mob action by the mysterious silence out in the wintry lake and storm the fabled shed-castle of innocence and purity. They purportedly go to rescue the girl who's having a wondrous time with Merle, yet they go as an unconscious crowd to seize the cash. They take turns shoving and squirming into the tiny shed. Racist Nancy slaps black Carol in the face before everyone. Eventually her brother Terry seizes the cigar box which is frenziedly torn and passed from hand to hand "like a sacred relic"[25] until the wind flings open the Pandora box, the hundred-dollar bills blowing in the wind like a satiric rendition of Bob Dylan's folksong refrain, "The answer, my friends, is blowin' in the wind." Greedily, the community flails in the dark windy night on the slippery ice trying to snatch the crisp bills from the howling wind amid their antic mob-inspired lottery.

The concluding paragraph of the book,[26] projected in the voice of a local oral storyteller, highlights the question of chronology with its indeterminate and mysterious evocation of the present:

> He built another bobhouse the following winter, and as usual spent most of the winter inside it. He never spoke of the lottery money, and you can be sure that no one else ever mentioned it to him, either. Until now, that is, when Merle seems to have gotten over his despair and the others their shame.[27]

It is significant that Merle has built a new bobhouse because he had just finished repainting and redecorating the old bobhouse until it became a much remarked upon wonder in the trailer park community. He has discarded or destroyed his painstaking handiwork in an effort to help himself and the community to forget the legacy of shame. Merle was never interested in the money—the little interest he had in it was to help people he knew. The fact that Merle's clown circus finale of the airborne hundred-dollar bills, compared by Niemi to the climax of B. Traven's *The Treasure of the Sierra Madre*,[28] occurs shortly after the arson and abortion, makes the communal greed of the trailer park denizens doubly shameful. Their oblivious selfishness, laxness, and grotesque insularity make the subsequent murder of Bruce on the property less surprising and a more of fitting conclusion to the list of Gothic horrors that haunt the trailer park.

"What Noni Hubner Did Not Tell the Police About Jesus" recounts the rebellion of Noni against the tyranny and delusions of her mother Nancy. Traumatized by the abortion her mother insisted on, Noni turns to religion for solace, but her disorientated visions clearly indicate a nervous breakdown. Readers discover that she's seeing a psychiatrist who provides her, "with enough Valium to put her to sleep for the rest of her natural life."[29] Despite the zombie state her medication enforces upon her, she can no longer endure her mother's denial that her father is dead. Of course, the bizarre propagandistic conversations about how Nancy had loved her husband when Noni knows that was not true, remind Noni that she had loved Terry this past summer. Her mother's denial of her husband's death also reminds Noni that she can't forget killing her own child in the womb. In a desperate effort to end this abusive derangement and unconscious psychological persecution, she ties her mother up, drives out to the cemetery and begins to wield a shovel, but the police show up before she can complete the exhumation of her father to prove to her mother that her husband is dead. What the reader wants to hear is what the psychiatrist has to say about this incident, but the reader is left to play that role. The comparison of Noni to a lady slipper that blooms in June presents a clear allusion to the bloom of her first love affair and the pregnancy, but the bloom of the lady slipper is long gone by the early New Hampshire autumn and Noni has become a wilted, half-dead stalk frozen under winter snow.

"Dis Boy, Him Gwan" recounts the end of Bruce, the correspondence college student and local marijuana dealer. Bruce is a walking cartoon cliché, a naïve yet corrupt parody of the early seventies counterculture, a small-time opportunist ubiquitously found floating on the skein of the counterculture movement. Bruce's *profit motive* cynicism remains as shallow as counterculture affectations. His unthinking valorization of black people carries as much racism as empty-headed stereotype.

Terry gives Bruce the worst possible advice in handling the drug dealers who are after him by telling him to beg for his life rather than take any aggressive action to preserve his life. At this point, Bruce should just head north, stay at a few motels for a month, then relocate somewhere else, but he appears to be committed to staying at the trailer park because of his casual affair with Nancy. When the two drug dealers appear, Terry just walks away, knowing the Jamaican will kill Bruce; he washes his hands of Bruce's life and the community to which he doesn't belong. He doesn't call the cops or even note the license plate of the killers because he doesn't want to be involved in life's messy problems, whether it involves his girlfriend or business partner.

At the end of the story, Terry lies to his sister Carol (who doesn't know Bruce is dead) about having recently seen Bruce, and one can presume he will not give an iota of information to the police, which casts a retrospective *frisson* of irony on the title of the following story in *real* time (which occurs the previous spring) about innocent Noni not telling the police everything about Jesus, who prosaically turns out to be the mysterious Merle shuffling around the pond in the wintry gloom without speaking.

While Merle becomes a ringer for Jesus in Noni's eyes (and there's some ironic truth to that hysteric vision) and presides over a Barnum Bailey Ringling-like circus spotlight with his lottery winnings, he's also the meditative center and moral conscience of the narrative. His name indicates the narrative technique Banks employs in the story collection—what in Homeric scholarship is called ring composition,[30] whereby related digressions in time and space create links between stories, as in a chain of linked rings. Such linking of thematic or especially plot rings creates associative memory guides for the oral storyteller, becoming a marvel for the audience, which wants to hear the tale more than once to savor the intricacy of the related rings as they jangle in echoing ironies. Homer remains the undisputed and legendary master of this technique yet Banks's adaptation of the ancient technique to a contemporary American Gothic that presents Americans with a cultural critique on greed and racism that achieves marvelous resonance.

While it may be considered an extraordinary act of hubris to recreate Homeric technique in rural New Hampshire, the proof is in the pudding and this book is quite a pudding with varied layers of flavor. As for Homer and rural considerations, it may be worthwhile to recall that Homeric society was still primarily rural (the great city population booms happened a couple of centuries later), and that in the *Odyssey*, Homer told a rural story about a particular family dynasty in a somewhat remote corner of the Greek world that Ionian city folk knew nothing about. In his poem "Epic," Patrick Kavanagh noted Homer's transforming link between the local and the universal when a writer appropriates the Otherworld, "Gods make their own importance."[31] Although there's no Iliadic time-warp fantasy offering theogonic sci-fi excerpts of gods disputing in *Trailerpark*, the clay-footed denizens of the community experience the *deus ex machina* of the double-lottery-win as a community event that exposes their clawing greed. The image of impoverished Americans chasing windswept hundred dollar bills though wintery New Hampshire woods provides a ghostly, haunting image that is perhaps more resonant today than when Banks completed his masterpiece.

As in the underclass fiction of Nelson Algren, most of the denizens of the trailer park have self-blindingly constructed their own inferno. The anthropologist from *The Book of Jamaica* had engineered his own more *sophisticated* hell through his alcoholism like many Algren characters. The near-underclass ambiance of the trailer community also recalls the underclass boarding house community of Algren's masterful collection of stories, *The Neon Wilderness* (1947), where boarding house life receives a fatalistic muckraking portrait in gut-bucket prose. The theme of boarding house life was revisited by James T. Farrell with less shocking sensationalism but more empathy in *Boarding House Blues* (1961),[32] a collection of short stories about dead-end lives that more subtly stressed sociological environmentalism in its portrait of seamy unemployed bohemians during the Great Depression. Brigit O'Dair takes over a rooming house on Chicago's north side and she provides a mechanism for linking the stories of roomers together, just as Marcelle functions in *Trailerpark*,[33] which combines both the fatalism of Algren and the sociological environmentalism of Farrell, synthesizing both approaches to storytelling. The collection contains six stories of environmental sociology: "The Guinea Pig Lady," "Cleaving, and Other Needs," "Black Man and White Woman in Dark Green Rowboat," "God's Country," "Politics," and "The Right Way." Complementing them are six stories of dour fatalism: "Dis Boy, Him Gwan," "What Noni Hubner Did Not Tell the Police About Jesus," "Principles," and "The Child Screams and Looks Back at You." The concluding story, "The Fisherman," combines the sociological environment of the trailer park with bleak fatalism, but Merle incarnates the hero who, in his stoic generosity and seventeenth-century wisdom, rises above both the surrounding sociology and his victimization by the community.

The composition of *Trailerpark* has been carefully planned around five tragedies: the suicide of Tom Smith, the insanity and arson of Flora Pease, the abortion and subsequent nervous breakdown of Noni Hubner, the money-theft riot, and the murder of Bruce Severance. The various sexual affairs, Marcelle Chagnon, Carol Constant, Doreen Tiede, Tom and Buddy Smith, and the Captain provide connecting threads in the Gothic tapestry. The concluding farce, like a Greek satyr play, concerning Merle's lottery winnings, highlights the central theme in the novel of life as a meaningless provincial lottery, updating Jackson's dour Puritan parody of small-town New England life in her anthropologically satiric story "The Lottery." Banks's story about Merle, who placidly accepts his role as a communal scapegoat, is democratically anarchic, the antithesis of the traditional New England authoritarianism mocked by Jackson—Banks's lottery story may have been conceived as a gentle comic parody of Jackson's great story, but more importantly as a sociological update of the changes in rural New England since Jackson published her story about communal morbidity in *The New Yorker* on June 26, 1948.

When Banks had experimented with the Gothic in "The Caul," the end result was a witty academic performance that had nothing to do with contemporary society, something that he later objected to in his review of Oates. While the stories in *Trailerpark* squat firmly in New Hampshire ambiance and landscape, the characters (except perhaps for Bartleby-like Merle) have a more universal resonance in American society—many of the inhabitants' stories might have happened in nearly any trailer park from Florida to Montana.

Among the Gothic horrors unearthed by the collection, readers find the exhumation of child abuse, traditional Puritan prejudice, and rural anomie (these are cast in the past) augmented by the corrosive presence of racism and the pursuit of narcissistic hedonism (the present horrors). While Banks's previous books focused upon individual problems of alienation and cultural dissonance, *Trailerpark* represents a social advance in constructing a broader and more relevant social commentary; *The Book of Jamaica*, outlined the limits of a liberal intellectual who thought he was above racism, while he clung to the traditional hubris of European thought. *Trailerpark* marks a turning point in Banks's writing as he begins to probe larger social panoramas, yet the dense Homeric irony will be abandoned for a looser yet more accessible narrative, opening his writing to a larger audience.

7

Mainstream Realism and Zombies: Continental Drift

> And, as his strength
> Failed him at length,
> He met a pilgrim shadow—
> "Shadow," said he,
> "Where can it be—
> This land of Eldorado?"
>
> —Edgar Allan Poe, "Eldorado"

In 1981, Russell Banks began researching and writing a historical novel about Franklin Pierce and Nathaniel Hawthorne, lifelong friends, who met at Bowdoin College, where Pierce was a year ahead of Hawthorne. Hawthorne later wrote a short biography of Pierce when he ran for president in 1852.[1] In October 1981, Banks read a newspaper article that stirred his imagination and changed the direction of his writing. The article profiled a tragedy involving a smuggler, the U.S. Coast Guard, and a boatload of Haitians off the Florida coast near Palm Beach. Banks told Janet Maslin, "You read things backward in your imagination sometimes. I instantly knew how the Haitians got there in some way, and I also knew how the smuggler got there—God only knows how he did, but I knew how one *could* get there."[2] Banks conjured in his imagination two stories: one of a man from New England and one of a woman from Haiti whose stories would collide. The seed for his novel *Continental Drift* (1985), which garnered the John Dos Passos Award for fiction, was planted. Banks felt that the theme of immigration had a more compelling, contemporary relevance than the book he had begun.

That inspirational seed of the newspaper story recalls the working habits of Nelson Algren and Richard Wright. In the 1962 introduction to a reprint of *Never Come Morning* (1942), which explores the psychology of criminality with some empathy, Algren mentions how he used newspaper accounts of a particular case to stimulate his development of the novel as he wrote.[3]

The prospect of a newspaper article diverting a novelist's direction echoes what Algren had said in a noted interview about his most famous novel, "I told them I was going to write a *war* novel. But it turned out to be this *Golden Arm* thing. I mean, the war kind of slipped away, and these people with the hypos came along."[4] Despite being Algren's most poetic novel, it was the only Algren novel to enjoy substantial sales; the early drafts focused on an army veteran card-dealer with a "golden" arm, but Algren shifted the focus more into the present as he portrayed the effects of lingering drug addiction due to war wounds.[5]

Banks had previously written of characters from deep introspection. Now he had to develop a more distant mode of narration because he could not presume to know what occurred in the mind of a Haitian woman—his residence in Jamaica had at least taught him that. Algren had been able to delve into the minds of his underclass characters because he was familiar with their sociology; there were no real cultural impediments and he had great mimetic ear for reproducing underclass dialogue. Banks had to put aside his postmodern inclinations to make sly experiments with narrative and adopt a more traditional storytelling posture, closer to conventional realism:

> In this case, it seemed to me that the material had to be explained much of the time, the way [Charles] Dickens often had to explain, the way [Theodore] Dreiser explained "Sister Carrie" or Sherwood Anderson explained "Winesburg, Ohio." The behavior is only the surface of the character's inner life and you're dealing with people who are essentially inarticulate, that's their main characteristic. Their lives are more complex than they seem. So you have to articulate for them, and do it without condescension. I hate the kind of fiction that makes the reader feel superior to the people who are being revealed.[6]

Banks needed to invent a narrator more removed from intimate participation in the narration, a narrator who projected a more neutral point of view, perhaps like a windowpane. Banks cites Anderson whose realism of the grotesque he had handled in an neorealistic manner when composing *Trailerpark*, yet the citation of Dreiser, a naturalist (a later development of realism), rings with more relevancy for this new book. Traditional realism ambled in the mainstream of popular reading, as the journalist and novelist Tom Wolfe was later to vociferously argue.[7] Despite Banks's grittier naturalistic strain of realism in the manner of Stephen Crane and Theodore Dreiser, *Continental Drift* became Banks's first book to go through more than one printing and the subsequent printings of the paperback edition went into double digits. Reviews of the book were unusually exuberant and Banks began to reach a wide reading audience as he wrote in the spirited working-class tradition that Nelson Algren, author of *A Walk on the Wild Side* (1956), had once encouraged him to pursue. Banks's novel presents a descent into a doomed underworld that Algren so eloquently and dramatically limned for Americans in Chicago; yet locating this underworld in the Caribbean context offered a subject not much touched upon since Zora Neale Hurston's novel *Tell My Horse* (1938), which explored voodoo.

Continental Drift opens with what appears to be an apparent anti-invocation, summoning not the traditional Western muse of memory ("nothing here that depends on memory for the telling"), but an impassioned prayer to the Yoruba West African god Legba to come forward! Legba, the Benin horned god of virility and fate, the youngest son of the supreme god Lisa and his consort Mawu, the moon goddess, functions as the messenger god who moves between the all-father sun god Lisa and the earth, warming and fertilizing the earth, much like the Celtic sun god Lugh who was incarnated in the rays of the sun. Roman Catholic missionaries considered Lugh to be a prototype of Jesus Christ, and Legba to be a gatekeeper prototype of St. Peter or St. Anthony. Like Lugh, the inventor of the alphabet, Legba is the god of language, versed in all human languages.

The invocation conjures the mouth-man, the tribal narrator, to come forth with the story that provides "an accounting to occur, not a recounting, and a presentation, not a representation."[8] Legba stands at the crossroads and gives permission to speak with the spirits of Guinea, that is, other West African gods or any departed souls (like the Greek god Dionysos, nicknamed Christos). While *Trailerpark* imitated Homer's technique in the narrator's casting of events through the prism of the storyteller's echoing memory rings, here the narrator conjures the fateful and lusty present dark mysteries to carry the story more in the manner of an entrancing tribal recitation than the Western concept of art as mimesis (imitation of life) because the story presents an account of a real life story. Legba is asked to permit the story of a dead man, Robert Dubois from Catamount, New Hampshire, to be told.[9] Above all, the religious sense of Voodoo offers a process of self-discovery,[10] recalling the wandering leitmotif addressed to the anthropologist in *The Book of Jamaica*, "You will see what you want to see."

And yet the Western traditions of both realism and naturalism portray an imitation of life as the artist conceives it. Is the voodoo incantation itself a colonial cultural appropriation in the hands of a New Hampshire writer? Is it just rhetorical window dressing? The novel shuns the colonial view of voodoo as a base superstition, presenting voodoo as a living, dynamic religion, something that opposes the traditional agnosticism or atheism characteristically found in realistic or naturalistic novels. Here the nonwhite world finds itself portrayed as a vital transcendent world subject to much suffering; the reader experiences shock at the end of the novel when a white man suddenly experiences suffering at the hands of evil, which no race or people are free from. The universal theme that all people should live with dignity binds the colliding black and white worlds together in the novel. Rather than answering all questions with an imperial discourse, the book challenges the reader to ponder issues of cultural prejudice and cultural insularity in the greater tragedy of our common humanity.

The approach that Banks takes to voodoo (the word is derived from the Fon language of Dahomey and means spirit or god)[11] is akin to that of Hurston's in *Tell My Horse*, which is to present Voodoo as a sophisticated and legitimate religion.[12] Both attempt to rescue Voodoo from the sensationalism of the white entertainment industry[13] or the prejudice of previous white writers. Each chapter of Banks's novel features a simple but relevant line drawing in the traditional style of drawings reproduced in Alfred Métraux's book *Voodoo in Haiti* (1972). Since no attributions appear, it seems the drawings are the work of Banks, who as a young man, once thought he might be a painter.

Robert Raymond Dubois, who works as an oil-burner repairman for the Abenaki Oil Company, drinks with Doris Cleave (with whom Robert has been conducting a casual affair), recalling the intimate but distraught ambiance of the bar scene from *The Book of Jamaica* when the anthropologist converses with the prostitute Yvonne. Like Algren, Banks excels in handling such scenes with a nuanced deftness, his only contemporary working-class rival at the time in such authentic narration being some stories by Raymond Carver, author of *Cathedral* (1984). The first section of the first chapter, "Pissed," concludes with a biographical précis in the manner of Ivan Turgenev who kept profile files on his characters before beginning his novels. Banks's employment of the paratactic *he* in the biographical slide conveys a forceful and effective musicality that transcends its simplicity. Robert feels stuck in his dead-end job with the burden of bills to pay in order to support his wife and two children. At 30, Robert begins to undergo a precocious mid-life crisis. Robert's surname functions as an ironic reminder of the intellectual and activist W. E. B. Du Bois who aided the plight of African Americans. No intellectual, Robert Dubois will be guilty of aiding a mass murder of Haitian immigrants.

The beginning of Robert's story finds its setting during the Christmas shopping season, as in "The Fisherman" from *Trailerpark*. Robert's claustrophobic amid the New Hampshire, the closure of family life's duties, and the repetitive routine of his job, experiencing the paranoia confinement induces. Except the suburban setting is not Southern midsummer, but midwinter depression in below zero New Hampshire. Robert, after a few too many rounds of drink, vents his repressed rage on his own vehicle, smashing his station wagon windows with his fists before driving home in a snowstorm. The second part of the first chapter begins with Robert realizing that the Horatio Alger American Dream of a success ladder presents a mass delusion enhanced by the entertainment media and he's bewildered that, "everyone in America seems to believe in it."[14] In a *tour de force* of self-pity induced by drink and paranoia, Robert concludes the segment with an embellished fantasy of being transported as a prisoner in chains across nineteenth-century czarist Siberia. Some Americans just don't know what they have. Ironically, this hallucinated fantasy probably derives from the entertainment media he professes to loathe and which he later rails against in the following scene with his wife. This reprise of a Walter Mitty-like fantasy that first appeared in "With Ché in New Hampshire" achieves an inconspicuously droll and deft execution.

At home with his wife, Elaine, Bob confesses he broke the car windows. Bob talks about former friends who have left New Hampshire, finding a comfortable living in Florida. Elaine gets the hint and agrees to a Florida move and they make vigorous love. Readers now realize why Bob never had an orgasm when he made epic love to Doris before coming home. Elaine tells him that she could never forgive him if he were ever unfaithful to her. Bob denies ever thinking of the subject. Our first impression of Robert Dubois paints a slightly unhinged womanizing liar who's tired of the routine of crawling under pipes and who fantasizes paradise as elsewhere. Bob's motivation for moving to Florida is also a way of saving his marriage, for it will sunder him from divorced Doris Cleave before his wife finds out about the lengthy on-going affair. Bob's humiliating daily submission to pipes (a phallic image) appears to endow him with a wooden (his surname) phallic potency that women can't resist.

Chapter two, "Battérie Maconnique" (Macerating Battery) opens with the kind of geological vision that informed chapter two of *Hamilton Stark*. Banks presents an epic humanitarian meditation in the tradition of Michel de Montaigne, an influential writer from the French Renaissance, comparing waves of tribal migrations to the global sea currents that shift the continents and create their mountains, thus signifying the book's title. Like Montaigne, he enlivens the picture by developing anecdotes about people caught in the drift of historical migration and cultural clashes, yet limns all this with the pessimistic image of planet Earth creating and recreating itself like an uroborus, which functioned as a central image in *Hamilton Stark*, thus raising the question whether history has a purpose for human suffering that humans can discern with any consolation. Banks reverts to explaining the cultural fatalism of history's victims around the globe and their folkloric consolation in *feeding the loas*, the spirits of dead ancestors. Survivors of natural and cultural catastrophe discover solace after calamities like hurricanes in remembering that, "it is we who live for the dead and not the dead who live for us."[15] This is the same ancient global folk wisdom that unites seventeenth-century England (as in *The Relation of My Imprisonment*) with Haiti, China, Vietnam, Celtic culture, Yoruba culture, and innumerable other cultures on the globe as they cope with the imprisoning closure of the uroborous. *We* are victims of the waves that move continents and *we* drift on the drifting surface of those continents, unaware of the staggering eons of time or the unconscious forces that operate within our own small lives. This fatalistic and engaging meditation on culture presents a more sophisticated, far-flung, and more intimately linked eloquence to the novel than the offhand experiment of glancing environmental determinism found in *Hamilton Stark*. Banks revisits some of his earlier philosophical preoccupations with a more relaxed and vibrant prose more integrated to the action of his novel. Robert Dubois may be said to be suffering from uroborus phobia.

An extended anecdote lands us in Haiti where the second thread of Banks's bifurcated narrative, first pioneered by Homer in *The Odyssey* (with Telemachos and Odysseus) and imitated by James Joyce (with Stephen and Bloom) in *Ulysses* (1922), brings us to the story of Vanise Dorsinville.[16] The influence of Joyce's bifurcated narrative structure (two separate narratives that collide and resolve, not merely two plots) has had a significant influence on

American fiction in the second half of the twentieth century, influencing writers like Tom Wolfe, Cormac McCarthy, and T. C. Boyle, yet it is also a device that Mark Twain employed in *The Adventures of Huckleberry Finn* (1884) with Huck and Jim. In Banks's novel, two separate character stories about immigration to Florida collide. Bob Dubois has fled voluntarily from the boredom of New Hampshire and has sold his house, boat, and effects, arriving by station wagon with his wife and two children without a job yet with an embedded contact (his brother Eddie) and a still relatively prosperous standard of living. Vanise Dorinsville arrives with no financial assets or contact and two children, emerging from near-servitude. Motivated by American cultural greed and privilege, Bob dreams of getting rich; Vanise finds herself forced into immigration in order to save her children from near-certain extinction.

The hurricane that has battered Haiti has overturned a food supply truck. Vanise's nephew Claude discovers the van with the driver dead inside and steals a large smoked ham, bringing it home for a family feast. This section of second-person plural narrative appears to be spoken by a lover of Vanise's through the authorial liberty of American English. Young Claude will not tell where he got the ham until it's half eaten. Then the paranoid gamut of possible reprisals descends upon the family after they have consumed most of the stolen meat; it's decided that Vanise, Claude, and her infant Charles (by the local police chief Aubin, owner of a general goods store) should flee with money sent by Vanise's husband who had been smuggled to America.

The smuggling operation works as a scam, the immigrants being deposited on North Caicos Island, nearly 600 miles from Miami. While some immigrants suffer bewilderment and are shortly rounded up, Vanise, who has nothing, gives young Claude a stone to suck on to assuage his hunger, but the ham bone with some meat left on it becomes offered up in sacrifice to Papa Legba and they are *saved*—she gives the ham bone to a mangy three-legged yellow dog which they follow home. The owner, George McKissick, a small-time marijuana grower, discovers attractive Vanise and realizes that he can take advantage of the desperate Haitian. He keeps her in a shed, feeding her in return for sex. Here sex functions as a mode of mere survival, contrasting with Bob's sexual adventures for recreational pleasure.

Bob's migration also lands him in a pickle. His wheeler-dealer brother Eddie offers him the job of running a liquor store he owns. Desperate for a job, Bob takes it, but has to work the cash register for nearly 70 hours a week for off-the-books small pay in a job instead of making the *killing* he dreams of. The new job provides more boredom and less challenge than his former plumber's job. Both Vanise and Bob have been taken advantage of upon their arrival, but Bob's problems are minor compared to Vanise's. Bob has an elderly African American stock hand (whom Bob in his oblivious racism doesn't think of as trapped), whose daughter Marguerite he eventually takes advantage of and seduces, "but like most white men, he's not imaginative enough to believe that being a woman is extremely different from being a man and being black extremely different from being white."[17] Yet this affair becomes more serious

Mainstream Realism and Zombies: *Continental Drift* 77

than Bob's liaison with Doris Cleave, while Vanise has no interest at all in her forced *relationship* with McKissick.

Bob dislikes carrying the gun he's been given to make the closing night deposits to the banks, disobeying that cautious instruction. His apocalyptic paranoia about Florida materializes in a robbery as he goes to the store to use the phone after his car breaks down. It becomes clear that the shotgun-wielding robber, egged on by his maliciously voyeuristic sidekick *Cornrow*, will pull the trigger unless Bob magically conjures up the day's take, Bob reaches for the pistol and shoots the robber in the shoulder. The shotgun blast narrowly sails over his head and showers him with gin and icicles of glass. Inspired by television cop shows, Bob gratuitously shoots the robber in the mouth, killing him. Cowardly Cornrow fouls himself from fear as Bob indifferently lets him escape while he calls the police (only to regret letting him go later). Bob gulps down half a bottle of whiskey as he awaits the cops while drenched in blood. But this apocalyptic incident had nothing to do with Florida culture—ironically, the car plates of the robbers were from New York State (an alert reader should have identified the gunman's accent). Bob made a killing, but not the big score imagined in his Horatio Alger dreams.

Bob's family finds itself ensconced in a mobile home docked at a trailer park. With Elaine pregnant, he's deeply in love with Marguerite, or so he tells himself, while his family is expanding. Daydreams of joyfully fathering a boy proliferate, but he doesn't arrive for the birth because he's making love to Marguerite. Bob finally ruptures his working relationship with his brother Eddie, who flounders deeply in debt to loan sharks. Fearing for his life after he had spotted Cornrow, Bob chased him down, lost him, and in his frustration almost shot an innocent bystander in a bar, and then nearly shot Marguerite because she had innocently given Cornrow, a distant relative by marriage, a lift in her car. He doesn't trust himself to handle a gun anymore, so he quits the store. While the rupture between the two brothers makes difficulties for both of them, Bob remains determined to claim his independence and sanity. The portrait of Eddie, Bob's brother, caught up in financial scams, looms pathetic and chilling—predictably, fast Eddie's character presents a cantankerously ugly portrait of the *American Dream* as a slime-slide in the sunshine.

But those difficulties can't hold a candle to Vanise's struggle to survive in the chapter "Grand Chemin," the great road. (Mention of the *Grand Chemin* appears to be required on a Voodoo passport.[18]) To get his job back, McKissick's former underling Robbie conspires to aid the Haitian captives. In Cockburn Harbour, Robbie puts the Haitian family aboard a boat to Bermuda (they don't have the faintest idea of their 300 mile destination) where Vanise finds herself brutally raped by the rusty hulk's crew as well as the paying Haitian men passengers in the stuffed hold. So begins her ferried Charon-like descent into a hell peopled by the living dead—zombies, both white and black, those ghosts who have no conscience, no sense of right and wrong, the place where one finds, "all those sorry souls, / who've lost the guiding Principle of Mind."[19] Like a lurid zombie movie,[20] these pale ghouls prey on Vanise's flesh as if she were a common pot to eat from. On an immigrant boat, a nonpaying female passenger acquires the status of bottom-rung prostitute.

Banks never employs the word zombie (the word derives from the Kongo *nzambi* meaning "spirit of a dead person"[21]) and never falls prey to the melodramatic hysterics of the over-the-top genre. His restrained subtlety enhances his wild-side realism, evoking a horror far more real and terrifying than the comic, stylized play-acting of the zombie genre. Worse than the grim terrain of John Steinbeck's migrating Oakies in *The Grapes of Wrath* (1939), Banks evokes sympathy and pity with the plight of the Haitians, for without money, what can they do but be victims in transit? Between bouts of forced sex, Vanise is described as "an animal resting."[22] To the crew, Vanise is just a cunt and the family hunkers in steerage, conjuring images of chattel slavery. Claude and Vanise cling to the base of the hold ladder as if they are manacled to it.[23] In this dire situation, prayer to the Haitian gods, especially Agwé,[24] the voodoo *loa* (divinity) of the sea, during the nightmare of a sea storm provides the only thread that enables Vanise and Claude to retain their sanity amid these devilish ghouls who have lost the capacity of their intellect to be aware of any possible goodness. Even young Claude suffers the humiliation, degradation, and physical pain of being raped during the two-day journey. Painting such scenes of horror without condescension or sensationalism, Banks's neutral narration daubs a contemporary *Inferno*.

When the boat arrives at Nassau in the Bahamas, the city appears deserted and the plan consists of walking unobtrusively to Elizabethtown. Perplexed that she can't take her bundle of clothes with her, Vanise stands catatonic; she's pulled off the boat and deposited on the pier after being told it's better not to have her bundle. We get a farewell ironic glimpse of two of the zombie rapists, boss and captain:

> The white man came forward and joined him. *It's pathetic, ain't it?* He flipped his long hair away from his face and lit a cigarette.
> The captain nodded. *Dem Haitians, mon, dem worse'n Jamaicans. Live like dogs, mon. You cyan deal wid 'em like dey was normal people.*
> The white man smiled as if the captain told a joke. *Ain't that the fuckin' truth, though.*[25]

Vanise, Claude, and the infant Charles move on with Claude trying to comfort Vanise by saying that *Les Invisibles* are with them always and everywhere as in Dante's *Divine Comedy*. Although they evade the police, Vanise ends up enslaved as a prostitute in an upper room over a bar. Claude escapes through a window and nobody cares that he's gone, but after a while he returns, possessed by the god Ogu,[26] to kill the bar owner with a machete, liberating Vanise and baby Charles. But they are still in hell, their middle passage not over.

The fourth part of "Grand Chemin," where Vanise will get her west wind to take her to America, features an anthropological slide explaining the psychology and sociology of why some men and women among the exploited

Mainstream Realism and Zombies: *Continental Drift*

population of the tourist trade become attracted to the Voodoo gods, due to the despairing duress of their lives. Such a connection to the divine offers not only consolation, but a way out of the masochistic paralysis that grips both mind and body—that living connection to the invisible world which transcends their debilitating physical world. Here Voodoo finds presentation as a positive force for good that contrasts to those nonbelievers in society who reject its spirituality and at the tipping point of their frustrated despair enact drunken violence or other self-destructive nightmare scenarios. This exposition, unobtrusive in its passing, prepares the reader for the following scene wherein Vanise finds herself mounted by the *loa* Agwé in an episode of divine possession.

But Claude pays for the ritual from the money he earned after he escaped from the bar-bordello. He cannot use any of the *blood money*, that large roll of bloody bills he had taken from the bar owner he killed, because tainted money can have no efficacy in the spiritual world. The mambo (female shaman) thinks the ritual is to be performed for Claude because he's paying for the goat sacrifice, yet Claude says no to her, that the ritual is to preserve Vanise's life, not his, as he points to his aunt. This becomes a significant detail in the plot.

Readers are situated at the point in ritual sacrifice before the historical separation of religion and theater. The ritual *barque* is loaded with flowers and sacrificial offerings to be sent adrift into the ocean:

> The *houngenikon* sang as loudly as ever, with the energy of someone discovering her voice anew, and the drummers beat on as if they had found lost drums only a moment before, and the mambo, apparently finished with Vanise, stood at the mast and waved about her head a pair of white chickens held by their feet and chanted and prayed to Agwé and his mistress Erzulie la Sirène. The passengers, awash with sweat from the heat, their bodies stilled by it, nevertheless sang along with the *houngenikon*, keeping up the joyous pilgrimage despite the heat, the work and discomfort, the long hours it was taking.[27]

Readers see the ancient rite of a chorus leader guiding the participating audience into the ecstasy of music and song, then the cathartic possession of Vanise transformed into the visage of Agwé wearing *the very face of history* as he views the boat passengers with *infinite compassion* while scalding tears flow down the face of Agwé—Vanise. In this brief but eloquent passage, readers witness the primitive miracle at the birth of dramatic tragedy, for the Greek word literally means goatsong (the song sung at the goat sacrifice). Here Agwé breaks the linear boundaries of Western historical time, incarnating himself briefly in Vanise. The pilgrims have entered the Otherworld outside of mundane time.

Because the narrator remains outside of Vanise's consciousness, the mystery and dignity of the transcendent ritual is preserved. In contrast to the first-person narration of the incompetent anthropologist character of *The Book of Jamaica*, the anthropological work here is sober, accurate, and sound, but it has been transformed into compelling art, conjuring the primitive origin of drama Aristotle alluded to his *Poetics*.[28] Everything regarding Vanise up to this point constitutes what Aristotle calls the involvement, those incidents leading up to the transformative change. That transformative change lies in Vanise's possession by Agwé. Everything after the possession scene becomes what Aristotle labels the unraveling of the plot—Vanise's salvation effected by the ritual. For postmodern literature, the conjoining of the climax with religious ritual remains a highly unusual synthesis, a synthesis as daring as remarkably successful, a marriage that incorporating both classical heritage and living reportage from an anthropological lens. The scene captures the mystery, the genuine atmosphere of invoking the gods with passion and pathos as well as the otherworldly strangeness of the ritual in all its poetic detail by people who have nothing, sacrificing what little they have to implore the gods both as individuals and as a group.

Meanwhile, Bob is about to embark on his boat crossing to his own hell. His former high school friend Avery Boone, the callous seducer of Bob's wife back in New Hampshire, offers him a job piloting his boat, the *Belinda Blue*, which Bob had run a few times in circles up on a New Hampshire lake some years ago. Bob, having just quit his job with sleazy brother Eddie, little knows he's out of the pot and into the frying pan—Avery's after the big money through smuggling drugs and illegal aliens. Bob naively thinks the profit comes from taking ignorant dorky Americans with beer logo hats and their wives who don fashionable sunglasses to disguise their crow's-feet eyes out for tour rides on the boat. Avery will buy a new boat and run it to smuggle drugs on his whimsical schedule.

Bob consents to work for the man who had seduced his wife. In contrast, Vanise submits to the divine will without condition or remuneration. The climax of Bob's monetary decision remains in the Western sense rational and quietly personal, a capitulation to needy circumstances based upon a dubious friendship, which occurs in the humdrum light of late afternoon. Vanise's climax appears, on the other hand, primitively and ecstatically irrational, as well as a public ritual of prayer and song conducted at twilight with candles and fire.

"Selling Out" paints a deeper portrait of anti-hero Bob's confusion, denial, and anger. His fishing-excursion job as boat captain turns out to be a part-time gig reducing the family to subsistence at a trailer park rental because he sold the mobile home to buy a one-quarter stake in the boat. He makes a habitual pass, this time at a trailer park neighbor, but when it's accepted by the older woman with a wig, he backs out in panicked embarrassment, telling himself that he's trying to be good, yet this event clearly unravels his psyche, destroying his self-image. Bob runs into the retired baseball player Ted Williams and behaves like a tongue-tied child instead of asking him out on the boat to get a candid snapshot that he can use for promotional purposes. When told his thumb-sucking daughter Ruthie has been diagnosed as mentally disturbed and that they will need more money to address this situation, he's initially in denial (the way he first treats all his problems), then trashes the trailer, destroying crockery and lamps. Bob arrives at the frustrated brink of beating his wife Elaine as she holds the baby, losing the respect of both his family and the reader, yet Banks has provided a believable psychological portrait of how a struggling working-class man arrives at dysfunctional despair. His wife Elaine takes an evening waitressing shift at the Rusty Scupper restaurant.

Bob romps with Avery's girlfriend Honduras (in the kind of spontaneous comic sex scene Grace Metalious made famous) after she seduces him with marijuana and cocaine. He talks to his older brother Eddie on the phone and finds out that Eddie's wife has taken the kids away, his epilepsy has returned, the liquor store has closed, his new boat repossessed, and he's facing foreclosure on his house in a few days—unless he comes up with big money, he will forfeit his life to loan sharks. When he asks his brother Bob for the loan of a six-figure sum, Bob laughs uncontrollably, and Eddie hangs up. Bob decides to drive up to see his brother a half hour later at 4:00 a.m., only to find his brother has committed suicide. Yet amid everything, Bob remains true to character, brimming with his Mittyesque flights of fancy, assuring himself that he's not a failure like his brother. While Bob's flights of nostalgia for his brother's youth are understandable, Eddie's wife's bitterness offers a shocking economic perspective, especially since it was her purchase of the yacht that caused Eddie's economic house of cards to collapse.

The death of Eddie unveils an economic determinism at play in the novel whereby the failure to pay bills leads to the destruction of some American families. Such basic honesty rarely appears in American literature after Steinbeck. The economics of the American system usually finds itself conveniently ignored by authors because unless the writer distracts the reader with entertainment, book sales will suffer. It's presumed that if one can afford to buy a book, one soars above society's economic pitfalls. It's also true that there isn't a character in Banks's novel who would ever read a novel. Banks provides a social portrait of both the virtues and vices of his working class subjects, avoiding sentimentality, Lucretian philosophy,[29] and Marxist ideology as he critiques the persistence of the Horatio Alger infection:

> It's not bad luck, Bob knows, life's not that irrational an arrangement of forces; and though he's no genius, it's not plain stupidity, either, for too many stupid people get on in the world. It's dreams. And especially the dream of the new life, the dream of starting over. The more a man trades off his known life, the one in front of him that came to him by birth and the accidents and happenstance of youth, the more of that he trades for dreams of a new life, the less power he has. . . . This is how a good man loses his goodness.[30]

While sympathizing with Bob's plight, one understands he's locked into that old existentialist box with no exit.

When the plots of Bob and Vanise meet on Haiti during the pickup of illegal aliens (Bob being assisted by Avery's Jamaican Tyrone), Vanise is "trying to exchange an absence for a presence, a condition for destiny."[31] From the third-world perspective, there can be no destiny until they can enter the capitalist market, which argues a denial of alternative Marxist possibilities. Before they leave Haiti, the seer *mambo* looks into Tyrone's eye and decides he's a bad man, a feckless opportunist who will do anything, a correct assessment that prepares the reader for what Tyrone will eventually do.

Spotted by a U.S. Coast Guard cruiser, Bob begrudgingly consents to Tyrone's advice to dump the Haitians in rough seas, Tyrone carrying it out at gunpoint. When Bob sees they are drowning, nothing can be done. Eventually, 13 of the 14 Haitians die, the only survivor being Vanise, who stumbles ashore half-unconscious. Due to the death of her child and nephew, Vanise has become a zombie teetering at the border of death. Vanise, delivered to her brother in this state, attends a voodoo ceremony in order to get her soul back. At the ceremony the *loa* Baron Samedi (Baron Cemetery is married to the Irish fertility goddess Grann Brigitte) takes her after Agwé gives his permission. Vanise is revived and saved, but she believes that the *loa* Ghede, the god of death, allowed her to live merely because she was the one who fed the others to him. The theme of "Feeding the Loas," the title of the last chapter, carries the tragic mode throughout the novel as it relates to those around Vanise, Eddie, and ultimately Bob.

Upon docking, Bob, somewhat to his relief, discovers himself detained by the Coast Guard. Bob thinks that he will be charged for murder of the Haitians, but they are only interested in searching his boat for drugs because Avery has been nailed for selling uncut cocaine to a narc agent. Bob, as Avery's associate, is searched, but in an unusual, somewhat magical, hole for a realistic plot, they fail to find the bulging wad of bills in his trouser pocket. Bob tells his wife Elaine she should quit her waitressing job, offering her some money, but she's deeply suspicious of the money's source, rejecting it as ill-gotten drug money. She keeps her job and declares she's now the family breadwinner.

Haunted by his unrelenting guilt for the death of the Haitians, especially after he reads a newspaper account of the 15 deaths, Bob cruises the dive bars in little Haiti, desperately searching for Vanise. He wants to give the cash he was paid by the Haitians to her in a gesture of expiation, but in her bewilderment she cannot accept such blood money and "refuses to remove the sign of his shame."[32] In this dangerous Miami nighttime neighborhood, Bob finds himself set upon by four thieves (the four directions of the compass). When he refuses to turn over his money, they summarily slaughter him with knives. The *loa* Samedi has used Vanise to feed Ghede as a return gift for accepting her from Agwé. The conclusion locates itself in the religious and mythical morality of voodoo at hands of *Les Invisibles* rather than the more commonplace world of cops and crime one would encounter on television.

Perhaps Bob's guilt marks him as a potential penitent, but he has despaired of life, despaired of living for his family because he lost any hope of any self-redemption. If Bob had thought more of his children rather than his dignity, perhaps he would have remained alive to help them. At bottom, Bob has the character of an overgrown, insecure child. His ignominious end appears to be an enactment of the rough street ethic he participated in when he became an accomplice to killing the 15 immigrants. Ironically, the Jamaican Tyrone, a more guilty man, finds himself deported back to Jamaica.

The concluding "Envoi" speaks of its 41-year-old common man Bob as, "one of those who perpetrate crimes becomes one of those who are the victims of crimes."[33] Readers are told that books written on the subject of people like Bob or Vanise will not set the world free, that such knowledge or empathy for the world's victims changes nothing amid indifferent nature. The goal of the book has been *sabotage and subversion*. The author prays that his book will "help destroy the world as it is."[34] The final wisdom consists of passion not knowledge. Unlike the philosophy of Plato or Lucretius, knowledge remains futile when set against the random continental tides of human history. Only the mysterious mythology of passion has the power to unlock the dark secrets of freedom, which dwell more in aspiration and prayer than in nature.

The *deus ex machina* conclusion appears inevitable yet more tragic because we were privy to Bob's ambivalence about the Haitian operation, his genuine concern for the welfare of the Haitians once they were aboard his boat, and then the reversal when he dumps them. One hears the final wisdoms of his ruminations on life before the sordid fate of his sudden death. Any other conclusion to the story of Bob Dubois would be gratuitously self-indulgent on the part of the reader and author. Vanise remains a cipher uncontaminated by the Horatio Alger fantasy as well as any blood money. She is free to struggle, whether to swim or drown, in a culture she knows nothing about. Her religious debts are for the moment paid and her journey to live the secular life in America will begin as she leaves mythical time and enters the historical time of recorded migrations. Freedom continues to be complicated and it arrives with a great price, something Bob realizes only just before he dies.

This bifurcated narrative belongs to the category of tragicomedy, an unusual genre, because most bifurcated narratives are either consistently comic like Joyce's *Ulysses* or bleakly tragic like Euripides's *Heracles* (416 BC), although one might argue Homer's use of bifurcated narrative in *The Odyssey* constitutes the first example of tragic-comedy. In providing a bifurcated tragicomedy, a blended genre that rose to prominence during the Continental Renaissance and advocated in England by the literary criticism of Sir Philip Sidney in *A Defence of Poesie* (1595),[35] Banks valorizes the third-world underclass over spoiled Americans of the working-class who (like privileged children) don't realize just what it is they have, one of the leitmotifs concerning poor Selena in Metalious's working-class novel *Peyton Place*.[36]

A similar use of a bifurcated tragicomedy plot with a parallel sociological perception akin to Banks's critique of greed in American culture can be found in Boyle's *The Tortilla Curtain* (1995), a novel about immigration set in southern California, which charts the intersecting lives of two couples rather than two characters. Banks, Boyle, and Metalious all embrace the kind of tragic-comic vision pioneered by Virginia Woolf in her satiric first novel, *The Voyage Out* (1915),[37] although in general American writers project far more sympathy for the trials and tribulations of the working class.

Banks presents a rebuking critique of the Alger rags-to-riches fantasy in Bob Dubois, but this in itself does not constitute a critique of the American Dream. As Banks points out in *Dreaming Up America* (2008), the American Dream was one of immigrants working for generations to climb the economic and social ladder generation by generation through hard work:

> It was the millions of Americans who worked on the assembly lines, in the mines, in the fields, in the shipping yards, on the docks and the railroads, and so on. They were the ones who changed the world. That's why I'm still talking about the American Dream. Because there is an ongoing battle for the right to restore that dream or see it replaced by empire.[38]

The problem of Bob Dubois was that he gave up on that dream—he was not willing to sacrifice his fantasies of Disneyland riches so that his children could go to college and become teachers or lawyers or even postal workers. He becomes the self-indulgent victim of the dream, searching for the easy way out. Bob thought of himself and never of his children, except in self-indulgent moments of daydream delusion. Bob gambled on the short cut and lost. Our identity as a nation of immigrants was not one identity but many identities, but what was shared was that work ethic, "to sacrifice and build."[39] Banks points out that the dream of empire nurtured by John D. Rockefeller, Andrew Carnegie, and Henry Ford was not the goal of the citizens who made this country great. The strength of this country lay not in its financial hierarchy but in the workers who created those noted captains of industry. What Banks once declared about Algren's *A Walk on the Wild Side* (1956) applies just as well to *Continental Drift*, "the novel is at once a radical critique of the American economy and a grief-stricken portrait of its victims."[40] While Banks investigates a smaller and less bitter cast of characters than Algren, he plumbs the interior life of his working-class characters with greater depth.

At the end of the novel, Vanise arrives as a penniless immigrant. She will not realize the American Dream herself, but perhaps her children's children will be arguing a case in court or managing a small chain of stores. There's no quick fix, no magical scam, to create the American Dream. The dream of instant riches and sprawling mansions offers a zombie dream that afflicts some Americans—no doubt enhanced by whatever's playing on the idiot box. The genius of U.S. President Franklin Delano Roosevelt and writers like James T. Farrell, Algren, Studs Terkel, and Banks consists in understanding that the sociology of the American Dream remains built from the bottom up and not from the top down. The fantasy of Northerners entering the borderlands[41] of the South for imperial conquest exposes them as quixotic conquistadors caught in a geographical undertow they cannot comprehend. The novel's concluding "L'Envoi" aspires to demolish the preconceptions of a naïve cultural arrogance Americans often exhibit on the global stage.

Daniel Simon notes that Algren's method of writing consists of a process of accretion, much like a painter applying varied layers of paint to a canvas.[42] In many ways *Continental Drift* represents an accretion of Russell Banks's obsessions: bar scenes, geographical metaphors, anthropological considerations, meditations on death, examinations on motivations concerning sexual infidelity, the provincialism of American culture, the salutary yet sometimes delusional role of religion, and the restless questing that squats like a cure or cancer at the heart of life. All these elements become problematic in the search for freedom that his characters undertake. The accretions of these previous signature characteristics appear in *Continental Drift* with a new synthesis, at once more accessible, mysterious, and evocative.

The genre of mainstream realism in American fiction continues to be uniquely adaptable and accessible to the American public, and that is one reason why *Continental Drift* achieved success both on a commercial and a critical level. While the novel presents a more translucent and supple narrative than Banks's previous novels, the style brims with what the Greeks called *energia*, that is, an energetic vigor conveying great immediacy and clarity. *Continental Drift* was a finalist for the 1986 Pulitzer Prize, yet found itself edged out by a popular nineteenth-century Western about a group of ex-Texas Rangers living on a border town penned by Ken Kesey's former Stanford classmate—Larry McMurtry with *Lonesome Dove*.

Banks's novel made the finalist list for the Pulitzer despite the uncomfortable topic of immigration, a brutally violent conclusion, a treatment of marital infidelity, a portrayal of voodoo as a living religion, and a plot about small-time drug smuggling; the novel critiqued what would become the greedy corporate mentality of the early 2000s that eventually brought the American economy to its knees; that such a novel would even be considered for a broad popular prize was in itself a remarkable achievement. The novel offered a too-honest probe into the cultural roots of American narcissism, working-class confusion, and frustrated anger. That tragic story Banks found outlined in the newspaper about smuggling illegal aliens ended up as a vivid walk on the wild side. Despite the passage of a quarter century, the dicey economic situation portrayed in the novel situates the novel as more relevant than ever, magnifying the novel's achievement.

8

Naturalism as Postmodern Parable: *Affliction*

> The tracks were there. He knew the sheriff's—the heavy, deep, deliberate prints, even in the rainless summer's parched earth, of those two hundred and forty pounds of flesh which wore the metal shield smaller than a playing card, on which he had gambled not only his freedom but perhaps his obliteration.
> —William Faulkner, *The Hamlet*

Three Chicago writers, James T. Farrell, Nelson Algren, and Richard Wright, were mutual friends as well as disciples of Theodore Dreiser's naturalism, but they developed in different ways. James T. Farrell, who advised Wright on his early work and tried to get Vanguard to publish him,[1] employed his studies in sociology to dramatize how people were trapped by the web of class and culture as well as youthful rebellion. Algren focused on people trapped by the seamy underside of the street, especially criminality. Wright dramatized how the delusional ideology of race supremacy created a debilitating fear and paranoia that destroyed dignity as well as society. Wright's approach integrated the influences of Dreiser, Farrell, and Algren, as it added a symbolic dimension to the poetic resonances of Algren's bleak lyricism.

After Wright introduced Algren to Simone de Beauvoir, the handsome Algren became her lover for a brief time,[2] but that experience was more traumatic than transformative. He continued to work in the naturalistic tradition of the street as if he was the American literary equivalent of the chanteuse Édith Piaf, changing only the locale for his last great novel *A Walk on the Wild Side* (1956) to New Orleans as he kept to the Depression era setting of his Chicago novels like *Never Come Morning* (1942), which charted the deterministic development of crime. Wright followed in Dreiser's urban footsteps with *Native Son* (1940),[3] examining the entrapping mechanism of crime with an explosive racial twist. After Wright moved to Paris in 1947, Wright became a good friend of de Beauvoir's long-time lover, Jean-Paul Sartre, with whom Wright collaborated on social causes.[4] Existentialism was attractive to Wright and he may have been employing it long before he discovered it, but he more self-consciously came under the influence of Sartre's existential philosophy in *The Outsider* (1953).[5]

In its historical development, naturalism in the works of Emile Zola and his disciples centered upon urban settings with their complex and sensational sociology. In America, Stephen Crane, Frank Norris, and Dreiser followed Zola's naturalistic, urban, deterministic, sociological approach[6] while the rural novel lingered in pastoral shade, unwilling to relinquish its romantic roots. Like Gustave Flaubert and Ivan Turgenev, William Dean Howells,[7] the grandfather of American realism, centered realism upon character studies. These writers were unwilling to renounce romantic themes in a rural context. Mark Twain's *Pudd'nhead Wilson* (1894) was grimly deterministic. Following Dreiser, Farrell, Algren, and Wright wrote of passion rather than romance in the orbit of urban sociological determinism. In Banks's *Affliction* romance appears ecstatic as in traditional pastoral, but the narrator surrounds romance with an atmosphere of frustration relating to his brother's job and ultimately *argues* anger as a motivation for murder.

Affliction compresses the naturalistic influences of Farrell, Algren, and Wright into a single masterpiece, adapting working-class naturalism to a postmodern rural rather than urban context. The sociological approach of Farrell finds explication in town and family history while the influences of Wade's job might be seen in the importance of working-class occupation as pioneered by Farrell in his second novel written during his Paris sojourn, *Gas-House McGinty* (1933). The depiction of the inside story on how a police officer arrives at flipping into criminality would, on the surface, relate to the sympathetic character portraits of underworld characters in Algren's fiction (especially *The Man with the Golden Arm*), but something much more complicated goes on in Banks's novel. The double murder-plot of Wright's *Native Son*, which Wright inherited from Dreiser's *An American Tragedy* (1925), will provide an element of Banks's sensational plot, but Banks prefaces the theme of an apparent accidental murder as an antecedent mystery murder before further murders.

The background opening of *Affliction* (1989) recalls the geographical metaphors invoked in *Hamilton Stark* and *Continental Drift*, but the origin of this technique, surpassed in Banks's more poetic execution (here playing as a recurring winter refrain) can be traced back to the opening of *A Walk on the Wild Side* with its briefing on the backwoods Linkhorn clan, emerging as it does in an urban context with Fitz the cesspool cleaner.[8] Banks penned a 1989 foreword to the 1990 reprint to *A Walk on the Wild Side*, acclaiming it an American classic alongside *Huckleberry Finn*, *The Red Badge of Courage*, and *Native Son*.[9] The poet Margaret Walker's 1988 biography of Richard Wright, *Richard Wright: Daemonic Genius*, emphasized the psychic wounds of his youth,[10] a theme found layered into Banks's *Affliction* with regard to disciplinary abuse (but not race). Father-son conflict had appeared previously in some of Banks's short stories, especially "With Ché in New Hampshire" and "Firewood," which contains the theme of a frozen pile of wood that appears in *Affliction*. Like Wright's Bigger Thomas of *Native Son*, Banks's Wade Whitehouse finds himself

Naturalism as Postmodern Parable: *Affliction*

trapped in an existential hell that places him amid the interaction of environment and heredity. For Bigger Thomas to think about consciousness leads to the risk of insanity or violence—Wade *apparently* follows in those footsteps.

Rolfe, Wade's younger brother, narrates the story of his older brother. Rolfe's monologue highlights the Whitehouse family's dysfunctional internal wars and psychic instability as well as the town itself. According to Rolfe, their father appears as an archetypal *Ahab* figure of wrath, heartily drinking Canadian Club like Hamilton Stark, pontificating on his apparently futile quest to make real men out of his boys. The opening epigraph of the novel quotes Simone Weil's existentialist observation, "The great enigma of human life is not suffering but affliction." That is, suffering can be more easily understood by rationality while affliction partakes of the irrational and absurd. *Affliction* meditates existentially upon the irrational and the absurd in the small New Hampshire town of Lawford where Wade will, according to his brother, transgress the law amid a variety of pressures. Although the novel presents itself as a murder mystery in a small town, the novel contains a deep parable of national significance. *Affliction* is a twentieth-century epic parable about a great American tragedy.

The opening scene of the novel occurs during Halloween, which the narrator disparages as an irrelevant holiday. While the historical interpretation of how and why past holidays cling to civilization's backwaters offers a sensible rumination, a reader might know that Halloween, All Hallows Eve, is a Christian label (celebrating the hallowed saints) for the pagan Celtic feast of Samhain, which usually lasted for three days and nights. During the feast, the boundaries of this world and the Otherworld break down—people don masks and behave outside the boundaries and morals of regular time. People might impersonate gods or become the incarnation of their ancestors. It provides a time to leave food out for one's ancestors in the hope of communing with them, asking their advice, or allowing their spirits to take on the burden of your problems. Since Banks employed a true understanding of Voodoo mysteries in *Continental Drift*, there's reason to believe the Halloween setting offers more than childish decoration. Such interpretation finds confirmation in Banks's use of allusion to John Montague's well-known poem "Like Dolmens Around My Childhood, The Old People" which features the line "Fomorian fierceness of family and local feud"[11] when describing the scene of marital discord between him and his former wife Lillian Whitehouse Horner. Fomorians were prehistoric invaders of Ireland, famed for their monstrous savagery in battle:

> His [Wade's] glance passed over the red granite war memorial next to the town hall. It stood in the pale moonlight like an ancient dolmen, and he saw above it, in the lighted window of his own office, his daughter, Jill, still wearing the hideous plastic mask [of a tiger], looking back at him.[12]

The names of Wade's two older brothers, who were killed in the Vietnam War, rest on the granite above with names from other American wars, going back to the Revolutionary War. The monstrous fierceness of feud refers to both family strife and national strife in the allusion to historical wars—the subject at the heart of the novel. The opening functions as a prologue setting down the novel's martial epic theme as well as bitter local atmosphere.

Ironically, Wade meditates on the destructive war pranks young teenagers perform during Halloween as he admits to his memory the desultory pranks he and his brothers performed on the town when young, marveling at the aggression he perpetrated with his brothers and the perverse humor of children. Yet Wade cannot make the connection an anthropologist would about a culture designed for warfare. New Hampshire deer hunting season begins on November 1st with shots echoing in the hills on that snowy morning[13] when Wade awakes alone in his trailer, owned by his boss Gordon LaRiviere, on the windy tip of a lake, one of a dozen trailers, as in *Trailerpark*. Rolfe, the university history teacher, remarks that Halloween means nothing, yet says that for snow to start falling November 1st is perfectly normal. In the Celtic calendar, Samhein (Celtic New Year) marks the beginning of winter, winter and night reckoned as anterior to light, as in many ancient calendars, including Hebrew.

Jack Hewitt, Wade's co-worker in well-drilling and snowplowing, appears as a potential double of Wade, younger, with a similar potentially angry personality, but determined to discover a way not to become another Wade. Wade's part-time job as police officer consists of working one hour a day in the morning during weekdays as the school crossing guard, a job he thoroughly enjoyed until his daughter Jill moved down to Concord with her new husband. The school bus now reminds him of her absence and how he longed to see her face in the bus, then see her wave—a mime theme later taken up in *The Sweet Hereafter*.

Banks's monologue technique converts the traditional repertoire of naturalism's strands and compresses them into an involved monologue, thus inserting a postmodern perspective that participates in postmodern relativism. While Rolfe concludes that Jack Hewitt was innocent, the reader need not reach that same conclusion. An ambiguous space, an absence, opens up as the reader becomes aware of the possibly prejudiced assumptions of the historian as a participant-observer in the narrative. While the participant-observer of *The Book of Jamaica* was delusional, Rolfe remains soberly sane, but readers need to examine carefully the facts as he presents them.

Rolfe first depicts Hewitt as shooting Evan Twombley.[14] Then Wade gets into the grader to plow. Another slide appears in which Twombley accidentally shoots himself, but in this version Hewitt devoutly hopes he's dead.[15] There's a long disquisition about Wade the dreamer, which if the reader thinks about it, sounds out of character for Wade. It is learned that Wade no longer hunts and hasn't fired a gun in many years and has never, even in the service, killed anyone. Wade asserts to Hewitt that he must have seen Twombley shot. Rolfe then places three fantasies in his brother's imagination. In the first two scenarios, Twombley accidentally shoots himself. In the third fantasy, Wade struggles with Twombley, who's supposedly madly seized by greed for the shot, seizes Hewitt's gun, and finds himself shot in the struggle.[16] Rolfe has presented differently imagined versions in a kind of *Roshomon* montage, but they are all his versions.

Naturalism as Postmodern Parable: *Affliction*

These three imaginings lead to the later incontrovertible conclusion that the death of Twombley was just an accident and that Wade killed his friend Jack to enact justice after Jack murdered his father. The divorce lawyer J. Battle Hand down in Concord, finds the story of Twombley's sudden death strange and suspicious. This is all the evidence the reader hears. One other detail: Wade has confiscated the murder weapon as evidence for his report, but since Wade disappears, so does the gun, the principal item of evidence. The only way anyone, not a state official, could get that gun would be over Wade's dead body.

Exactly midway through the novel when the story will turn more deterministic, at the opening paragraph of chapter 13, Banks creates a prose poem rendering of a telephone ring that echoes the famous opening line of Wright's *Native Son*, "*Brrrrrrriiiiiiiiiiiiiiiiiiinng!*" with its seven italic *r*'s and nineteen *i*'s imitating the ring of an alarm clock. Here Wright employs a typographical technique invented by the Russian Serapion Brothers circle.[17] In Wright's novel, the annoying mechanical clock announces a tragic *musical* prelude to a nightmare caught in the hands of time. Those awakened have no idea what time it is, any more than a slave once knew one's age, as Frederick Douglass poignantly pointed out on the first page of his autobiography—*Narrative of the Life of Frederick Douglass, An American Slave*. In Banks's novel, the oppressive ringing of the telephone conjures up a nightmare continuum between sleeping and waking:

> THE SHRILL RING of the telephone tumbled Wade from light and heat—a blond dream of a beach town in summer—tossed him into darkness and cold, a bed and a room he could not at first recognize. The wrangling jangle of the telephone: he did not know where the damned thing was; it kept on ringing, still coming at him from all sides; some kind of maddened bird or rabid bat darting around his head in the darkness.[18]

Wade had been sleeping during a snowstorm. Not knowing what time it is, LaRiviere yells at Wade to let him know that the 4:00 a.m. phone call is to let him know that he should have been working at snowplowing since 11:00 p.m. LaRiviere insults Wade for plowing his girlfriend instead of working. From this point on, Wade begins his descent into paranoia, as the plot follows the Dreiser-Wright pattern.

At Sally Whitehouse's funeral, after she has frozen to death, Banks offers a satire on Lena Whitehouse's born-again evangelicalism, including a bumper sticker that warns during the coming Rapture the driver of the vehicle may *disappear* at any moment. Niemi correctly notes that Banks's satire on religious zealotry recalls Dreiser's send-up of Clyde Griffiths's family in *An American Tragedy*.[19]

After the burial of their mother, Rolfe confesses he had convinced Wade that Hewitt murdered Twombley. Wade says that it makes him crazy that a man (Mel Gordon) can have his father-in-law murdered—nobody gets punished. Rolfe confesses that he wanted Gordon and Hewitt punished, but how could he be responsible for Wade's taking his "highly speculative theory"[20] seriously?

Rolfe only changes his mind about the conspiracy after the disappearance of his brother. It's highly ironic that Rolfe now sees his *wrong* theory as based upon flimsy evidence, but there's a sense in which his *wrong* theory turns out to be both right and wrong.

Do Wade's disappearing footsteps jokingly parody the mysterious conclusion of *Hamilton Stark*? Here the *absence as presence* motif of the disappearing footsteps invites the reader to construct an ending: Wade is dead as far as Rolfe and the town is concerned—that's the story he has labored to convince the reader of. But is he? There's only circumstantial evidence about what has happened to Wade.

Some reviewers complained that Banks does nothing to make Rolfe attractive to the reader. Robert Niemi quotes Fred Phiel's observation that he, "simply can never believe Rolfe can know all he's saying or execute this masterful narration; nor do I believe in or care about him as an individual character whenever he is roped into the plot."[21] But there may be a reason why Banks does not want the reader to identify too closely with Rolfe. Absurdly, Rolfe even provides his brother's dreams. Yet Banks is not a careless writer and one of his favorite postmodern techniques consists of employing confident narrators with limited perspectives. Some distance in identifying with the narrator may be a clue to the narrative. Although Rolfe concludes he has solved the events of his father's death, it may not be the case from a postmodern perspective.

Twombley, the first Catholic permitted to buy a house and land on the shore of fictional Lake Agaway (which excludes Jews and blacks), is murdered before he was to testify on mob connections within the construction industry. Jack Hewitt, either the witness or murderer, was murdered, closing the trail to the conspiracy. The witness or assassin finds himself murdered—an old story of a larger national story, the assassination of U.S. President John F. Kennedy, also covered up by an illogical and fatuous fiction, *The Warren Commission Report*. The novel offers a parable about a monstrous affliction in America by dramatizing the problem on the micro, rather than the macro level.

Affliction as a theme, operates on five levels in the novel: the scars of childhood abuse in dysfunctional families; problematic intimacy, sexual dissatisfaction connected to promiscuity, and spousal abuse; the tyrannical workplace with exploitative bosses; town and national politics abusive of its citizens; and the wounded narrator as a representative man. All levels interact to enhance paranoia, but I want to focus on the political, the most submerged of the levels.

There is no room for meaningless drift in a Banks novel where every concept and word finds careful placement. The apparently casual and contemptuous references to the Kennedy family in the conversation of the state trooper at the murder scene of Twombley, become prominent signposts of an American tragedy. Just as the American war machine got its reward of an expanded Asian war in Vietnam with the removal of Kennedy,[22] the mob-run construction union and LaRiviere get their way—a huge ski resort now dominates Lawford, a town that according to Rolfe has become unrecognizable with its past; its citizens possess an official history of lies that they can trot out

Naturalism as Postmodern Parable: *Affliction*

whenever asked. Such a local and national affliction appears less understandable than suffering—it has been our Native American tragedy since November 22, 1963. Just as a president is considered to be the living father of the country, the murder of a father provides parallel symbolism in the family. But was it Wade who really murdered Pop? That is Rolfe's guess, but the evidence remains suspiciously circumstantial.

As a reader or viewer, the most shocking element of the narrative is that the town police officer finds himself fired in the middle of an investigation because he apparently thinks a murder has been committed and his superiors will not let him talk to them—then he disappears and is charged with crimes. This appears to be something that Rolfe never questions because he knows of the family tension between Pop and Wade. The disappearance of Wade as a guilty party is based upon the circumstances that Wade was alone with his father, that he accidentally murdered his father then set fire to the barn, and especially that he knew where Wade was hunting, but then many people in the small town knew that. The barn burning might evoke the fiery incineration of a body in Wright's *Native Son* and perhaps the criminal destruction of a barn in William Faulkner's 1939 story "Barn Burning," which results in a trial to arrive at truth. Ironically, despite the murders, there will be no trial in Banks's novel. This barn burning appears designed to cover up evidence, but burning a barn never covers up a corpse. The barn may have been burnt to cover up something else.

Pfeil's enthusiastic but mixed comments on *Affliction* probe into the mystery of Rolfe's insecurity, his occasional *whiny* complaints as Pfeil calls it.[23] While Pfeil remains puzzled and annoyed by some of Rolfe's asides, they make more sense if we consider Rolfe himself suffering from an affliction he really can't identify. Rolfe's anguish lies in his difficulty and shame stemming from accepting Captain Asa Brown's official account of what happened and Rolfe's subsequent inability to discover hard evidence to contradict Brown's official report. Rolfe's narrative remains suffused with pain and his tone reveals a man trying to convince himself, more than others, of the terrible story. When at the end of the novel, Rolfe describes the whole tragedy as an ancient paradigm (father-son conflict), might one not wonder if Rolfe has the right paradigm in mind?

If a reader accepts Rolfe's conclusion that Hewitt did not shoot Twombley, it is still possible that Hewitt saw someone shoot Twombley and Hewitt became too cowed to speak out, finding his silence rewarded with becoming the new town cop. Twombley's gun contained a key piece of evidence. Was it ever fired? Did the shell caliber match? It is extremely difficult—quite an acrobatic feat—to shoot yourself in the chest with a rifle. Rolfe's conclusion in the epilogue applies equally well to the Warren Commission, "The evidence, all of it, was incontrovertible. What was not scientific was logical; and what was not logical was scientific."[24] Rolfe's afflicted monologue swaggers circular reasoning without evidence, his main piece of evidence being a newspaper clipping that declares Wade missing and under suspicion. The epilogue brims with the odd timbre of Banks's deeply oblique and ironic humor, "It is easier to understand diplomatic maneuvers in Jordan, natural calamities in the third world and the economics of addictive drugs than an isolated explosion of homicidal rage in a small American town."[25] It remains possible that someone has murdered Wade Whitehouse to prevent Wade from making a public ruckus, and then murdered his father who witnessed the murder, set the fire, disposed of Wade's body, murdered Hewitt, and used Wade's boots for the footprints leading to nowhere, thus making Wade the patsy, just as Lee Harvey Oswald was made the patsy. The conclusion of the novel offers no closure:

> there will be no more mention in the newspapers of him [Wade] and his friend Jack Hewitt and our father. No more mention of them anywhere. The story will be over. Except that I continue.[26]

Rolfe, a kind of surviving Ishmael, feels damaged by the whole story and wonders if some day he could become normal and have children like his dead brother Wade. Both Rolfe and the town are linked as victims in this story. In any case, a historian never cites the absence of evidence as *incontrovertible* proof of anything, but that psychology was what the Warren Commission provided. Absolute assertions without evidence beg questions. Since the evidence is so circumstantial, a number of scenarios might be worked out by a thoughtful reader—so, too, with the Kennedy assassination.

The year before the publication of *Affliction*, Don DeLillo published his novel on Oswald, *Libra* (1988). DeLillo concluded that Oswald could not have been a lone assassin, but the single gunman theory and magic bullet theory were the two absolutes the Warren Commission hammered, asserting them over and over, despite the lack of evidence. DeLillo was fascinated by Oswald's reactive pliability and passivity in the face of his handlers, and he has commented that, "Because the Warren Report is crucial to most meditations on the case, it becomes the book's [*Libra*] background radiation."[27] For Banks, the Warren Report provides background radiation to even small town politics. Banks also remains fascinated at how the American public accepts conclusions through assertive narrative.

In chapter 21, Rolfe provides a series of tape transcripts as documentary evidence of Wade's last two days. Some of these interviews were not immediate—Hettie Rogers's occurs six months later—and the official story might serve to prejudice some of those interviewed. Rolfe never questions whether everyone tells the truth in these transcripts. Captain Brown's transcript is a contemptuous collage of lies. First of all, Wade was not drunk, but merely had a swollen jaw from his toothache and he had not been in a fight. Brown says that Wade came by to ask him if he could become a state trooper at the age of 41. This is patently ridiculous. Rolfe says that Wade was smarter than he and that Wade could have passed the test for state trooper at any time. It's preposterous that Wade as town cop would not know basic regulations. So why did Wade stop by to talk to Captain Brown, a man whom he did not like and who did not like him? Obviously, to report his theory of murder and conspiracy since Chub[28] Merritt would not even talk to him. But what happens if you spill the beans before the wolf?

Naturalism as Postmodern Parable: *Affliction*

Captain Brown was the first man at the scene of Twombley's murder, "For a second Wade entertained the notion that the police captain, Asa Brown, was somehow involved, but then dismissed it: he only thought it because he did not like Asa Brown personally and wanted him somehow involved."[29] If Twombley was murdered on behalf of the mob and if Jack Hewitt did not do it but witnessed the murder by Captain Brown, Jack would be shocked and might have been cowed into silence. Brown later gives Twombley's gun to Hewitt when he gives Hewitt back his hunting license, making him the new town cop. When Wade offers evidence and his theory, he would want Brown to try to get a confession from Hewitt. To protect himself and the conspiracy, Brown must murder both Wade and Hewitt. Margie Fogg's confession of guilt at the end fails to account for the fact that once her loaded car was seen leaving town, it left Wade defenseless against his enemies.

If Brown rode out with Chub to arrest Wade on some trumped-up charge, Wade would have defied him and Wade would have been murdered. Pop would have witnessed it and would have to be done away with. If there had been a struggle or some shots exchanged, then burning down the barn would destroy evidence. Wade's body could have been stuffed into a body bag. Brown could have taken Wade's rifle; Chub could have driven Pop's truck, both of them driving out to Parker Mountain where they knew Hewitt was hunting. Brown could have put on Wade's boots and shot Hewitt with Wade's gun. Chub could have driven the car up to Canada, secretly disposing of Wade's body on the way. Captain Brown discovers Hewitt's dead body on Parker Mountain—the investigation leads to Wade and the case is closed.

Wade wanted Hewitt to talk. The last thing he wanted was a dead witness to the murder or the murderer dead because that would impede exposing the larger conspiracy. With Hewitt firing Twombley's gun (perhaps never fired before), the prime piece of evidence disappears (like the government's destruction of JFK's limo within 24 hours), then the witness is murdered. Pop's death was an accidental casualty of the conspiracy. Wade has never ever killed a man, not even in the army, and it would be out of character for him to do so, much less kill his father, even if he wished his father would die.

Serial murderers often leave telltale signatures. The fact that two men were killed roughly at the same spot holding the same gun indicates the telltale rhyme of a hermetic pathology. A government representative has colluded with the mob, resorted to murder, in a conspiracy to ensure land development, just as Kennedy was assassinated by the government with help from the mob because he opposed American corporate land development in Cuba and Vietnam.[30]

Perhaps this conspiracy theory remains as far-fetched as the numerous speculations surrounding the Kennedy assassination, but the argument offers a counter to Rolfe's presentation, which consists of more fantasy than fact. As a storyteller Rolfe remains afflicted because he cannot know the whole story with any certainty any more than a citizen of this country can, or probably will, know the whole story of the Kennedy assassination. Banks's concept of affliction extends beyond the parameters of the small town and records a national malaise. Such uncertainty recapitulates in a larger social context the existential mystery that concluded *Hamilton Stark*.

Paul Schrader's movie version hews closely to the naturalist elements of the novel, but wisely drops the subterranean political theme connecting the story to the Kennedy assassination, an aspect of the novel that cannot be filmed. Instead, it concentrates on the Whitehouse family saga and provides a parable about child abuse from the point of view of the wounded narrator, Rolfe. The film presents a sympathetic focus on Wade until the reversal, the accidental murder of his father in a fit of retaliatory rage imagined by Rolfe. The film manages to keep Lawford's corrupt politics in its crosshairs, letting the viewer know that the conspiracy between Mel Gordon and Gordon LaRiviere (linked by their names) succeeds and makes them very wealthy.

Besides the deep character layering and background, one aspect of the book that is not translatable into the film remains the novel's occasional bursts of unexpected humor, like this passage concerning marriage, explaining why Wade and Margie become engaged to marry:

> The way to make a marriage work, they both believed, was to improve your character and take advantage of your luck. The first they believed they had control over; the second you took your chances with. So that when one agreed or refused, to marry a person one loved, one was making a statement about that person's character and was expressing his or her attitude toward luck at that particular point in his or her life.[31]

While the novel relies more on narration—Banks's great strength as a writer—the dialogue leaps off the page because of the way it embodies conflict and tension, which is what makes the novel so easily translatable into film along with the deeply etched images in the novel.

One small difference between the novel and film consists of the way the confrontation between Jack and Wade is portrayed. In the film, Jack shoots the tires to LaRiviere's truck which Wade is driving; in the novel Jack's armed standoff occurs on ice, his truck leaving while Wade's sinks. Jack's behavior in both displays a terrified guilt and cannot be explained as innocent behavior. Also, the fact that he's not fired for what he has done to LaRiviere's vehicle—he suffers no consequences at all—stands out as a significant clue that points to conspiracy, but the brutality of both novel and film, the manic intensity of atmosphere and narrative drive, emotionally bludgeon the reader or viewer, making the postmodern interpretation of collusion less apparent, more resembling the resonating image of the sunken truck or the shocking deflation of the bullet-ridden tires.

Another aspect of the book not translatable into film remains the total atmosphere of small pond enclosure made famous in *Peyton Place*, but the atmosphere of the novel more approximately resembles Faulkner's *The Hamlet* (1931). The conspiracy to build the new ski resort on the part of LaRiviere and Gordon bears resemblance to Snopes-style social climbing but in a more Northeastern way with mob involvement as city money begins to exploit the New England countryside. At the bottom of Faulkner's novel lay the obsession with land and its ownership—just as in Banks's novel. Wealth in the land appears somewhat delusional in Faulkner (the theme of buried treasure), but it is real in Banks's novel as LaRiviere and Gordon become ski resort millionaires. Corruption occurs from the bottom openly working its way upward in Faulkner, while in Banks it occurs as secretly working its way down from the top.

Banks's portraits of Lillian and Hettie present northern types more reserved than Faulkner's Eula and Yettie, especially in their sexual manipulation of men for their ascent in social status, although bright and scheming Lillian remains virtually barren compared to the ignorant and sensual Eula. Just as the promiscuous Yettie and Mink Snopes appear at first to have an ideal sexual relationship, readers learn that is not the case. Likewise Jack and Hettie arrive on stage as a happy couple, but readers learn at the end that is not the case. As in Faulkner's novel, the depiction of sexual relations remains problematic for both couples and married people. The observation that "Faulkner's major characters lived and moved upon a marital and sexual landscape that was in shambles"[32] might well apply to Banks's novels, especially *Affliction*; even the ecstatic sexual moments of relief that Rolfe depicts between Margie and Wade cannot hold them together. The sylvan backdrop found in both novels provides menace—Faulkner offers more sexual irony in his lush paradisial landscape while Banks's Nordic hellfrost more directly contributes to a crunching determinism. Faulkner presents more vulgarity, even descending to bestiality,[33] while Puritan reserve cloaks Lawford's secret sins with closed doors and uptight hypocrisy. The Gothic element of family legacy wedded to brutality depicted in *Affliction* is not a whit inferior to Faulkner's southern sociology, although race plays an integral role in Faulkner's novel.

The Hamlet achieves the general effect of presenting its characters as so mentally unbalanced that a reader begins to question the sanity of humankind. In like manner, the anthology of Rolfe's audio transcripts at the end functions to question the sanity of all the inhabitants of Lawford and permits a reader to wonder if all these characters are indeed representative of the human species. In contrast, Wade appears saner than the town's other inhabitants. Fyodor Dostoevsky achieves similar eerie effects in several of his novels, especially in *The Devils* (1871) and *The Brothers Karamazov* (1880) where at the end the state is revealed as the villain who confiscates the wealth of its citizens. While Dostoevsky employed realism in his narrations, he permits relative interpretations of the narratives: as commentary on contemporary events; considerations surrounding the progressive evolution of a new Christianity (its final expression being Zosima and Alësha Karamazov); the Slavic rejection of delusions inherent in Jean-Jacques Rousseau's Western Romanticism that he delineated so trenchantly in *Memoirs from Underground* (1864) and presented in all his subsequent novels where philosophy and art become inextricably intertwined; the pedestrian pleasure of events appreciated as mere melodramatic *tableau*.[34]

While Banks does not offer any mystical philosophy, like Dostoevsky, Faulkner, Algren and Wright, he delves into the pathology of local and national culture.

The existential quality of Banks's novel subsists at odds with the sober historicism of the narrator's facts. As a narrator, Rolfe believes that facts don't tell the whole story, but that he has a special insight into the story because he knows his brother and family so well. In Dostoevsky's novels such a presumption about perspective would be an absurd relic of the classical world where family cohesion was more necessary for survival and perhaps even then romanticized. Both the *Odyssey* and *Affliction* dramatize deep problems in the health of family and state—murder, conspiracy, and betrayal—although in Homer, the identification of evil remains obvious. Rolfe's concluding fantasy of his father attacking Wade with a pipe and Wade murdering his father, presents the antithesis of the conclusion in the *Odyssey* when father and son fight their enemies side by side. The elimination of Pop and Wade would make the probability of their property being sold for development, yet Rolfe stubbornly retains the property for unconscious reasons, admitting he's seriously tempted to sell the homestead for condo development.

To accept Rolfe's narration as the literal truth, conjures Camus's category of the absurd, while to accept a non-literal interpretation invokes the social commentary embedded in Faulkner's approach. The genius of *Affliction* consists of the simultaneous compatibility of both lenses that produce greater vision.

In a general sense, the novel belongs to the detective genre, influenced by the dense enigmatic puzzles of Jorge Luis Borges or the brutal Gothicism of Edgar Allan Poe's stories like "The Fall of the House of Usher" where the narrator has naively and unwittingly become an accomplice in the murder of his host's sister. Part of the burden and pleasure of the novel consists of unraveling evidence, an integral aspect of didacticism in the detective genre:

> Every detective story depends upon and reinforces many values: most of them require us to believe that crimes should be and generally are punished, that puzzles should be pursued to the bitter end, regardless of consequences, and that the troubles of society can be attributed to a small number of evil characters who can be purged from our midst.[35]

Family violence remains a problem in American society, yet when it becomes symbolic of the larger violence in our society, the psychological and sociological impact upon the reader finds itself doubly enhanced.

The nightmare of affliction in America continues because we do not know for certain the murderer of President Kennedy any more than the reader of the novel can be certain of who was behind the murder of Twombley, why Glenn Whitehouse (a coy combination of Kennedy's favorite hero, John Glenn, and the presidential residence) disappears, and why Hewitt is murdered. The gigantic antlered buck Hewitt kills and guts becomes insidiously symbolic of a dead tribal leader. Both Lawford and the nation remain afflicted with the menacing conspiracy of men who will stop at nothing to achieve their dreams of revenge and wealth—it has become a cultural trait of New England life. Rolfe remains afflicted with the riddle of his brother's fate. Clyde Griffiths and Bigger Thomas go to their execution in the respective naturalist novels about them, while secret action by the mob leaves the historian and the public in the dark. The white serial murderer, the embodiment of law and order, goes free. Banks's previous penchant for inventing parable in short stories has matured with this parable about a small town, which resonates with a postmodern frisson of national affliction. Affliction within a family, which Schrader's excellent film highlights, remains easier to understand than affliction in a nation.

9

OEDIPUS IN THE ADIRONDACKS: *THE SWEET HEREAFTER*

> ... one feels in the *Philoctetes* a more general and fundamental idea: the conception of superior strength as inseparable from disability.
> —Edmund Wilson, *The Wound and the Bow*

The Sweet Hereafter (1991) offers a jury novel that reflects the structure of a trial with the verdict left up to the reader, as it engages in narrative crossing.[1] The novel contains five chapters focused upon four characters, the first monologue by the bus driver Dolores Driscoll being divided into bookends. Four interlinked monologues, an anguished polyphonic quartet, featuring two female and two male voices, two survivors and two observers, supply differing interpretations of a traumatic school bus accident. Dolores, the effervescent character at the wheel during the bus accident, comes across as one of the most sincere and caring people one might encounter in literature, a motherly type full of earnest observation, capable of unexpected eloquence, "It's just that you have to love a town before you can live in it right, and you have to live in it before you can love it right. Otherwise, you're a parasite of sorts."[2] She goes on to say, "Fixing motives is like fixing blame—the further away from the act you get, the harder it is to single out one thing as having caused it."[3] With such discerning skepticism it comes as no surprise that Dolores has no religious inclination, though she sometimes puts in an appearance at a local Methodist Church for social reasons. She's an optimist who on principle says she acts like a pessimist, choosing caution whenever possible. The school bus accident with her at the wheel results in the death of 14 children amid a hugger-mugger community of New Englanders in the Adirondack town of Sam Dent whose inhabitants scrape by, making little more than subsistence living. Dolores is hard-working, cheerful despite her burdens, and as consistent and caring a person as any parent would want for a school bus driver. Like any good prosecutor, Banks opens his case with the most sympathetic witness.[4]

The novel's title refers to gradual resolution of survivor's guilt among those involved in the accident:

> All of us—Nichole, I, the children who survived the accident, and the children who did not—it was as if we were the citizens of a wholly different town than now, as if we were a town of solitaries living in a sweet hereafter, and no matter how the people of Sam Dent treated us, whether they memorialized us or despised us, whether they cheered for our destruction or applauded our victory over adversity, they did it to meet their needs, not ours. Which, since it could be no other way, was exactly as it should be.[5]

Accidents happen in life and people struggle to find answers for them, but the overriding question conjures up religion or philosophy: Religion in the Western tradition usually interprets accidents as a manifestation of a *Divine Plan*, while philosophy usually sees them as random events that illustrate the lack of any intelligent order amid our tears.

The cause of the accident is said to be a red dog fleeing across the road or perhaps the ghostly perception of one that was the phantom echo of a real garbage hound that had minutes ago run before the bus. The red dog image projects various implications: There's Clifford the Big Red Dog, familiar to parents and children alike as an American cultural icon of trust; The ghostly ambiance as to whether there was a real dog at all on the road at the time of the accident dredges up the image of the red herring invented by the Elizabethan satirist Thomas Nashe;[6] the old Elizabethan trope that God is dog spelled backwards in a mirror, which illustrates an atheistical joke; or the philosophical tradition connecting dogs to cynics (dog lovers who argue human love an impossibility, dogs being the only faithful companions in life).[7] The ghostly second dog conjures a symbolic double—as in Germanic folklore once the double is seen, death follows, yet Sigmund Freud in "The Uncanny" argues that any faith in the double springs from a well of primary narcissism,[8] which would accord with Dolores's apology and Nashe's comic psychology.

The novel plays with relative ambiguity: Who was responsible for the death of so many innocent lives? God? Dolores daydreaming or hallucinating at the wheel? The bus manufacturer or parts supplier? The state guard rail? The local town's neglect of the sand pit that became a sink hole at the bottom of the cliff? The seat belts that chained the children to their drowning deaths? And how do people, or the community as a whole, cope with the adverse aftermath of such a devastating tragedy?

In researching the book, Banks indicated how he approached the material:

> I thought of myself as a lawyer deposing these characters. And the form of their monologues was the deposition. In fact, I modeled them on actual depositions that I read in researching the book. A lawyer friend provided me with a lot of depositions that he had taken.... I invented myself as a lawyer deposing the lawyer Stephens, deposing Billy Ansel the mechanic, deposing Nichole Burnell the girl, and deposing Dolores Driscoll the bus driver.[9]

In that way the reader receives four self-portraits and becomes a juror who may debate the book with others who've read the book.

Like Banks's story "Survivors II" from his first book, *The Sweet Hereafter* presents a meditation on sudden accidental death from multiple perspectives. Each of the four monologues permits time dislocations in a casual, ruminatory manner packed with the energy of the manic affliction that the tragedy has effected upon the characters. The immediacy, variety, and clarity of the four monologues convey an eclectic apology for the minor flaws of each character as the focus upon the same tragic event from completely different perspectives gives the reader a larger perspective not available to each character. Yet that larger perspective does not necessarily bring the reader any closer to any form of consolation, but rather multiplies the central anguish, each monologue reifying the ultimate fact that there remains no easy explanation for life's cruelest jest, death, and the void that it can and will produce in those who love.

The second narrative, by Billy Ansel, widowed father of twins, who follows closely behind the big yellow school bus in his pickup truck as he waves to his twins, provides poignant contrast to Dolores's monologue. Billy sounds as bitterly practical as Dolores's monologue sounds idealistic and rambling. His philandering carnality vividly differs from Dolores's companionable sublimation for her wheelchair-bound husband. While Dolores sees from the perspective of her husband's debilitating stroke, Billy, a veteran of the Vietnam War, sees death as haphazard, an inevitable absurdity. Billy's traumatic experiences in Vietnam foreclosed any interest in religion:

> The Christians talk about God's will and all—that only made me angry, although I suppose I am glad that they were able to comfort themselves with such talk.... It was enough to listen to Revered Dreiser at the twins' funeral. He wanted us to believe that God was like a father who had taken our children for himself. Some father.[10]

The bitterness of Billy's atheism and passivity finds subtle reinforcement by the use of Theodore Dreiser's name—one of America's great fiction writers whose atheism swelled sourly against organized religion. Billy's chief consolation in life was his children, then secondarily sex, but with his children gone, he has even lost interest in sex. He lives in the land of the dead as an observant ghost. Describing the school bus, he calls it a leviathan, "a beast that had killed our children and then in turn had been slain by the villagers."[11] He rejects the offer of help from the lawyer Mitchell Stephens. Billy has no interest in dredging up the painful memories of the past and takes to drinking. He also knows a trial will not raise the dead and he reserves his dignity to resent any unwarranted intrusion into his destroyed life. Having regularly followed the school bus, Billy has no reason to blame Dolores whom he likes. Moreover, Billy, unlike others, possesses a realistic awareness about the limits of the law.[12]

The lawyer Mitchell Stevens conducting the investigation acts as a focused laser beam of rage, anger being his only elixir in life. He seeks revenge against those who calculate their greed at the expense of life. Much of his angry frustration derives from having lost his daughter to drugs and promiscuity. He can't understand why this is so:

> In my lifetime something terrible happened that took our children away from us. I don't know if it was the Vietnam war, or the sexual colonization of kids by industry, or drugs, or TV, or divorce, or what the hell it was; I don't know which are the causes and which are the effects; but the children are gone, that I know.[13]

Banks offers a similar trenchant and gloomy assessment of what afflicts our relationship with progeny in *Dreaming Up America*:

> We've ended up colonizing our own children. We're now engaged in a process of auto-colonization. The old sow is eating its children.... We've become the conquistadors of our own children.... We're seeing something different take place now, something altogether new on this planet—a fascist plutocracy presiding over a world population of disenfranchised and distracted consumers and would-be consumers.[14]

But such abstract analysis on the macro level doesn't dive into the microscopic drama of a novel. Amid a wound of irrational alienation between himself and his daughter, Mitchell's sole consolation consists of finding someone to blame for negligence or greed, thereby discovering and proving a cause for evil amid the welter of pain and confusion in his life. Ironically, his hysteria on some unconscious level must be fueled by a similar greed. His daughter continually scams him for money to spend on drugs as she aimlessly drifts about the country, her favorite scam being money for an airline ticket home that has him waiting for flights she's never on. As an observer and lawyer, Mitchell's observations are firmly grounded in the psychology of people—their nuances and the motivations behind their behavior.

The confrontational scene between Mitchell and Billy finds itself visited again from Mitchell's perspective and we learn that Mitchell was trying in his sly way to antagonize the not-so-sober Billy, whom he didn't like in his snooty city estimation, in such a way that Billy would not hire him or especially any other lawyer because he wanted to subpoena Billy as a neutral witness. Billy being the witness who would confirm that Dolores was not speeding, yet readers know that since Billy was on the phone with his mistress Risa at the time of the accident, he literally doesn't know how fast Dolores was driving. But the lawyer is betting on Ansel to support what Dolores had said to the police, 50 or 55.

When Mitchell interviews Dolores after a Roman Catholic funeral (where he displays some anti-Catholic contempt), she says 50 to 55 is what she *told* the police. She herself does not know what's true—maybe she was going 60 to 65, but no more. Dolores's wheelchair-bound husband decides they will not join the lawsuit of the lawyer. Her participation is not crucial but an attempted safeguard by the lawyer. Mitchell's monologue concludes with his

Oedipus in the Adirondacks: *The Sweet Hereafter* 105

phone call with his daughter Zoe who has a vitriolic compulsion to hurt her father as deeply as she can. The question of why a girl so young acts like this hangs in the air like a gaping lacuna in the novel.

Nichole Burnett's narrative exposes her father's sexual abuse—in the car, bathroom, and tool shed. The 12-year-old is confused and damaged by it. She finds some solace in religion and she has taught class in a local Sunday school, but bound in her wheelchair, she sees herself as a Frankenstein, except that Frankenstein could walk. Her notion of Frankenstein clearly comes from movies—she has not read Mary Shelley's novel *Frankenstein* (1818) whose central subject is atheism and the deranging possibility of humankind without religion. Nichole's naïve mentality finds emphasis in her ideas about the 36-year-old Marilyn Monroe's death—Nichole believes the government propaganda that she died from vodka and pills when Marilyn was, in fact, murdered through forced injection, probably at the behest of the government. This allusion functions as an example of the ideological colonization of children, but not exactly of the sexual colonization that Mitchell conceives—something more political and deeply sinister[15] like the brooding concepts behind Shelley's great novel whose subplot includes the execution of the innocent young Justine Moritz. Ironically, Mitchell himself appears to be the one guilty of *sexual colonization*. While Nichole has naïve qualities, it's also clear she's outgrowing those sensibilities and begins to resemble the Philoctetes of Greek legend whose superior strength appeared inseparable from his disability. The real charm of Nicole's humorous narration lies in her burgeoning adult sarcasm which filters through her efforts not to see herself though the lenses of self-pity, despite the fact that she suffers from survivor's guilt.

The detective novel aspect of this story leaves the reader some wiggle room for skepticism, yet the story is not nearly as coy and open-ended as *Hamilton Stark*. Many readers might be so traumatized by the visceral effectiveness of the haunting monologues that they will not want to think things through. The ghost dog apparition that Dolores conjures is an obvious red herring. There was no dog and she must have been going 60 to 65, cheerfully hitting the brake a tad too hard. The reader endures the temptation to imagine a list of red herrings that lead to dead ends, although one could make a case for a relativist religious allegory with classical dimensions.

The town was decidedly negligent in one way: It did nothing to fix the sink hole it had created, yet who could have foreseen such an accident? The town does as a whole bears some burden of guilt, the town that ostracizes the Otto family because they are transplants from New York City—the Otto's are derisively called hippies, dress differently, live in a strange dome house they built themselves, and have adopted an Indian boy, the charming Bear, who dies in the accident. By the novel's conclusion, any reader cannot but feel sympathy for the small Adirondack town's tragedy and cannot blame anyone.

As in a Greek tragedy, a stunning reversal occurs near the end—the root of evil is unveiled and a remedial solution found. Wheelchair-bound Nichole, who has been presented with a lose-lose situation and whom everyone regards as virtually incapable of being anything other than an empty-headed beauty queen with "movie star" potential, discovers a way to thwart the seemingly inevitable. In her room resides an iconic photograph of Albert Einstein, master of relativity. She thinks about how the lawyer will construct her case. Although she likes the accomplished seductions of the lawyer Mitchell and the laptop he has given her, she'd like to toss the whole case out because she knows it was an accident and not anyone's fault. But most of all, she'd like to send a message to her father that his sexual abuse is over, and that she's a new person. Through a lie, based upon a relativity of observation that no one else can prove or disprove, she finds a way to heal herself to a certain extent as well as revenge herself. She provides a mechanism for the town to move on by blaming Dolores, and so thwart the circus of lawsuits about to be inflicted on the town. Ironically, most of the town is destroyed anyway as many families move away, but the lawsuits would have engendered more bitterness rather than less. Moreover, Nichole's lie that Dolores was speeding at 73 mph arrests attention to the ultimate Greek taboo—incest, the subject of Sophocles's *Oedipus Rex* where the community finds itself punished before the king admits his guilt. The problem of incest in America is not confined to small communities but constitutes a significant sociological scourge. The subject can be explicitly written about today, but was repressed by the book's editor when Grace Metalious attempted to place it in the rural New England setting of *Peyton Place*. The reversal happens because of the looming emptiness of Nichole's life, a poetic renewal from the nothing that renovates life, as mentioned by Emily Dickinson in the book's epigraph. Yet her clever solution inflicts an injustice against Dolores.

The concluding monologue by Dolores at the local demolition derby presents an epilogue a year and a half after the accident. At the derby, both Nichole and Dolores make their first public appearance since the accident. Nichole discovers herself hailed as a local hero and with the help of booze, Billy manages to tell Dolores how Nichole fended off the plague of lawyers and so saved the town from the desolation and division the lawyers would wreak on everyone. Stunned, Dolores slowly absorbs the shock, yet feels slightly better when Billy concedes that the speeding accusation was not true. Billy rejoices that the lie brilliantly got everybody off the hook and back on the road to a semblance of community, yet Billy's public drunkenness becomes symbolic of a damaged self and diminished community.

Like Merle Ring from *Trailerpark*, Dolores shoulders the role of scapegoat—the tragic ending remains only partially redemptive. Banks notes that, "Dolores is alienated, and the community is reintegrated in a reconfigured way. Nichole Burnell is raised up as a kind of holy virgin and the townspeople all fall in line behind her and around her. But it's at a considerable price, which Dolores is made to pay. She's essentially excommunicated."[16] While both Merle and Dolores display the generosity of forgiveness, Merle continues to act as the center of the community, yet Dolores finds herself exiled to the wounded past.

The novel's conclusion eulogizes the old New England self-sufficient work ethic of the rural countryside as opposed to urban economic opportunism

Oedipus in the Adirondacks: *The Sweet Hereafter*

where greed substitutes for morality. Since the novel unearths so much searing pathos, the gritty comedy of the demolition derby—one jalopy bears the moniker "Rule of the Bone"—provides an appropriate anthropological ritual where community and reader experience catharsis, a purging of individual and collective pain in a bitter laugh that promises survival amid a community hardened to endure the bitter snows of winter.

As a parable of the exile from Biblical Eden, this story contains no idolatrous Serpent Cult to blame for the fall. Dolores as the *Old Eve* has fallen due to an accident and did not succumb to a temptation, which argues the traditional philosophical skepticism if not atheism. Nichole as the crippled *New Eve* offers hope of a temporary redemption through the principle of relativity. Banks's parable avoids the Roman Catholic paradox of the fortunate fall as well as the traditional pseudo-Pauline[17] notion that blames women in general, while the story identifies male (Adam) sexual predation through incest as the traumatic and wounding sin within the fallen condition of humankind. While Nichole's father must hide his shame in secrecy, the damaged women endure, as in the case of Nichole. The exile from Eden dramatizes the difficult circumstances under which all citizens of the world must labor and get on with their solitary lives within a diminished communal framework.

In the 1996 film version of Atom Egoyan's adaptation of the novel, the cinema reduces Banks's four perspectives to two, those of the lawyer Stephens and Nichole. In effect, the film becomes an *agon* between the lawyer and young Nichole. In Margarete Johanna Landwehr's article on the movie, she notes:

> If Stephens represents human law and justice (and its inadequacies), then Nicole's perspective portrays the redeeming value of art as a source of comfort and wisdom in the midst of suffering, a perspective, I believe, Egoyan wishes to share with the viewer.[18]

The film concludes with Nichole's rather than Dolores's perspective. Egoyan reaches for a statement about art, while Banks provides a tragic mimesis of death without meaning to the parents, as represented by and articulated by Billy:

> The only way I could go on living was to believe I was not living.... So for us [Risa and him as well as the other parents and survivors], it was as if we, too, had died when the bus went over the embankment and tumbled down into the frozen water-filled sandpit, and now we were lodged temporarily in a kind of purgatory, waiting to be moved to wherever the other dead ones had gone.[19]

Egoyan's superb film offers a traditional Hollywood glimmer of hope with regard to healing and the future, even if that remains in the context of a nontraditional (to Hollywood) consolation through art. In contrast, Banks's novel nearly offers the no-exit despair that traditional Greek tragedy provides, except that he draws back to create a small relativist ray of hope. Ironically, Egoyan's *technique* of presenting a legal versus poetic *agon* remains closer to the dramatic structure of Greek tragedy. While Banks's pluralistic perspective remains more accommodating to postmodern philosophical constructs of relativity and problematic skepticism, whereby readers may arrive at a conclusion of their choice.

The idea of art as providing a magical consoling role in life is, of course, an aesthetic Romantic construct and the Pied Piper version of the German fairy tale Egoyan appropriated for the film comes from Robert Browning, who was a Romantic, feminist poet in his subject matter, but whose technique appropriated and embodied the new trends toward Realism in his own day. Banks offers a choice of interpretations: the more religious and traditional explanation of purgatory as a metaphor and reality, the atheistic aspect of accident as the outcome of a random universe, and the psychology of revenge against an abusive patriarch who employs the romance of art as an element of his sexual seduction. The latter explains the outcome and the defeat of the lawyer Stephens and the triumph of Nichole over her father. As in some narrative poems by Browning, patriarchal monsters, like the narrator of "My Last Duchess," discover unexpected ironic defeat.

Landwehr observes, "the medieval music that infuses a sense of timelessness in the film shapes the story into a medieval fable,"[20] something that finds reinforcement by the local carnival motif, which is itself a medieval remnant awkwardly askew in the postmodern world. While Banks sought to revive the timeless pathos of Greek tragedy, Egoyan concentrated on timeless themes of circularity associated with medieval time—for example, the opening car wash scene which is not in the novel. Washing implies circularity and the comedy of the postmodern machine breaking down indicates a hidden deficiency in the postmodern world. The repeated phone calls (not quite dramatized so much in the novel) between Stephens and his daughter employ high-tech cell phones but the *conversations* contain a circular stasis until his 22-year-old daughter discloses that she's HIV positive. At this point it might not be clear to the reader why Stephens finds some release from the tormenting burden of his relationship with his daughter. The dramatic moment when Stephens asks Nichole's father why his daughter would lie the way she does achieves a shocking poignancy—it's a single triumphant lie as opposed to Zoe's repeated, futile lies.

The abrupt cinematic shifts between interiors with their discussion of tragedy and the looming white-capped mountains depict a breathtaking *Otherness* beyond any human emotion, reducing the tragedy to the eternal fate of man within the confines of either an inexplicable *Nature* or a *Nature* that offers an inhuman panorama of transcendental beauty rooted in the perception of either humankind or a God. Finally, the tape recorder and stenographer who has so laboriously documented the tragic accident, become irrelevant in the face of a simple lie whereby human whim or cunning brings the whole legal operatus and its whirling machines to naught.

In her conclusion, Landwehr nearly hits the nail on the head:

> The similarity between Sam Burnell and the Sam Dent of Egoyan's film implies that the town as a whole may have failed their children. Although some couples

provided stable homes for their children, others have committed adultery. This parallel in names implies that Sam Dent, like the town of the Pied Piper, is guilty and that the children's deaths constitute retribution for transgression in the tradition of the fairy tale.[21]

The town is not a pastoral paragon. Risa has committed adultery with Billy and the town appears to be layered in dysfunctional lies, but Sam Burnell has committed incest not adultery. If there is a traditional retribution for transgression in the fairy tale (from the point of view of a moralistic reading), then it is the perverted subplot of incest that causes retribution to be visited on the town—much like the retribution of plague visited upon Thebes in Aristotle's favorite play, *Oedipus Rex*, where incest leads to divine retribution and the retribution becomes a public rebuke of one guilty man, the leader of the community. In Banks's novel, it is the father, the leader of the family. Banks's cast of mind has always sought out the great classical models when presenting metatexts behind his own writing. Here that metatext is most certainly *Oedipus Rex*. Stephens, like Oedipus before him, conducts an investigation of a crime that leads to the problem of incest and he implicitly accuses Nichole's father, Sam, of his crime when he asks Sam to ponder the riddle of his daughter's lie. Stephens appears as a solicitous conjuror who can cast a spell to make anybody but Nichole say what he wishes. About Stephens and his daughter, Banks notes, "that relationship between a male parent and a child—especially a male parent who is both threatening and supportive and nurturing—that combination is really a powerful one, a dramatic one, I think."[22] By the end of the book, Stephens disappears like a demon banished to the concrete jungle. The bravura performance of actor Ian Holm in the film ably captures that eloquent Faustian quality of Stephens. As a viewer, one wanted to put the eloquent *djinn*, brimming with rage, back into a bottle whenever he appeared infallible, soaring, and unstoppable.

As is his habit, Banks somewhat modifies the metatext he employs—in this case the incest occurs between father and daughter, not mother and son. Egoyan remains scrupulously faithful to Banks's novel in this most important matter as he piles on his medieval, Romantic, and Victorian overlays. When Sam and Nichole first appear in the film in a shockingly effective scene, the viewer presumes that they are lovers in the barn romantically lit with candles that are dangerously supported by flammable bales of hay. It's an incendiary image. In an amusing and muted cameo, Egoyan symbolically casts Banks as the novel's Doctor Robeson, the surname being a tribute to the great singer, actor, and social activist Paul Robeson—the creative artist as social diagnostician and healer of local tragedy.

While Egoyan created a different kind of work of art out of the novel by wisely eliminating religious and philosophical considerations, he kept very close to the plot and physical setting of the novel; he replicated the tragic plot. Nichole, as the victim, grasps at a new solution that will mitigate the narrative of her victimization, at least in terms of self-respect. Her solution provides an element of revenge and rejection toward her father which may perhaps eventually find opaque sublimation in her future songwriting. While it's not in the novel, the film, through mere visual innuendo, allows Nichole to transfer her romantic longings from her father to another older man, Billy, which makes perfect psychological sense and illustrates a process of healing in her psyche. Although the film deletes the delicious demolition derby that concludes the novel, it keeps a carnival ending, visually emphasizing the circularity of a Ferris wheel and the hope of happiness that a carnival invokes as it displays a smiling Nichole, yet that very image of circularity imply an eternal repetition in the carnival of abuse. Banks's novel exposes the gossipy limitations of small town life, while it affirms the joys of knowing local characters in an intimate manner as it provides a parable about a town's exile from its once happy past, since the people and town change irrevocably after the accident.

As a parable of the fall set in America, *The Sweet Hereafter* ranks in achievement alongside Zora Neale Hurston's 1926 dialect story "Sweat."[23] While Hurston's serpent becomes symbolic of male infidelity, brutality, and the exploitation of women under a double standard, Bank's serpent exposes a crime just as old and even more horrible. Hurston's parable presents an ironic tragedy dyed in crass sexism, while Banks provides an anguished tragicomedy, ending with the hope that women can transcend the seductive limitations men ruthlessly impose in the name of love.

Both novel and film provide remarkable works of art in different mediums. The novel contains more depth, humor, and wry nuance than the film, but the film retains an unusual authenticity to the novel that remains both commendable as well as independent. It supplements the novel with stunning poetic visuals and subtle implications through camera work and remarkably effective montage. Steven Dillon aptly describes the film as a "film/poem" that works through montage rather than plot.[24] Both novel and film continue to be worthy of multiple contemplations that invoke thoughtful and complementary comparisons on the nature of accident and tragedy in life.

10

Rambling Picaresque: *Rule of the Bone*

> Then I sat down in a chair by the window and tried to think of something cheerful, but it warn't no use. I felt so lonesome I almost wished I was dead.... Then away out in the woods I heard that kind of a sound that a ghost makes.... I got so downhearted and scared I did wish I had some company.
> —Mark Twain, *The Adventures of Huckleberry Finn*

While *Rule of the Bone* (1995) appropriates various themes and motifs from James Fenimore Cooper, Herman Melville, Mark Twain, Willa Cather, F. Scott Fitzgerald, and J. D. Salinger, its story retains great originality and its narrator's voice projects a vibrantly nuanced, vividly contemporary idiom, as it artfully provides a weedy blend of slang and adolescent argot under an ironic tropical umbrella. The arc of its plot and the depiction of the young narrator's mental states, vacillating between bluffing boast and pitiful insecurity, cast a near-seamless spell on the action. The voice and difficulties of the narrator become more memorable than those of neurotic, nerdy Holden Caulfield and as compelling as the younger, adventurous Huck Finn. This coming-of-age extended monologue bridges Banks's background in New England with his Caribbean visitations and themes. Its focus fixates on Banks's obsessive theme of an irresponsible father and the quest for a substitute father so common among alienated adolescents, with tragic consequences, but the narrator's voice eventually projects the tone of a wise survivor like Melville's character Wellington Redburn from the novel of that name.

Rule of the Bone, a first-person narrative in a realistic vein that dabbles with improbable coincidences, opens with 13-year-old *Chappie* (his actual name is Chapman, the diminutive of the first English translator of Banks's favorite author, Homer) Dorset immersed in a fog of marijuana and sardonic adolescent attitude. As with Twain and Salinger, there's an intimacy to the narrative as well as fragility—by the end of the chapter Chappie exhibits a traumatic psychological meltdown and we witness him nearly kill his beloved cat Willie with a gun. The safety catch is on, and when he unlocks it, he falls into a trance, pumping rounds into his stepfather's and mother's bed, an action heavy with symbolic anger. The scene presents the reader with a vivid hook, a psychological mystery to be revealed in due time. Chappie flees home, crashing at his friend Russ's house. The use of the name Russ for the 16-year-old who dabbles in petty crime provides a rather curious touch—as if the author comically reproves his own ego for unattractive elements in his own adolescence. Chappie left home because he had been caught stealing, selling his stepfather's valuable coin collection for pocket change and recreational weed.

Because Russ is a good two years older than Chappie, Chappie thinks Russ has much to teach him, yet Russ packs a drifting blank of opportunism with nothing to teach. Chappie voyages on a quest for a father figure; his relationship with his stepfather Ken lurks in an underworld of alienation and anger. Just as Huck Finn has serious problems with his drunken, low-life father, Banks's will explore similar father problems. Like teenage Finn's adventures in small coastal towns on the Mississippi River, Banks's novel will wallow in a small town underworld of Adirondack New England before it departs for the purgatorial island of Jamaica where more magical and terrible events will occur.

Fairy tale motifs often employed in chapter headings work well, serving to anchor the younger and sentimental side of Chappie/Bone's fragile ego while reminding the reader in a subtle way of Chappie's troubled childhood. The use of fairy tale motifs in a picaresque novel remains original.

A preoccupation with the underworld of trickery, crime, and justified revenge has characterized the picaresque genre since its inception in sixteenth-century Spain when *Lazarillo de Tormes* first appeared anonymously in 1554. The novel exposes varied aspects of social corruption and difficult relations with a stepfather. Some notable later examples of picaresque novels include: Hans von Grimmelshausen's *Simplicius Simplicissimus* (1669), Alain-René Lesage's *Gil Blas* (1715), Daniel Defoe's *Moll Flanders* (1722), Henry Fielding's *The History and the Adventure of Joseph Andrews* (1742) and *A History of Tom Jones* (1749), and William Thackeray's *The Luck of Barry Lyndon* (1844) as well as Mark Twain's *Adventures of Huckleberry Finn* (1885). More recently, there have been Jaroslav Hašek's *The Good Soldier Schweik* (1923), Henry Miller's *Tropic of Capricorn* (1939), J. D. Salinger's *The Catcher in the Rye* (1951),[1] Saul Bellow's *The Adventures of Augie March* (1953), Gunter Grass's *The Tin Drum* (1959), John Kennedy Toole's *A Confederacy of Dunces* (1980), Jay McInerney's *Bright Lights, Big City* (1984), and Dave Eggers's fictionalized autobiography *What Is the What: The Autobiography of Valentino Achak Deng* (2006). The father-son enigma in plot provides much of the suspenseful tension and often drives the narrative of the picaresque genre. As in English literature's most famous picaresque, *Tom Jones*, the riddle of parentage underlies the architecture of the seemingly pell-mell plot of incidental satire on an institutionalized culture of self-indulgence.

Banks addresses problems in contemporary racism though the kaleidoscopic lens of a confused young teenager in flight. Being slightly older than Huck, Chappie's worldview constitutes a more cynical and alienated take on society. Similar to Twain, Banks's main character entertains advanced insights into how racism functions in society while remaining emotionally childish by throwing occasional tantrums, yet the tantrums dramatize a surface clue to the disturbing mystery surrounding his childhood.

Chappie runs away, becoming a small-time marijuana dealer to a local gang of bikers, Adirondack Iron. His friend Russ clerks part-time at a video rental store. Chappie sleeps on the ratty couch of a local biker's communal apartment (where Russ rents a room) in exchange for providing free marijuana. Briefly reunited with his mother and stepfather when he's caught shoplifting at the mall, Chappie resumes his vagrant underground life. At the mall, he spies an older man with a malnourished young waif. He dubs the older man a Canadian porno king. While the Canadian label provides merely a pretext for his prejudice, it appears that the nine-year-old girl has been sold to Buster for drugs or drug debts; their actual relationship remains murky to the reader and is perhaps best left that way. This episode presents the emergence of a *catcher in the rye theme.* Like Huck who wants to liberate Jim from slavery, Chappie wants to liberate the young girl from sexual slavery.

Chappie wants to rescue the young child, but unlike Holden's ineffective dreamy posturing, he will eventually do so. The childlike and the precocious mix in Salinger's Holden, along with his intelligence, makes Holden compelling— Holden has advanced opinions on various works of literature (naively stated) yet his central fantasy of saving thousands of little kids (*catcher in the rye theme*) locates itself on the map of malapropism:

> "It's 'If a body *meet* a body coming through the rye'!" old Phoebe said. "It's a poem. By Robert Burns."
> "I know it's a poem by Robert Burns."
> She was right, though. It *is* "If a body meet a body coming through the rye." I didn't know it then, though.
> "I thought it was 'If a body catch a body,' " I said.[2]

This kind of aural slip remains more characteristic of a 10-year-old than an adolescent, but remains believable.

The choice of the name Russ for Chappie's Sawyer-like companion provides an odd timbre—as if Chappie were the stronger and wiser alter ego that the writer wished he had when younger. Russ begins skimming from the video store till until he's caught and fired. Meanwhile, the bikers have become wholesale middlemen for stolen computers and high-tech electronics. Against the advice of Chappie, Russ crosses the bikers and begins stealing VCRs. The bikers interrogate, tie up, and imprison Chappie (in Twain's novel Huck's father imprisons him). Chappie would have been killed on the spot if not for the intervention of the one good biker, Bruce, who postpones the killing. He suggests that Chappie wiggles as bait for Russ, the guy they really want for revenge; Bruce doesn't want Chappie killed at all.

Despite imprisonment, Chappie manages to alert Russ from the window of Russ's room. Russ climbs up the fire escape to rescue Chappie, but on the way out a curtain ignites from a space heater and the rickety clapboard house quickly flares to flame. From a nearby abandoned building, they watch the murderous bikers flee. The fire department arrives with ladder and snaking hoses, yet Chappie gazes in horror as Bruce, thinking to save Chappie, plunges into the flames while the other bikers yell for him to come back. The roof collapses killing Bruce, the good thief, a theme quite typical of the picaresque novel, which often dramatizes how good people are expunged from the nightmare underworld in which they find themselves. In Mark Twain's autobiography, he mentions being haunted by the specter of having lent matches to a tramp who burned to death in the local Hannibal jail. In Twain's memoir, hideous dreams about the tramp appear to rebuke him for "a hundred nights afterward."[3] Although Chappie regrets Bruce's death, he feels no responsibility for it, which slides off his back like water off a duck, further illustrating Chappie's narcissistic tendencies.

Both Chappie and Russ are presumed dead from the fire, just as Huck enjoys posthumous life after faking his death with a pig, axe, and the pulling out some of his own hair.[4] Chappie and Russ hit the road just as Huck and Jim light out on the river. Russ steals a running pickup truck at a convenience store when the owner is inside the store buying cigarettes, and they are off in the stolen pickup truck to Vermont. Russ knows of an abandoned school bus where they crash. It turns out this school bus is the same bus from *The Sweet Hereafter*.

> Richard was going on about how him and his brother and sister used to ride the bus to school every day but this one time him and his brother stayed at home sick and that was the day the bus went off a cliff and crashed in a quarry. A *shitload* of kids were killed, man, but my sister, man, she was okay, he said. Well not okay, she got busted up pretty good, broke her back and everything and now she's in a wheelchair and all that. But check it out, this fucking bus, man, me and my brother James, we wasn't *on* the bus that fateful day, so this bus was like good karma for us and bad karma for my sister Nichole and bad karma for practically every kid except me and James in the whole town of Sam Dent.... We just needed a place to party and all.[5]

The deadbeat brothers don't look out for their young sister Nichole (there's no mention of older brothers in *The Sweet Hereafter*), but enjoy the overripe fruits of their idleness by desultory drug dealing at the nearby college where they dropped out. Ironically, they speak of *karma*. To describe the death of so many friends or acquaintances as a *shitload* lies beyond insensitivity and transgresses into blasphemous horror. They party in the bus that crippled their sister and killed many of their childhood friends. Chappie aptly nicknames them the Bong Brothers. Through these narcissistic brothers, Banks hinges the plot of this novel as a comic sequel to the heart-wrenching tragedy of *The Sweet Hereafter*. This peculiar link functions more like a satire of how other writers link novels.

The lay about brothers wallow in a debased parody of the counterculture. At the hands of an ignorant rabble, the counterculture did provide cover for self-indulgent dereliction. The Bong Brothers, narcissistic opportunists of epic delusionary highs, appear to be literary descendents of the two menacing drifters from the 1970 Woodstock concert portrayed by Ken Kesey in his memorial essay on the death of Beat icon Neal Cassady, "The Day After Superman Died,"[6] where Kesey issued an alarming and prophetic report of how the counterculture might be co-opted by crass underclass opportunists. While Kesey's portrait of the tattooed drifters remains more menacing, the Bong Brothers (perhaps inspired by the series of Cheech & Chong comedy movies) provide a paragon of irresponsibility and insensitivity veering off into petty criminality.

Appropriating Melville's *Typee* (1846) tattoo theme of acquiring magical protective icons, Russ and Chappie acquire tattoos to celebrate their new underground identities. Russ sports a black panther cover tattoo to disguise his Adirondack Iron biker tattoo, while Chappie opts for the regressive Captain Hook crossed bones without the skull on the inside of his left forearm, thinking buried treasure, that X marks the spot, and as in "Malcolm X like in the movie":

> You got the *bones!* He said to me. I could tell Russ was wishing he hadn't gotten panther now but it was too late.
> *That's* what your name oughta be, he says. Bone. On account of your tattoo. Forget Zombie, man, it sounds like you're into voodoo or some kind of weird occult shit like that. Bone is hard, man. Hard.[7]

Chappie attempts to assume his new identity as a hardened underworld adult, yet finds that more difficult than he imagined. Russ, to Chappie's disgust, chooses the name Buck as in the Buck knife company, but Chappie mentally puts him down for a Buck Rogers escapist fantasy-man, confirming Russ's commitment to a continued Zombie adolescence. It will turn out Chappie was not wrong in his assessment. For Chappie, the eponym Bone indicates a new super-ego that idealizes his desire to be an adult who will handle the traumatic core of his family background. Henceforth, Bone will attempt to rule his own life, the development of both his future and fragile identity lurking behind the cold mask of his cool piratical nickname.

On the bus to Keene, New Hampshire, Bone indulges in the fantasy freedom of his new disguise. Unlike Holden's contempt for all that's phony, Bone revels in the spontaneous art of the counterculture goof, the prankster put-on. During his bus ride to Keene, he tries to convince another passenger he belongs to a special Israeli Mohawk tribe. While it's not completely clear his audience believes Bone's absurd rap, it's evident Bone has made an impression upon his listener as a far-out dude. Departing the bus, Bone proudly unhoods his faint stubble of the Mohawk haircut he previously sported. The scene scintillates with charm in its wild goofiness, dramatizing the exhilaration of Bone's newly assumed freedom.

The fugitives crash at a plush summer house not far from Russ's New Hampshire home, a neighbor's summer house. Russ has occasionally done some odd summer jobs like lawn mowing for these well-to-do neighbors, the Ridgeways. In an exhibition of puerile adolescent anger, envy, and contempt, they trashed the house with litter, devour cans of stocked food and boxes of pasta, pile up dishes helter-skelter, and burn the expensive Adirondack-style furniture in the fireplace. Although Bone and Russ hail from the Adirondack area, they remain ignorant of the furniture's cost, unique aesthetic, and regional history. Russ deserts Bone as summer approaches (Russ knew the owners would soon return) and returns to the Buck Rogers safety of his planet Earth home. Bone finds a gun, but unlike Huck with a stolen gun, he decides to irresponsibly assert his new menacing Bone identity.

Banks emphasizes the narcissism of this initiation ritual by having Bone stand before a mirror while addressing himself in a rambling monologue on his new identity, depicting himself as his own schizophrenic best friend.[8] In a dramatic scene, he *kills* the immense picture window—the splaying, shattered shards symbolizing the death of his identity as Chappie and the confirmed ascendancy of Bone's new and dangerous ego that seethes with contempt for those who live the life of privilege. But unlike the doomed narrator of the novella *Family Life*, Bone will escape the curse associated with shattered glass. The episode of the shattered glass presents the crossing of that threshold which every hero must walk through. But as with great heroic narratives, once that threshold is crossed, "One has only to know and trust, and the ageless guardians will appear."[9] And so they do. They put Bone on the right path rather than the looming wrong path.

Bone the drifter hits the road with his thumb out. The picaresque genre traditionally indulges in the improbability of unlikely chance meetings and this novel is no exception. Buster Brown, in a van with a young pixie, picks up Bone. Buster calls the girl Froggy. Froggy was the echo character from the Andy Devine show (*Andy's Gang* on NBC from 1955 to 1960) who would spinelessly assure the host that he was always right in a witty comic routine that parodied the need for ego massage. Like Devine's yes-yes puppet, Froggy has no opinion on anything from sunrise to sunset. (Buster Brown shoes sponsored the show, although Bone, and most readers, would be too young to know any of this.) It turns out that Buster dabbles as a small-time band manager and his band has a gig at the state university in Plattsburgh, but he owes the band considerable backpay and there's the matter of other financial negotiations. He has a backpay stash that he was going to let Froggy hold because he doesn't want to enter the bar where he's meeting the band with the money in his pocket, but Froggy is a little slow on the uptake of anything, so he entrusts the money to Bone for safekeeping. Buster enters the bar; a little while later there's a brawl with the fight spilling out into the street. Bone sees his opportunity and splits with both the money and Froggy, returning to the abandoned bus. In a reversal of age motifs, Froggy appears as his new guardian, a waif Beatrice with not a thought in her head.

Instead of the despicable Bong Brothers, there's a Jamaican Rasta living there. I-Man, as he calls himself, becomes the youngsters' substitute father. The derelict communal bus now becomes an example of how the true counterculture commune may have sometime operated in the unnoticed rural world. Impressed by the informal gentility of I-Man's religion (as well as the continuous

Rambling Picaresque: *Rule of the Bone* 117

supply of I-Man's weed), Bone falls under I-Man's tutelage. Bone marvels that I-Man takes religion seriously and is not a hypocrite, except in the small, practical details that concern survival. Waking up in the morning to all the plants dripping dew inside the bus, Bone describes the bus as a Garden of Eden. The odd trio enjoys a peaceful Edenic communal interlude before reality wrenches them back to its obscene playbook.

Through a helpful telephone information operator (back in the days before robot computers took over communications), Bone eventually finds the phone number of Froggy's mother, a chain-smoking Nancy Riley in Milwaukee. Froggy's name is Rose, Rosie. Bone calls the disinterested mother who attempts to shake him down for an air conditioner, then puts Rosie on a bus to Milwaukee from Albany. Hitching back from Albany, Bone gets a ride from a sporty Turbo Saab—it's the pleasant Ridgeways whose house Bone has trashed with such abandoned glee. While trying to strike up a suitable conversation to impress them, Bone lets the name of his friend Russ Rodgers slip out. Oh, they know Russ very well! In an amusing and suspenseful scene, Bone struggles to hide his identity as he gets a lift from the generous people he has so egregiously abused. Since Bone, under I-Man's tutelage, has now developed the requisite sincere heart that all heroes must have beating under their chest, guilt prompts the anti-hero, now lolling in a lotus land of sweet marijuana, to change the direction his life.

First, Bone returns home to discover that his cat Willie has been run over by a car. He mounts a final confrontation with his stepfather when he arrives. His mother has left his stepfather and the house reeks with the rancid scent of empty beer bottles rolling under foot. Amid this squalor, his stepfather Ken attempts to rape Bone in the ass—Chappie claims there has been a long history of sexual abuse, whereby Ken had forced him as a young boy to perform oral sex on him. To defend himself, Bone pulls the gun from his backpack. Chappie waits longingly for one more insult from Ken to pull the trigger but Ken collapses unexpectedly onto a couch in tears. Having for once triumphed over his stepfather, Bone departs with his momentary dignity to visit his mother at work.

In the chapter "Red Rover," he finds his mother at work and wants to tell her the dark secret about Ken's abuse, but can't spit it out. He argues that his mother should divorce Ken. When she defends Ken, saying Chappie is the problem, he finds himself reduced to a childlike state of tears. He begins yelling that she should choose right now—either Ken or him, comparing the choice to the children's schoolyard game of Red Rover:

> I was remembering how when I was a little kid in the schoolyard we used to play Red Rover. . . . I'd let go of the hand of the kid on either side of me and I'd step out there in like no-man's land between the two lines all alone and exposed and everyone looking at me and I'd wind up and start running straight at the line opposite as fast as I could. . . . I was secretly glad to be captured. I never wanted to be the big tough kid who ended up on the other side all by myself and unable to say Red Rover, Red Rover, let even the littlest kid in the school-yard, let Chappie come over.[10]

Chappie's insecurity stems from his physical smallness plus a fear of being singled out, hinting that his relations with other kids were problematic in terms of status and perceived popularity, yet one must posit that Chappie's self-regard was impaired by the dark secret of sexual abuse. *Red Rover* is also the title of an 1827 novel by Cooper that depicts a notorious pirate who goes underground with a secret identity, much like our nicknamed hero Bone who imagines himself a secret pirate because of his crossed-bones pirate tattoo and his heroic stealing of treasure from the porno king. Like the hero in Cooper's melodramatic tale, Bone can't murder his evil antagonist (his stepfather or even later his biological father) because of the delicacy of family ties. Cooper's pirate hero Captain Heidegger is an honest, good man caught like Bone in an absurd situation. I-Man's proverb that, "every honest man is an outlaw"[11] applies equally to I-Man, Bone, and the biker Bruce who sacrificed his life for Bone, but it appropriately does not apply to those other multitudinous outlaws in the picaresque underworld of Banks's novel because they are not men of good heart.

Who will his mother choose to *come over*? Bone calls Ken a pervert, saying choose either me or the pervert. His mother thinks the accusation *pervert* an outrage, a vicious and false accusation prompted by over-the-top, angry rhetoric. She chooses Ken, telling her son to leave. So the door swings shut, closing his relationship with his mother. Her Chappie just can't utter the abuse accusation in detail because he knows that the situation would be his word against his stepfather's and that she will not believe him. His self-respect will not permit such humiliation. He departs for a visit to his grandmother, the chapter melodiously entitled "Over the River and Through the Woods."

Grandma lives alone in a small apartment. Glad to see Chappie, she's puzzled by his sudden appearance. Chappie, who thought he could tell her the story of his abuse at the hands of his stepfather, discovers that once more his lips cannot utter the obscene story. Engrossed in his alienation and narcissism, he imagines himself a human mirror walking down a road and all everyone can see is a reflection of what they think of him, not his true self. Such Gnostic yearnings underscore the burden of his humiliations. His grandma senses something's seriously wrong, yet all she only manages to wring her hands helplessly, unable to think of a way to let Chappie open up. He begins to think of himself as the rotten fruit fallen from the family tree, while the reader will eventually know the rotten fruit to be his biological father. Grandma and Chappie manage to talk a bit and Chappie hears that his biological father was a cocaine addict, something Chappie refuses to believe. After seeing a photo of his father, he imagines his father resembles the young U.S. President John F. Kennedy. Grandma has no money to help Chappie. He realizes how much he would hurt his beloved grandmother if he spills his dark secret, so he doesn't. He departs, romanticizing his biological father, walking out into a dark rainy night, thinking of himself as "Mister Yesterday" (the next chapter's title), a Mr. Nobody despairing of a future, humming Jimmy Cliff's version of the song.

Caught between aspirations to adulthood with his experiences of sexual abuse and dreamy marijuana, Bone sometimes reverts to the language of childhood fairy tales, the idyllic period of his life before he became the victim of sexual abuse. The experience of abuse at the hands of his stepfather flails at the frail center of his ego which threatens to collapse when he's under pressure. This frailty finds intense dramatization in his frantic trance-like nighttime attempt at suicide. A vivid depiction in the pelting black rain, after the near-murder of his stepfather and failure to connect with Grandma, supplies a climax of renewal. Despising his immaturity at not being able to pull the trigger of his gun on his stepfather, he fears that he cannot live with his sense of impotent shame and decides to commit suicide by jumping off a bridge. Readers might recall that even Odysseus, amid his varied sufferings, at one point contemplates suicide after his crew unleashes the bag of winds that Aiolos provided for guidance:

> Awakened by the turbulent storm,
> I had no idea what to do:
> Whether it was better to leap overboard
> and so end the trials of my vagabond suffering,
> or to carry on in silent humiliation,
> making the best of the situation.[12]

Likewise, Bone most seriously contemplates a final plunge into turbulent waters.

The depiction of Bone hanging from the bridge over the chasm with the roiling river below during a nighttime storm as his arms ache may recall for some readers a similar situation with Odysseus when he hangs over the whirlpool of Charybdis, although Homer treats the episode of the mature warrior with a giddy daylight humor:

> When the west wind had ceased and a south wind blew,
> I realized I was being carried back to unthinkable Charybdis.
> I saw Scylla's high rock and my keel began whirling
> into that dreadful vortex when I leaped up into the air
> to grasp the branch of a tall fig—
> clinging on for dear life like a bat!
> There was no place I could get a foothold,
> for the rock had been worn smooth by water
> and the roots of the tree were too far away.
>
> So I hung hummocking with both hands and feet,
> waiting desperately for the keel's remnants to be spit up.
> When you long deeply for something to happen,
> it often seems it will never occur,
> and for as long as it takes an experienced judge
> to sit on his bench, hearing frivolous and tedious
> lawsuits brought by quarreling young men,
> while he daydreams of returning to wife and dinner,

> so I hung there suspended in air,
> debating and judging my own strength—
> it took that long for the stern's splinters to reappear!
>
> Then I let go and dropped, plunging between two timbers,
> which I quickly pulled together and mounted,
> paddling away with both hands and praying fervently to Zeus,
> as I struggled to make headway, that Scylla not spy me—
> otherwise, I wouldn't be able to escape extinction![13]

Homer's metaphor of a bored and exasperated judge presents a witty, humorous incongruity to the perilous situation of Odysseus hanging upside down like a bat to the salvific fig tree. The scene retains an unusual and memorable comic aplomb, despite the proximity of death. Banks at first treats the episode of Bone's suicide attempt with the grim realism it deserves—a searing pathos more suitable to his young Telemachos's age, a frailer Telemachos embracing an imaginary heroic father rather than the Telemachos who had to cope with living up to the reputation of a true legend, a Telemachos far younger and much more inexperienced about life. Both characters swim in the self-pitying insecurity of having to grow up without the desired proximity of a father. Bone decides to commit suicide, but the bridge runs slippery. Amid the downpour, the biggest fear welling up inside him is that he will slip off and become an accidental suicide rather than asserting the dignity of a deliberate suicide. While obviously panicked and disoriented as he hangs from the bottom of the bridge, Banks's description of Bone imitates Homer by also adding an incongruous metaphor to the scene:

> But when I turned, my right foot slid off the edge of the post and my left followed and for a second I was floating in the air and then I flung out both hands and grabbed at the darkness and found the iron bars of the bridge railing. I clamped on and hung there with my whole body dangling below the bridge while the steady gush of the rain above and the overflowing river far below filled my brain like that classical music from the Burlington station I heard once on a car radio when I was hitching home to Au Sable from the mall. The music was real mellow and relaxing and all, with violins and clarinets and hundreds of other instruments playing this smooth powerful song that rose in spirals and fell and swirled around and rose again like it could do that forever or at least for a very long time.[14]

What makes this scene intensely compelling remains the way Banks allocates Chappie's rational stream of consciousness to the background, while in the foreground Bone lurches as an emotional animal running on sheer instinct, something Odysseus remains aware of but not Chappie. The once-heard music serves as a healing distraction, relaxing and inspiring Chappie to endure, just as the comic anecdote of the judge helps Odysseus to weather patiently and hang on. In both cases the authors employ images familiar to their audience, metaphors standing for the stability and security of civilization that support their heroes in a difficult struggle to outlast the perils of extinction. To think of civilization and its delightful music or its attempt at just law amid petty squabbles conjures the hope of returning to civilized life. With teeth chattering, Chappie picks up his backpack and, like Odysseus, attempts to make the best out of a humiliating situation.

But the next morning Bone, the hardened side of his new personality, decides (ironically) the music that saved him was evil and not his decision to attempt suicide, that the eternity the music intimated was the eternity of death, that classical music was the tempo of a dead civilization—reggae being the *only* real music. Bone has a different interpretation of Chappie's experience—the Chappie/Bone dichotomy in his personality signposts that the narrator suffers from bipolarity. Bone also regrets that weaker Chappie gave the sweater Bone stole from the Ridgeway house to Rose when he put her on the bus at the Albany bus station, despite being with the Ridgeways shortly thereafter.

Bipolar disorders often generate the kind of behavior that Chappie/Bone has manifested: his stealing and selling his stepfather's coin collection, his fantasies of murdering his stepfather, and possibly even the story of sexual abuse on the part of his stepfather. This could possibly be a transferred memory of sexual or physical abuse on the part of his biological father whom he extravagantly romanticizes. Male bipolar children who have been abandoned often romanticize their biological fathers in extreme ways.[15] Ken may be no prize but compared to his biological father (whom the reader has yet to meet), he may appear in retrospect less sleazy if he has not been a sexual abuser. The ultimate reason he doesn't make the sexual abuse charge may be because it's not true. Stepfathers often become the victims, bearing the brunt of repressed memories associated with biological fathers. That would make Chappie's mother and grandmother's attitude more understandable than the apology Chappie/Bone offers the reader as he defends his own irrational behavior with justified narcissism. This observation presents a speculation not sanctioned by the literal plot, but what alienated early adolescent does not exaggerate or lie, especially those dwelling with a stepfather they disdain and perhaps even harboring unconscious memories of abuse or merely severe self-pity from abandonment at the hands of their real father?

Arriving back at the bus, superman Bone declares he feels like a newborn baby as he admires I-Man dancing while smoking weed. But Chappie's body has a severe fever and he remains in bed for several days as I-Man plays nurse, acting as both mother and father to self-created Bone. (The autochthonous fantasy appears quite often among adopted bipolar children.) During his chills over several days, Chappie watches I-Man's dancing to reggae as if he were a curing shaman at his bedside. To Bone's delight, I-Man tells Bone he's on the path to righteousness. When Bone recovers in late July, a bountiful harvest ripens for them to smoke and sell. I-Man tells Bone he would like to return to Jamaica.

Bone then listens to I-Man's Jimmy Cliff soundtrack tape from *The Harder They Come* (1972), thinking how great it would be to see the film. The movie tells the folkloric story, based upon real events, of a notorious Jamaican drugdealer who guns his way to wealth, publicly defying and eluding the police with insouciant bravado. While the colorful onsite film supplies amusing comic entertainment, it recounts the story of a descent into the criminal underworld by a charmer who ultimately meets his violent doom—not exactly a promising road for young Bone. The mention of the movie prefigures the dangerous path Chappie/Bone has embarked upon. Bone decides to fulfill I-Man's ambition to return, like Odysseus, to his home kingdom, offering to pay for I-Man's flight from Buster's wad of bills.

I-Man proudly declines Bone's generous offer, yet they both end up with one heart at the airport bound for Jamaica, which I-Man portrays as their New Jerusalem while Bone imagines a Peter Pan Neverland and where he hopes to find his shadow (biological) father. Although Bone doesn't have a passport to buy his ticket, I-Man assures him that will not be a problem. Bone's new Virgil-like guardian works his mojo at the airport. In an incident that is not believable in any realistic sense (but who questions the outrageous coincidences of picaresque novels like *Gil Blas* or *Tom Jones*), I-Man hypnotizes the ticket clerk and they both receive their tickets to a new life. Here readers leave realistic narrative behind and plunge further into the improbable fantasy world of the picaresque *deus ex machina* where a mere wave of the authorial wand conjures improbable plot acrobatics, catapulting the action to Jamaica.

I-Man's connection at customs blandly waves them though. In "Sunsplashed" Bone briefly enjoys the beach, retreating inside the labyrinthine *ant farm* compound to sprawl and get stoned. He spies a spider web and positions a candle underneath it, frying the golden web and flaming a spider. His guilt, near to tears at his wanton destruction, evokes a famous passage from Jonathan Edwards's 1741 sermon, "Sinners in the Hands of an Angry God":

> The God that holds you over the pit of hell, much as one holds a spider, or some loathsome insect, over the fire, abhors you, and is dreadfully provoked; his wrath towards you burns like fire; he looks upon you as worthy of nothing else, but to be cast into the fire.... You hang by a slender thread, with the flames of divine wrath flashing about it, and ready every moment to singe it, and burn it asunder.[16]

In Bone's petty pantomime, a reverse parody of Edwards, Bone plays the role of Edwards's angry Puritan God as he sunsplashes the spider. Bone returns to the beach in catatonic stupor to savor the feckless loneliness of his life until dawn. I-Man joins him at sunrise to comfort him; back at the compound I-Man introduces Bone to his posse in the ganga business. Bone notes they bear a passing resemblance to the Adirondack biker gang in the histrionic way they gesture and boast.

Bone, bored and poor, takes to begging at the market, on the lookout for white tourists to whom he might sell some weed. Suddenly, he recognizes his biological father who slouches into a Range Rover with a white Rasta woman and speeds away. Bone excitedly chases in pursuit, exultantly clothed in dust. Such unlikely meetings furnish and fuel the traditional picaresque. I-Man relishes his amusement in discovering that *Doc* is Chappie's real father, mockingly calling Chappie Baby Doc and his father Papa Doc. Doc is a drug kingpin and his girlfriend sails under the moniker Evening Star. They take a gasping green bus to his father's estate signposted Starport, as if Chappie's traveling in a science fiction fantasy. Chappie has an attack of nerves that is bolstered by the loud music blasting from speakers, but they are greeted by the Venus goddess herself in her flowing green, red, and gold gown, flanked by two guardian dogs. I-Man speaks up for tongue-tied Chappie and one learns Doc's first name, Paul. Evening Star politely listens to I-Man, departing to locate Doc while I-Man contemplates a painting of the "The Peaceable Kingdom." (Later readers will learn Doc's a lion who ravages lambs.) Chappie listlessly watches a flight of crows (iconic companions of fertility goddesses). Doc happily acknowledges his Chappie Dorset, embracing and hugging him. Dad enquires about Bone's tattoo and gives his little budding devil an enthusiastic double hug.

Bone provides a sociological analysis of Jamaican tourism beyond his years, especially on the topics of recreational sex and the economics of exploiting Jamaican youth, yet Banks's teenage idiom remains so savvy and convincing that Bone's critique poignantly succeeds. Dubbing Starport the Mothership, Bone notes that Evening Star pays all the bills, provides the delicious buffet spread, and attracts a steady tourist clientele from America of Southern middle-class women vacationing from their husbands. Doc disappears for a few days of the week to work his mysterious doctoring.

I-Man opens up a major branch office at the pool to sell weed, recruiting others to sell in town. Bone takes to the beautiful Evening Star from New Orleans as a substitute mother because she chats with him, letting him help her with cooking. Doc occasionally packs Bone along for educational field trips to score cocaine or make illegal currency transactions as he teaches his Chappie how to grow up more Bone. During these excursions, Doc tells Chappie if hadn't been for his mother, he wouldn't have left him when he was five, making the apology persuasively cool by addressing Chappie as Bone. Doc claims he had to leave the country because he would have ended up in jail for not being able to pay alimony and he didn't want Chappie to grow up under the indignity and shame of having a father who was a jailbird. He was planning to send Chappie a secret stash of money, but never could figure out how to do it without the law finding out, so he's been waiting all these years for Bone to find him. Chappie gobbles up this family feast without a taint of Bone's weary cynicism.

After an arduous day of observing Doc's criminal activities, Bone, restlessly stimulated by cocaine, grooves to the Bee Gees under the winking stars. Evening Star explicates the mystic wisdom of astrology to Bone, extracting from Chappie his Leo sign and birth date, which turns out to be in three days, so his 15th birthday party is planned. On the afternoon of his party, Bone accompanies his father who wants to buy a gun for a native hanger-on, so he can perform a revenge killing, but they can't locate the contact. Bone says he doesn't want a birthday cake, but Chappie shoulders mark disappointment when a cake doesn't arrive.

When most of the stoned and drunk guests depart, Chappie notices some strange noises emanating from the laundry room; he opens the door to find

Evening Star and I-Man making love doggy-style on a cot with their clothes on. Chappie's angry about his father's absence from the party while Bone stumbles around stoned and sloshed; Bone heaves a beer bottle into the dark night, which smashes on the tiles surrounding the pool. When one of the dogs yelps after stepping on glass, Chappie feels sorry for the dog. Lonesome, Chappie wanders around in moonlight feeling sorry for himself, the sound of the wind nearly making him sob.

Defeated, Chappie heads for his bedroom and hears his father call him from the living room. Desperate to communicate with his father, Chappie indiscreetly mentions Evening Star's indiscretion. Dad casually declares he'll have to kill I-Man because he owns Evening Star. Panicked, Bone conjures a red-herring location for the deed. While Dad searches for the impetuous sensualists, Bone tells I-Man that Doc's carrying his gun and wants to kill I-Man who decides to split for the Cockpit country featured in *The Book of Jamaica*. Bone cheerfully departs with I-Man, discarding tattle-tale Chappie. Unlike Fitzgerald's *The Great Gatsby* (1925), there's no car accident and no dead body in the pool at the upper-class mansion, yet the parallel between illegal bootlegging and illegal drug dealing as a source of income holds, as well as sexual jealousy.

Like Melville's nautical hero Redburn in *Redburn* (1849), Chappie has "learned to think much and bitterly before my time."[17] As with Redburn's and his fascination with exploring barbarous countries, Chappie finds himself seduced to explore Jamaica with his mentor and substitute father, I-Man. Unlike Redburn's travails at sea with dirty jobs and seasickness, Chappie, now Bone, discovers in Jamaica a seeming paradise with which he will be disillusioned into adulthood. Like young Redburn, Bone will be tempered by adversity and grow wise beyond his age—it is precisely this perspective and tone that make both these coming-of-age novels so taut, magical, and enthralling. Although Melville's critique of the world remains more eloquent and articulate on some levels, especially in his sardonic fillip about Adam Smith as an apologist for the upper classes when Redburn reads *The Wealth of Nations*, "I read on and on about 'wages and profits of labor,' without getting any profits for my pains."[18]

Bone notices how the hard work of the marijuana growers retains a similarity to slavery and that most native Jamaicans have few options—even the option of coming to work in the land of the *free* America becomes for the typical aspiring Jamaican a condition of slavery. This is illustrated by I-Man's experiences as an apple picker in New England when he was subject to living in a work camp, insecticides, and a diet that was against his religion.

I-Man stations Bone at a bamboo hut in Cockpit country to water and watch his marijuana crop where he meets some of I-Man's close friends, including Terron Musgrave, I-Man's cousin, the character depicted in *The Book of Jamaica*. Along with Rubber, they take Bone to a secret cave and smoke some special weed. Bone has a vision of a slave auction, a sugar factory, and a slave rebellion. As in Willa Cather's *Death Comes for the Archbishop* (1927) where the Stone Lips cave over a subterranean river employed for Indian ceremonies and vision experiences contains both a terribly awesome and politically practical aspect

Rambling Picaresque: *Rule of the Bone*

that impresses Bishop Jean Marie Latour, Bone likewise is fearfully shaken. With the initiation ceremony over and in rustic contrast under moonlight, they load bulging bales of ganga into a small plane headed for Haiti, but I-Man is not paid. Nighthawk proffers a yarn about the backer being held up in customs.

Next morning I-Man and Bone hitch a ride on a beer truck to the ant-farm compound where they expect to get paid for the weed. I-Man wanders off inside the compound. Nighthawk appears with his Uzi and another black dude, Jason, from the Mothership with a gun as well as a white guy in a safari jacket that Bone had never seen before. The three thugs flutter in panic mode. They are lost inside the labyrinth, unable to discover the exit. Bone suddenly realizes they've just killed I-Man. They want directions out before they whack Chappie, who tells them to keep making left turns (as Jorge Luis Borges advises). Bone attempts to argue for his life and shows them out when Jason recognizes Bone. Nighthawk spares helpless Chappie because he's white and he doesn't want the *tourist board* to start an investigation. The disgusted white overseer says okay, do what you want—I'm off the island tonight. Chappie is spared on the basis of white skin privilege. Chappie searches and finds the bloody, bullet-ridden corpses of I-Man and Prince Shabba. Bone decides to flee, picking up I-Man's effects, both his box and conjural Jah-stick. He begins hiking, but realizes that he's not particularly wanted by the Maroons. He crashes into unlocked cars as he contemplates his guilt. Bone had grown dreadlocks, but Chappie hacks them off when he can't get rides hitchhiking.

Bone extracts a phone credit card from an abandoned purse after a purse snatching, then calls up Russ back in Vermont. Chappie finds out his grandmother had died ten months ago and that his mother and stepfather moved out near Buffalo where his stepfather found a job as a prison guard. Chappie begs Russ for plane fare back to the states. To Bone's horror, Russ declares he'll sell his car and fly down to aptly named Montego Bay for a spree. Chappie calls Rose only to have her mother tell him she's died. As an illegal alien and foreigner, Chappie sees no option but an orbital return to Mothership where Bone can avenge I-Man's death like a wrathful waif Odysseus sneaking home.

Chappie calls out but finding the house deserted, he decides to play one of the CDs he stole from the Ridgeways in Vermont. Bone conceives of Charles Ives as a cool white Rasta because of titles like "The Unanswered Question" and "The See'r," so he spends a couple of hours listening to Ives, including "General William Booth Enters into Heaven." Through the music he imagines I-Man addressing him as a new superego:

> even though I was a white kid I could still become a true heavy Rasta myself someday but only as long as I didn't ever forget I was a white kid, just like black people could never forget they were black people. He was telling me in a world like ours which is divided into white and black that was how you finally came to know I.[19]

Bone's enjoyment of Ives's arrangement of Vachel Lindsay's poem "General Booth Enters Into Heaven" provides a fitting memorial piece for I-Man and an accusation against Chappie's biological father: Lindsay's poem celebrates "General" Booth, the founder of the Salvation Army, leading a band of underworld refugees (*vermin-eaten saints*) and convicts into heaven, those unrecognized saints "washed in the blood of the Lamb," victims of social violence, and inequality like I-Man. Chappie's father, the man behind I-Man's murder, is hardly among those heavenly elect.

Bone has finally come into the awareness that white is a color, something that whites often deny, either consciously or more commonly unconsciously. If white people adopted such an I-and-I consciousness, they would not presume to trample on the consciousness of others. This epiphany of Chappie/Bone marks the first real step into an adult psychology that moves beyond his flailing adolescent opportunism and self-defensive narcissism. He precociously enters adulthood, seeing people as others, with everyone needing moral guidance and ideals.

When Doc, wearily strung out on speedballs, and Evening Star arrive, she excitedly embraces Chappie while his Dad behaves like a spoiled adolescent, limply shaking his *pick'ny's* hand and vehemently expressing his intolerant hatred of Ives's music. Evening Star displays concern that Bone was involved in drug deals and asks him to tell her everything because she heard I-Man was murdered because he tried to rip off a big American dealer. Bone helps Evening Star prepare dinner and boldly asks her if she'll relieve him of the burden of his virginity. Since Doc lays zonked on the couch, they retreat to the laundry room and happily have sex. Postcoital conversation reveals Doc has another family in Kingston, with two young boys.

Bone sees his father slumped on the couch and decides that he's evil. With sudden inspiration he removes the stuffed woodcock he had taken from the Ridgeway house and stuffs it with a note trailing out: "THE BONE RULES, NEVER FORGET-TEE!" Resting the bird on his father's stomach, the beak nearly touching his nose, Bone departs in triumph, unconsciously turning the Maltese-like falcon where he had hidden Buster's money into an impromptu Edgar Allan Poe prank. Bone takes out his machete to deal with Jason and avenge I-Man. In a deliciously comic scene without resorting to violence, Bone manages to freak out Jason at the grill. Jason ends up seriously burned with Bone pushing him into the pool and departing. Through the sheer luck that drives the picaresque genre, Bone lands a job as cook on a tourist excursion boat about to leave.

By the end of the novel, Bone, like Redburn, appears to have escaped his doomed family background, but how this will be accomplished remains obscure, embedded as it is in the confident tone of Bone's narration. The reader closes the novel with a wondering hope as to where Chappie/Bone is now and what he is doing with his life. With the resolution of Chappie-Bone's father problems, the optimism does not seem strained, yet to a certain extent the conclusion begs for a more pedestrian epilogue or even a sequel novel to its soaring poetic meditation on starry fate.

Leslie Fiedler argued the circularity of Twain's ending to his picaresque, as the novel concludes with the possibility of once more refusing adoption and opting for flight from the evils of civilization, so that the reader becomes forced to ask the question the novel refuses to answer: "What will become of Huck if he persists in his refusal to return to the place where he has been before?"[20] In an article on Twain and Banks, Jim O'Loughlin notes Ernest Hemingway's critique that such a vague ending conjures cheating. O'Loughlin defends Twain's ending by observing that the dual tension of adoption or flight offers "a cautionary reminder of the limitations of individual heroism."[21] O'Loughlin argues Banks follows Hemingway[22] in that his ending rejects the civilized possibility that Bone's white skin has served in saving his life. Twain's probability of ending with Huck becoming diminished offers a more trenchant social critique, and that Banks's ending preserves Bone's heroic status as white rebel and outsider in contrast to Huck's humiliation of being repatriated to civilization, despite his resolution to *light out.*

Yet O'Loughlin does not mention the ironies surrounding Bone's situation, nor does he put the ending in the context of Banks's other work, or the picaresque genre. First of all, Huck and Bone are not the same kind of character. O'Loughlin judges Banks's conclusion a failure because O'Loughlin interprets Bone's poetic dream of a new map as a fantasy of transcendence, yet such an interpretation fails to locate it in the context of Chappie/Bone's character. From the start Bone has been a more thorough anti-hero than Huck. From a psychological point of view, Bone suffers from deeper psychological afflictions than Huck—Bone's immersed in the culture of drug consumption and he's mentally unstable, probably bipolar. In the concluding monologue, Bone, atop Ave's excursion boat, ruminates on the stars, but a flight of poetic fancy never solved anyone's problems. Captain Ave from *Continental Drift* operates as a smuggler of drugs who ends up doing serious jail time. What indeed will happen to Chappie/Bone adrift in the Caribbean?

The novel ends with a young disturbed teenager at night trying to commune with the grateful dead, attempting to digest what I-Man has taught him. Just as Huck has rejected slavery, Bone has rejected the white hypocritical inclination to deny that color matters. Bone well knows that personal identity can to some extent be constructed but *not* transcended—that is the lesson Chappie learned when his white skin saved him from execution. Bone improvises a poem very close to prayer. He would like to embody his substitute father's ethical ideals— the resolution relates to resolving Bone's problem with the father, as many picaresque tales like *Tom Jones* achieve with their traditionally happy but improbable conclusions.

The conclusion of Banks's novel relates to the father-son problem, transference not transcendence, and not issues surrounding race, a problem that no novel can solve, even when it treats the problem. Furthermore, the resolution remains encased in danger. Bone appears headed toward a life of crime and Chappie appears unlikely to steer him back to *civilized* America, yet Bone has embarked (ironically) upon the American myth of building a New Jerusalem in his life. That thematic irony and Bone's unstable bipolarity provide a tension equivalent to Twain's. Bone is still likely to be the victim of American mythology no matter how intensely he rebels—that diminishes his heroism but not his aspiration. This dilemma is not Twain's, but Banks's dilemma for a different century. As long as discussions of race remain immured in American mythos, there can be no resolution, and no one can expect a novel to supply such a resolution. Bone would like to discard those myths, but it's not completely clear that he can. By the same token, Bone declares his father problem solved, and the reader has reason to hope that is so, but bipolar people retain a tremendous talent for dreamy self-delusion. Ultimately, the novel's story is that of a young teenager who thinks he has discovered a new map to the universe, but any adult reader will realize that the narrator still has much to learn and much to experience about life, despite his already precocious adventures. Most bipolar kids prefer their fantasies to reality, but such fantasies hardly provide a solution for bipolarity.

Other commentators like E. L. Doctorow go beyond Hemingway and judge Twain's ending to be an inappropriate muddle, a Southern minstrelsy of Tom Sawyer's devising that humiliates Jim and alienates Huck.[23] To be sure, ambiguity remains. Toni Morrison notes that Twain's conclusion does not remove the monsters the novel addresses and that Twain's unwritten sequel reunion imagines Huck, Jim, and Tom soaring in a balloon over Egypt,[24] a motif that Thomas Pynchon appropriated for *Against the Day* (2006). Banks's conclusion expresses the likelihood that Bone's father-son conflict is resolved, that the racial monster might at some future time be slain, but unlike Twain's Jim, there is no hope for dead I-Man, although his teachings live a resurrection in Bone's consciousness while white society forgets and even denies I-Man's Egyptian-Christian-Ethiopian spirituality. Bone's concluding monologue divulges serious maturity in its tone and Banks has said that Bone grows to one of his most mature characters.[25]

Although Banks prefers classical and jazz music, when he composed the novel he listened almost nonstop to grunge and alternative rock music to help him get the right tone, rhythms, and vocabulary for the young narrator.[26] For older readers closer to Banks's generation, it remains amusing that he concludes the novel with the theme of the Grateful Dead, one of the oldest folkloric motifs in literature and also the name of the band that invented acid rock. The Grateful Dead (grateful for the dead musicians whose tunes they reinterpreted), whose music defined a generation from the mid-1960s to the mid-1980s, held aspirations of communality and social justice parallel to I-Man's. One way of looking at the novel is that Banks transplants counterculture themes from the late sixties to the end of the century for a new generation of alienated students who suspect that there is something rotten about the American mythos. Banks updates and reinvigorates the counterculture advice to tune in and drop out, but for anyone who attempts it, it remains a poetic first step that leads to dilemmas rather than solutions. Teachers who use this very teachable book need to understand that young Chappie/Bone operates like most kids of that age—in a world of impractical daydream.

By the end of the monologue, readers don't know exactly what Bone's doing with his life, yet, that, like Telemachos, Chappie/Bone has come of age, become wiser and more seasoned after his revenge victory over Jason. Bone's renunciation of both evil fathers, his biological father and stepfather, has thrust him into premature adulthood and has validated his critique of cultural decadence. In Twain's novel, the reappearance of Tom Sawyer threatens to derail everything Huck has learned. Likewise, the reappearance of Russ in Jamaica and his boarding the Mothership threatens to pull Chappie/Bone back into civilization's orbit when he returns from the tourist excursion. Bone did not want to come back after I-Man's death: Chappie brought him back, while Bone achieved his inspired revenge. Chappie/Bone might return with Russ to America now that his mother and stepfather have moved. Bone's newfound wisdom makes him more self-confident than Huck, yet as a more deeply disturbed character with greater impediments, he faces immense obstacles in realizing his dreams. As in Twain, we conclude with a question, yet the poetry of the open road beckons more strongly in Chappie/Bone who at the end embodies the spirit of "Song of the Open Road" by Walt Whitman:

> Afoot and light-hearted I take to the open road,
> Healthy, free, the world before me,
> The long brown path before me leading wherever I choose.[27]

Hugh Kenner says that the errant instigator Ezra Pound always offered such Whitman-like advice to aspiring writers, urging them to conclude their books by "opening out" and rejecting "closing in."[28] Like most really good writers, Banks prefers to pose questions rather than answer them. The conclusions in the novels by Twain and Banks challenges readers to think about youth, identity, alienation, skepticism, and social problems.

11

Hologram Pics: *Angel on the Roof*

> I was accosted by the Angel of the Odd.
> —Edgar Allan Poe, "The Angel of the Odd"

The Angel on the Roof (2000) collects 22 previously collected stories with the addition of nine previously uncollected stories. The introduction contains a shortened version of "My Mother's Memoirs, My Father's Lie, and Other True Stories" from *Success Stories*, a book that received intelligent reviews along with adequate commentaries.[1] In "Success Story," Banks has changed the name of retired Captain Harry Heinz from Maryland to Captain Dewy Knox of "The Right Way" who had appeared in *Trailerpark*, thus linking the two stories by giving a deeper profile of Knox.[2]

Much of the lively Preface to the book cannibalizes one of Banks's autobiographical stories from *Success Stories*, "My Mother's Memoirs, My Father's Lie, and Other True Stories." This includes the part about his mother knowing all the principals in Grace Metalious's *Peyton Place*, especially about the incest theme (removed from the novel), and that she knew the girl who killed her father and buried him a manure pile. Banks never believed either that story, or the story of Metalious's characters from *Peyton Place* driving all the way to the Banks household in Barnstead once to attend their Christmas party. Banks provides several instances of known whoppers that his mother fantasized, including watching him on television with Dan Rather. The point Banks makes is that he grew up in a household of storytelling that stimulated his imagination, even if most of the stories told appeared as fantasy folklore.

The book's title refers to its epigraph, "Every angel is terrifying," from Rainer Maria Rilke's *Duino Elegies* (1922). Since an angel is a messenger, it refers to the inspiration of the artist as announcing the terrifying beginning of a new project; terrifying because an artist never knows if the completed work will live up to the inspiration. The Canadian writer Ted Bishop ran a riff on this concept in *Riding with Rilke: Reflections on Motorcycles and Books* (2005), which created delightful parallels between creative literary inspiration and his mania for the literal angel of a motorcycle by the name of Matilda which facilitated a lengthy hospitalization. Beginning a story conjures a dangerous trip.

Appropriately, the first story in the collection, "Djinn,"[3] offers a high-risk parable set in a nightmare Kafkaesque colony in Africa. The American protagonist works for a multi-national company producing rubberized sandals, protected by America's ability to bomb any country it wishes into submission. Everybody in the story appears to be a cog in the craw of the global economy. Promoted, the American returns to build a new factory but a strange experience at an outdoor restaurant changes his life. A man called Djinn (one possessed by a spirit), whom the narrator sees as mysteriously possessed by a divine wisdom and love, appears in the restaurant courtyard. While eating a special pie which tastes like pig, but he thinks may be bush meat, the American becomes fascinated by Djinn who climbs up the balcony of the next building. A policeman warns Djinn to stop, then shoots him. (In tropical cities people often sleep on rooftops.) Enquiring what happens to Djinn's body, he's told it will be taken to the police station. Next day the American appears at the restaurant, drinks a few beers in the courtyard, wonders why Djinn was killed. The waiter tells the American because he broke the rules. The American finds this ridiculous. Glad to hear that the American enjoyed yesterday's special pie, the waiter cheerfully apologizes that the pie had no bush meat but that green monkey works as a tasty substitute. Under a strange compulsion, the American corporate boss begins climbing the building just like Djinn did as if he were ascending a ladder. A policeman threatens to shoot him, but he feels nothing but love for the policeman. As the American puts his hand up on the roof, the policeman shoots, narrowly missing him, and he hurls himself up on the roof where he admires the stars all night long. At dawn, he climbs down: Time has apparently disappeared and he discovers the city deserted.

One may see the messenger and martyr Djnn as a personification of spiritual enlightenment, but one might also interpret the story as an allegory of how a conformist wonk in the manufacturing world awakened to individuality through breaking absurd rules. The American no longer works for the international conglomerate—at the beginning of the story he tells us that he now contentedly works at home. As a parable about individuality and the breaking of rules, it bears a passing resemblance to Vladimir Nabokov's favorite novel, his antitolitarian *Invitation to a Beheading* (1936; trans. 1959) where the writer-protagonist, imprisoned for being different, finds himself beheaded by an ax-man, then happily sets about destroying the cardboard stage world around him. The parables of Nabokov and Banks invoke the metaphysical desire to lay aside the ordinary world of repression and conformity to take up writing about the problems of freedom and identity.

"Xmas" recounts the story of a middle-aged political science professor who drives down from New Hampshire to Boston the night before Christmas. Gregory wants to impress his second ex-wife with fashionable middle-age gifts to show off how well he's doing. Susan, a gritty documentary photographer whose work has gone out of fashion, has three teenage children from her first marriage. Susan went to Brandeis University and married another Brandeis student; both became Weather Underground activists, a theme that foreshadows Banks's novel *The Darling*. Gregory recalls an intimate moment when Susan had once punched him on the shoulder in jest. Driving his Audi in the snow, he has a minor fender-bender in Susan's derelict neighborhood. Two black guys emerge from the storm and one punches Gregory in the mouth as he genially lowers his window to make a joke. Gregory spits out part of a broken tooth, sees blood on his shirt, and realizes several teeth sit loosely in his gums. His first reaction argues denial. Distraught, he pictures how Susan might see him now—helpless, undignified, and confused—might indelibly change her perception of him. He's a teacher of political science theory making his living on Marxist intellectual interpretations of the proletariat—one of his obtuse gifts to Susan is an expensive three-volume edition of Fernand Braudel's *Civilization and Capitalism, 15th–18th Century*. It is something that a photographer with three children would never have time to read even if she wanted to, but no American photographer would sit around reading thousands of small print pages about the European economic legacy over the centuries. Susan would be better off with the cash equivalent of the books. Gregory realizes that he is in some way a fool, a privileged voyeur. As a narcissist, Gregory remains worried only about his image. The idea that Susan would play mommy to him is what makes this unforgettable Christmas X-rated.

"Cow-Cow" offers an amusing and surreal rural anecdote. Two high school buddies remain living in a double wide trailer after one marries and has two kids. The wife who works a night shift is away at work. The guys sneak off to a local bar and have a few drinks, returning about midnight before the wife comes back. Larry, the unmarried friend, forgot to latch the fence post after feeding the cow, something he has a habit of doing. They blunder in the dark with flashlights looking for the cow (named Katie after the narrator's wife) as they jokingly name each year's cow (cannibalistically) after a member of the family. They fatten the "cow-cow," an ordinary cow, not some noted brand for autumn slaughter, butchering and storing the meat in the freezer. The narrator convinces Larry to bring along his gun in case the cow has broken a leg, but when they find the cow at the cemetery eating grass, he persuades Larry to shoot it. They haven't thought things through, yet Larry manages to wake up an old friend to come in the middle of the night with his yellow front-loader. Arriving back home at dawn and stringing up the cow, Larry volunteers to butcher the cow straightaway.

The narrator's wife Katie awaits the pair with crossed arms to announce that it's time for Larry to move out. Larry butchers the cow for them, moving out that afternoon. The laconic tension somberly lurking behind the comic narrative lies in its implication: The narrator knows that one more drinking episode will end his marriage. When he begins the anecdote, it's been "not quite a year" since this happened and he can't quite understand why his wife was offended by this particular incident. It's the story of how a man lost his best friend and lost his favorite recreation, making amusing small talk at the local bar. He blames himself for insisting that Larry bring the gun and demanding that the cow be shot, but it's clear he could be a happier man if his wife was more tolerant of his light-hearted peccadilloes. The narrator has become cowed; he's now the family cow everyone will devour.

"The Plains of Abraham" features one of Banks's more obtusely farcical characters: "Had he known everything then that he'd know later, Vann would have called it a coincidence, nothing more."[4] Thrice married and now unmarried, Vann can't get his second wife, Irene, out of his mind, if he can be said to have one. As doctors and nurses prep Irene for surgery, Vann smokes in his truck, sipping coffee while he recollects that four years ago shortly after their divorce, Irene had sent a package to his motel of an oil painting entitled "The Plains of Abraham." Overweight, Irene lies sprawled under the knife for an emergency heart operation as Vann, the superintendent plumber, checks the just installed air ducts for heating and air-conditioning in the new wing of the hospital for a compression test.

Irene had always been a mischievous jester. Vann likes the oil painting, but doesn't understand why, nor does he comprehend its sexual or political significance. In the foreground the painting portrays a flowing field of wheat of a late summer day and a towering mountain peak, Algonquin Peak, in the background. It was the abolitionist John Brown who named the small fertile plain. Vann had once seen the painting and admired it, until he discovered its expensive price. The sexual symbolism of the female pubic hair and phallic mountain are lost on Vann, as is the ironic reference to America's New Abraham whose large family dwindled, but whose Northern moral history retains monumental significance. Vann's marriage produced only one daughter. Irene's independent attitude toward Vann's unreconstructed sexism continues to be a mystery to Vann's opaque narcissism. Their 20-year-old daughter Frances anxiously sits in the hospital.

Instead of delaying the test (conducted three days ahead of schedule) out of respect for Irene's dangerous operation, he proceeds with disastrous effects, garbage and dust being spewed out of all the ducts in the functioning wing of the hospital. This results directly in Irene's death. Ultimately, this is the fault of the engineer, but as an experienced plumber, Vann should have noticed the connecting air duct between the two wings, which was noted on the blueprints. Vann appears to be more upset that he's going to lose his job, than about the coincidence of his ex-wife's death. He decides to give the painting to his distraught daughter, Frances, so that the painting will make her think of him and he can see it whenever he visits her. Vann remains the kind of dunce Molière ridiculed in his comic farces.

"Assisted Living" features Ted, another insensitive dolt, oblivious of his mother who has early signs of Parkinson's disease in her old age: "Emily loved Teddy and was grateful to him but sometimes felt he should just let things go, or let her go."[5] Ted, the custodial child with money, nurses the notion that his father used her. Installing his mother in a nearby assisted living community instead of a nursing home, he solicitously looks after her. On the one hand, mother is happy not to worry about things, but on the other hand, she's bored and misses her independence. Ted suffers from the incurable wound of having been moved from a small New Hampshire town to a Massachusetts suburb when young, the move being connected to a car accident his father Wayne, a shipyard welder, was in. Being close to his mother now, he wants to revisit his childhood grudge.

Ted wants to get at the truth of the move, but his mother says that since his now dead father was a compulsive liar and womanizer, there's no point in trying to excavate the past which they will never know, but Ted's self-indulgent obsession overrules common sense. The archeologist in him wants to construct a coherent narrative, the logical reason for the move. Was it because of his father's mistress, Brenda? Were there lawsuits or insurance reasons? Ted is surprised to find that the Somerset house was in his mother's name. His father, driving drunk, killed a 10-year-old boy; his mistress received a concussion from the dashboard as well as injuries to her neck and back from the sudden stop. Brenda lied at the trial to protect Wayne and secure his pledge to marry her, but he never divorced Emily. Later over the phone, Brenda threatened to sue Wayne for her injuries. And so the sudden move, displacing Ted from his schoolmates.

Ted remains furious that the move was a whim, not a logical event, and he cannot forgive his father if it was an illogical whim. Mother is understandably troubled by Ted's obsession and notes that he settled in a small New Hampshire town much like the one he left in his youth. She has an epiphany about Ted, "He was doing to her what his father had done to him, only softly and slowly, and the person he was lying to was himself."[6] Emily lies to Ted, saying Ted was right and that his father had his reasons. Ted sees her tears and apologizes but realizes that he has done something that cannot be undone, yet it's not clear he understands it was his mother who demanded the move. Ted cannot conceive of his mother as a person apart from being a victim and Emily at this point cannot afford to alienate him. She tries to comfort her little boy who in some ways never grew up. Emily provides psychological assisted living to her son.

In "Quality Time," the physician Kent, after a divorce (because of his wealthy wife's serial affairs) when his daughter was 15, receives a visit from his now almost 30-year-old daughter Rose. She is a sculptor with two one-person exhibits to her credit, one at her alma mater Skidmore College and one arranged by her new husband at the clock museum in Litchfield, Connecticut, a 150 miles south. Kent is 60, more of an administrator than physician, and he relishes the quality time he has spent with his daughter every other weekend and over summers for the past decade. Recently married, Rose considers herself to be a bohemian artist, rebelling against her father's scrupulous health habits. Arriving late at night after being out with old friends she finds boring, he asks her not to drink from the milk carton. After he washes her milk glass, he turns out the lights to retire but his feet crunch on a trail of birdseed. Rose had filled the empty birdfeeder. Her room is still lit, so Kent knocks on her door, asking her to clean up the mess.

Kent leaves for work early in the morning. They've arranged to meet for lunch. In anticipation, Kent stands outside looking for Rose's approach. He sees her endanger her life by needlessly swerving into an oncoming truck. Disturbed by her recklessness, he mildly reproves her. She explains that she likes to live dangerously and that is part of her identity. Rose does things like that because what her father does is *violent* and that makes her violent. Her father seems, "incapable of knowing that his kindness and intimacy draw her close to him, but only for him to reject her because of her sloppiness, her carelessness, her disorder. She reminds him of last night's confrontation over the spilled birdseed."[7] Rose tells him that all these years, he's treated her as if she was *him* that he did the same thing to her mother, and now has lost them both. She will probably never again return for a visit. She leaves immediately. This cranky, ultra-histrionic scenario of upper middle class prosperity delineates a representative problem of the well-to-do with their spoiled children. Rose is clearly concerned only with her self. Through the use of the name Kent, Banks calls attention to an artist (Rockwell Kent) concerned with society at large and common people in particular, the kind of people like the old friends Rose despises with a newly acquired aristocratic contempt. There's been no quality time between father and daughter since the daughter will not permit that. It's unlikely that Rose's sculptures have any artistic merit because she comes across as a decidedly petulant whiner, a dabbler.

In "The Moor," Warren has just participated in a 30-second-degree Masonic initiation in which he appeared as an Arab replete with blackface.[8] He has a touch of the actor and he takes pride in investing his role and the ceremony with theatricality, when most inductees would shuffle through the event with embarrassment. Warren Low's a plumber advancing his small business in a little New Hampshire town. Boosted by Warren's game performance, his friends accompany Warren to a Greek diner for a couple of drinks. All their kids have flown the coop, so they talk about them, their wives, and ex-wives. The Greek owner asks what's up with the grease paint and Warren jokes that it's a little theater group, fearing to say the Masons because the Greek is Orthodox, but the Greek knows what's going on. Warren notes an old lady, really *old* he thinks. The Greek says it's her 80th birthday and that her name is Gail Fortunata. Her two plump middle-aged sons attend her, but Warren notes her clear piecing eyes and how she dominates them. The name doesn't immediately ring a bell, but Warren says maybe he knows her from somewhere. His friends get a good laugh when one suggests she's probably an old girlfriend. As the Masons begin pulling on their coats to depart, Gail says to Warren, "I knew you years ago."

Gail asks about the blackface and Warren says he was just doing some theater and didn't have any cold cream to take off his makeup. She begins to introduce him to her family and grandchildren and the other two Masons depart. The snowstorm begins to rage rather than lilt, but Gail won't leave with her family. She tells them Warren will take her home. Gail speaks of when they were lovers 30 years ago, tactfully asking Warren if she had taken his virginity. Warren's embarrassed and thinks about lying, but admits yes, that at 21 Gail was his first lover. This makes Gail so happy, and Warren realizes that he has given her the perfect birthday present, the one no one else could have given her. He asks about her husband, discovering he died ten years ago. Warren inquires if he was her only lover and she says yes, although he doesn't believe her. Gail explains she thought Warren would go far as an actor; even though he's only doing small local acting, she takes some pleasure in that.

Warren drives her back home and walks her to her door. He gently kisses her on the lips "then a little more, and she kisses me back, with just enough pressure against me to let me know that she is remembering everything, too."[9] Gail steps away, smiles, notes the makeup and says she forgot to ask what play he was in. "Othello" Warren replies, casting Gail as an unfaithful Desdemona, yet Gail remains pleased that Warren played the lead role as the Moor. Warren then drives home through the snowstorm, unsuccessfully trying to think about work:

> Driving home, it's all I can do to keep from crying. Time's come, time's gone, time's never returning, I say to myself. What's here in front of me is all I've got, I decide, and as I drive my car through the blowing snow it doesn't seem like much, except for the kindness that I've just exchanged with an old lady, so I concentrate on that.[10]

Gail was the love of Warren's life. He's lied to her about his continuing his acting career, playing Othello. Meeting her again, he has acted his small part in an impromptu play by lying to the woman he most loved in order to make her happy. The irony of the Greek diner setting glows as a contrast to Warren's failed ambition to be a professional actor. At the end, like Othello, Warren finds himself in exile, a self-exile from the ambition he once had to be an actor, but nobody will track Warren down and kill him. Perhaps with Gail (the winds of fortune) as his muse, he might have made it to some degree as an actor. Warren's no grand Othello and the snowy, orgasmic flakes dancing mockingly before his windshield celebrate a pathos he finds nearly unendurable, but Warren, like everyone else, must concentrate on the road before him. The reader experiences cathartic sympathy for the rural Walter Mitty with some ambition, never rising above the fate of small-town life. Most of us never realize our most cherished secret dreams. Banks has turned an unexpected meeting into an encounter with memory, kindness, and the charm that sometimes shimmers in the great stories of that greatest of short-story writers—Anton Chekhov.

"The Visit" also offers another memory trip, but filled with more poignant recollection. A New York City professor travels to deliver a lecture at a small Pennsylvania university at the foothills of the Pocono Mountains near the Delaware Water Gap. Arriving earlier than he anticipated, he drives a farther 20 miles to a small town where he once lived for one year when he was 12. It had been the last year his parents stayed together in the impoverished town, a year of dislocation, tension, and hysteria for himself. He notices that a small bar his father once took him to is still there. Not knowing why, he enters the damp, dirty pit, and has a drink. Not a single thing in the bar has changed, except that it's more bedraggled. While there, he remembers that when he was 12 his father on a grocery expedition had brought his younger brother and him to the bar. While his father had a few drinks with a fat woman daubed with bright red lipstick, he and his brother had fooled around. An old man in the bar inquires about him and when told that he was here once and that he had lived in the town for a year, the man utters his surname. Astonished, the narrator warms to the old man, only to be rebuffed and mocked as a trespassing alien from an uncivilized and violent big city.

He drives a few miles farther to the house he once lived in and discovers that it is now a tiny restaurant. In contrast to the old man, the owner brims with hospitality, remembers his father, and ushers him about as he proudly discusses his remodeling, even telling him he can go upstairs to see his old bedroom (now his) if he wants. He declines. The owner thinks he declines out of respect, but that is not the case.

As a few snowflakes flutter, he stands outside and looks into what was his bedroom window. He recalls that on the way home from the bar, his father told him to lie, to say that they had spent some extra time in his plumber's office while he went over papers. Once home, he lies as requested, but his mother intuitively knows and smells the scent of the bar and the woman. A hysterical scene follows. When he goes to bed, his mother eventually pleads with him to tell the truth and he reluctantly does so. Then he recollects the beating his half-drunk father administered to him in punishment. The reader learns that he travels to all the many places he once lived when young to meditate on the beatings his father has given him or to the beatings he has given or endured at various bars, yet he does this as a kind of yogic act of catharsis to heal his nightmarish wounds. He revisits these places once. The little lecture he gives at the university finds a gentler and more genial reception than he thinks it deserves. An anecdotal story of redemption, the prose rises to the lilt of a peaceful meditation on drifting snowflakes and the contrasting memory of the heat and light that violence produces in the wounded brain. The story implicitly urges the reader not to repress truth, but to explore it in tranquility. The theme of drinking and lying to a mother had previously appeared in "The Right Way" from *Trailerpark*.

"Lobster Night" denotes the Thursday evening special at Noonan's Family Restaurant where a fickle waitress lands a summer gig. The story belongs to a medieval Irish genre about taboo, *geis*,[11] wherein the breaking of a taboo leads to situations of grotesque comedy and bizarre horror. Stacy, a winter ski instructor who once harbored the ambition to be an Olympic champion until she shattered her left thigh, has never told any man her dark secret. When 17 she was struck by lightning—the phallic god of lightning raped her—she must never tell a man. Sometimes she's been tempted to confess to men she's been intimate with, but has always been able to think of sudden distractions. Young Stacey finds herself reluctantly attracted to middle-aged Noonan's manly ruthlessness with its subtext of animal violence.

One Thursday night, Stacey expresses some disgust at the process of displaying the lobsters in tanks and then having them killed for the customers.

Hologram Pics: *Angel on the Roof* 139

Noonan[12] jokingly tells her that she should take up vegetarianism. Stacey replies she did when she was in college. Noonan inquires why she gave up skiing—because of an accident. He casually asks why she took up skiing to begin with and the rest is history. Noonan seductively extracts her thoughts about how being struck by lightning made her different from all mortals. Noonan then confesses he once had an analogous experience with a bear that changed his life. A bear tore down his camp in the woods. The trauma made him a different person—the next day as he lay dazedly immobile in the woods, a woman strolled by looking for her lost dog and he married her. But Noonan hints he's no longer happy and gives Stacey a hip bump before departing for the kitchen.

Later during an unusually busy dinner rush, the two young La Pierre brothers who wash the dishes for minimum wage quit at the height of the rush. Stacey and Gail—the other waitress sporting a homonym for Gael (Irish person)—work hard at trying to straighten out some of the chaos. When not cooking, Noonan juggles the dishes. He tells Stacey that as soon as they are alone, he's going to *take her down*. Stacey grows furious at the frank pass and follows Noonan into the kitchen to have it out with him. Noonan smoothly calms her down and conspiratorially asks if she'd want to split the last lobster with him when everyone leaves. She declines and Noonan mocks her. Noonan yanks the last lobster out of the tank and flails it in Stacey's face with its writhing antennae and claws, taunting her for her fear of the lobster and then plunges it into a boiling pot.

Loud exclamations from the diners reveal a bear ransacking the garbage out back. Noonan grabs his rifle, attacks the bear with his meager .22 caliber gun, finally killing the bear with the eighth hit at point-blank range after which the bear finally collapses before his feet. The crowd of rubbernecking spectators enjoys the thrill, but they depart in hurried disgust once the bear falls. Gail quits her job on the spot. Stacey enters the kitchen to see Noonan stuffing lobster into his maw, raving about the eight shots it took to fell the bear, obviously surfing a mad adrenalin rush from his near-death encounter. Stacey picks up the nearby rifle, asks if it's still loaded, and hearing the affirmative, she shoots Noonan in the forehead. Then turns off the gas stove:

> Never, in her life, never, had Stacey known the relief she felt at that moment. And not since the moment before she was struck by lightning had she known the freedom.[13]

The two LaPierre brothers hop off a cousin's truck. They joke about taking turns raping Stacey who's catatonically zoned out like a zombie on a kitchen stool. The reader can supply any ending, but Stacey, now freed from the taboo, faces the doom that many Irish literary heroes have faced: Freedom from the taboo comes at the price of freedom itself. The novelist William Kennedy most likely explained the genre to Banks after some bizarre dinner they shared. England judged the genre to be a form of ignorant superstitious barbarism, but eventually reinvented the Gothic genre nearly one millennium later on the foundation of sensational anti-Catholicism.

In collecting his best stories, *The Angel on the Roof* displays a bravura performance, a writer in command of varied approaches to fiction, expert at delineating character with a few short strokes of dialogue. While the angels' inspiration arrives intact, Banks challenges the reader to discover the deep ironies layered into his stories. Banks remains centered on his craft as he careens through a landscape of nuanced, narcissistic folly.

Banks's later stories appear self-confidently laden with profound psychological depth and nuance. "Transplant,"[14] an uncollected recent story that miraculously floats on sheer anecdote, manages to convey a strikingly memorable pathos. The style of Banks's late stories displays a lyricism of both language and deep metaphor, exhibiting the influence of Chekhov's psychological empathy, yet remaining a uniquely American voice.

12

Resurrection Dream: *Cloudsplitter*

> I've been to Palestine.
> WHAT DID YOU SEE IN PALESTINE?
> Old John Brown.
> Old John Brown.
> And there he sits
> To judge the world.
> His hunting-dogs
> At his feet are curled.
> His eyes half-closed,
> But John Brown sees
> The ends of the earth,
> The Day of Doom.
> And his shot-gun lies
> Across his knees—
> Old John Brown,
> Old John Brown.
>
> —Vachel Lindsay, "John Brown"

While Russell Banks labored on *Cloudsplitter*, a prolix yet beautifully penned epic on John Brown and his son Owen, he found the great opus interrupted temporarily by his sudden writing of *Rule of the Bone*,[1] perhaps Banks's most popular narrative. *Cloudsplitter* is a translation of the Algonquian Indian name, for the highest mountain in New York State, currently named Mount Marcy or *Tahawus*, meaning Cloudsplitter. As with the fictional Mount Job of *Hamilton Stark* and the encompassing geological metaphors of *Continental Drift* and *Affliction*, landscape and people morph in metaphor with greater splendor than Grace Metalious's use of the Indian Summer leitmotif in *Peyton Place*. While the tallest mountain in New York State splits clouds, its extended geological legend becomes a towering metaphor for John Brown as a cloud splitter—a man about whom many remain divided in their opinion. Many whites agreed with U.S. President Abraham Lincoln that Brown was "insane,"[2] while most in the African American community regarded Brown as an unequivocal hero, "To black Americans the leader at Harpers Ferry was primarily a symbol that gave them dignity."[3]

Countee Cullen called Brown an archangel in his poem "A Negro Mother's Lullaby,"[4] but the response among whites has been much more vexed.[5] Banks provides the first extended novelistic interpretation of Brown from within the New England abolitionist perspective, a general humanist perspective from which whites may be able to empathize with the great arc of Brown's remarkable life and heroic moral compass. By confining his need for experimenting to the challenges of a memoir (or epistolary novel), Banks once more adapts his tinkering postmodern sensibility to the realism of a novel with a historical setting. As the novel's Preface indicates, Banks writes fiction without dabbling in the genre of historical fiction.[6] Banks avoids the hopscotch focus that in an epistolary novel can become formulaic by casting the genre as an extended memoir. Rather than offer the wide scope of a historical novel, Banks takes mild liberties in expanding and romanticizing Brown's involvement at upstate North Elba (now called North Elbow) in the Adirondacks where Brown is buried. Banks writes to his strength—an inward confession of conflict that offers a virtual history confined to one character.

John's third son Owen, his lieutenant during the Kansas wars, now in his old age, living in California, narrates his apology. This finds precedent in the fact that his grandfather Owen wrote a family memoir as he neared 80[7] and that Owen himself kept a diary, some fragments of which, relating to the preparations for Harpers Ferry, have survived.[8] Owen's brother Solomon also left some writings. Here Owen, living an extra 11 years beyond his actual death, cooperates with Katherine Mayo, the young female assistant of a prominent scholar, so the biography of John Brown by Professor Oswald Garrison Villard would become a better book. This device gives Banks wiggle room to include information not in Villard's monumental 1911 biography, allowing Banks to omit material like Brown's work for the post office.[9] Villard's biography makes short shrift of Brown's brief stay at North Elba, mentioning it merely as the last business failure before Brown turned to be a guerilla fighter in the war against slavery. Villard concentrates upon Ohio, Kansas, and the fatal events at Harpers Ferry. Technically, Banks's novel belongs to the epistolary genre as a letter monologue recounting Owen's autobiography from childhood on. Much formative emphasis falls upon the North Elba lacuna in Oswald Garrison Villard's fairly definitive biography. Begging his father John's forgiveness throughout the novel, the story implants upon the reader the haunting, suspenseful drama of Owen's guilt: What dark betrayal lurks at the bottom of the narrative?

This fictional Owen recalls the treatment of Banks's early short story "Indisposed" about the wife of the cartoonist William Hogarth where Banks took major liberties about what we know of the historical character. This virtual

Owen, a complex psychological puzzle, even confesses to *intermittent* pacifism. Such confessions emerge slowly due to reticence as Banks notes:

> He [Owen] can only go so far in terms of sexual explicitness. He can only go so far in terms of his descriptions of violent acts, because he's got a certain amount of decorum that's necessitated by whom he's speaking to.[10]

Because of such decorum, a reader needs to pay close attention, especially with regard to sexual innuendo. While examining the Villard collection at Columbia University, especially the diaries and letters of Brown's children, Banks experienced the archival jolt that led to the convoluted reticence in his conception of his fictional Owen Brown.

Owen confesses three serious problems about his life, one religious, one psychological, and one familial, all of them united in a Oedipal Gordian knot. (A milder and happier Oedipal struggle had appeared in Banks's short story "The Defenseman.") Owen promptly informs the reader, "I did not believe in God, then or now."[11] Such thinking sundered him from his father who instructed his children to "mark God's perfect logic."[12] This breach never hobbled John's affection for Owen, but provided Owen with a lifelong wound separating him from a father, of whom he and other men stood in awe. Owen's perception of life remains the classic wheel of fortune turned with a skeptical heft. Owen observes the destitute conditions of slaves and indentured workers with rhetorical sarcasm, "Was this, then, that great cycle of birth, life, and death which my father spoke of with such admiration and belief?"[13] More importantly, Owen's atheistic rant proceeds to see no purpose in procreation, a violation of the central religious and biological imperative of life itself, an imperative even the atheist poet Lucretius embraces.

Owen's other difficulty is that he remains traumatized by the early death of his mother when he was only eight. At North Elba, 16 years after his father has remarried, Owen still whines about his stepmother, even though he has nothing bad to say about her. His awkwardness in accepting his stepmother, as well as his overly shy inhibitions in attempting to relate to women in general, is noted with compassion by John who appears acutely sensitive to this problem because his own mother had died when he was eight. John appears as a probing master psychologist in his relations with others and with his family, especially with Owen whose deep sexual frustration he analyzes in formidable detail.[14]

Owen's two problems are placed in the context of a third problem common to all family members—a sense of imprisonment by their towering father whose patriarchal brooding greatness towered over all members of the family:

> Forgive the Old Man, I would say to myself. Come on, now, grow large, Owen, and be generous with understanding and compassion. Yes, understanding, especially that—for when one understands a human being, no matter how oppressive he has been, compassion inevitably follows.... My thoughts, my questions, were blocked, occluded: by the absolute rightness of his cause, which none of us could

question, ever, and by the sheer power of Father's personality, the relentlessness of it, how it wore us down, until we seemed to have no personalities of our own, even to each other.[15]

Owen's imprisonment remains his haunting guilt at not only having let down his father, but also never measuring up to his father's sublime dignity, feeling himself small in his father's shadow. He locates this aspect in his childhood, especially with the trauma of his mother's death. Owen's and the family's problem with identity remains as much critique of patriarchy as it does a compliment to John Brown as an elemental force of nature. He is a looming Cloudsplitter, legendary for his ability to untiringly split wood and confound the expectations of both family and society with the consistency of his idealism as he holds himself accountable to it. Deep down, the novel's theme consists of exploring the role of conscience as an obsessive moral and social force.

It's somewhat ironic that Banks chose this trenchant theme at a time when America was about to abandon any notion of social conscience before the whole globe as it attempted to annex Iraq as a playground for American corporations, some of which would behave like the pro-slavery annexationists of Kansas. Behind Brown stands grandfather Captain John Brown of the 9th Company, 18th Regiment of the Colony of Connecticut, who, in 1777, gave up his life for the American Revolution "in a barn in New York."[16] While the Adams family of Boston, as depicted in *The Education of Henry Adams* (1918), saw itself as the landed proprietor of the American Revolution and its revolutionary heritage,[17] the impoverished Brown family saw itself as no less custodians of that *moral* spirit and they remained ready to pay the price for freedom, not just with their ideas, but with their lives.

When Brown's friend Ralph Waldo Emerson spoke at a fund raiser for the Brown family two weeks before doomed John's execution, he approvingly cited John Brown's words that, "he did not believe in moral suasion, he believed in putting the thing through."[18] Emerson thought it the height of absurdity that the governor of Virginia—a state Emerson regarded as governed by a reign of terror because of slavery—was forced to hang a man the governor declared, "a man of the utmost integrity, truthfulness and courage that he ever met. Is that the kind of man the gallows is built for?"[19] Emerson concluded his commemoration of Brown by allusively urging the people of Massachusetts to preserve their freedom by resisting the Federal government's unjust Fugitive Slave Law of 1850.[20]

Anthony Hutchison locates Banks's approach within the larger historical sweep:

> In his fictional portrait of Brown, Banks marshals all the intellectual energy of Puritan and post-Puritan New England as it moved west into ideologically contested antebellum territory. He does so in order to tell thestory of race and the American Civil War—a story that, as Alfred Kazin's characterization implies, cannot be detached from the Bible absorbed so thoroughly by heirs to the New England intellectual tradition as diverse as Ralph Waldo Emerson, Abraham Lincoln and John Brown himself. By carefully weaving in such strands in order to give a

powerful sense of Brown's intellectual life and context—that is, a powerful sense of his connectedness with the wider culture—Banks shows how, by Emerson's criteria at least, such a "madman" or "terrorist" accordingly came to constitute one of the era's "representative" men.[21]

Banks keeps a dramatic focus on the narrator Owen and his father John, although Banks's portrait of Emerson remains consonant with Walt Whitman's portrait of Emerson from the memoir *Specimen Days* (1882). Hutchison puts Owen's narration into the genre of witness literature (stemming from Samuel Taylor Coleridge) like Herman Melville's Ishmael and the monomania of Ahab respectively, yet such a reading of how Banks employs meta-texts fails to take into account the consistent counterpointing Banks performs when dealing with meta-texts. While Ahab's sanity is clearly impaired, John Brown's sanity is not; while Ishmael clearly has all his marbles, the reader will discover that despite his reasonable tone, Owen does not. While Ahab is possessed by a demon, Brown is not; while Ishmael is virtuous, Owen is a subtle monster more akin to Ahab. It seems to me that it's just as much the activist W. E. B. Du Bois in his portrayal of John Brown as Emerson who becomes a *representative* man.

Hutchison reminds us of the larger historical picture and how Banks's presentation accords with Emerson's valorizing perspective, although that perspective is modified by both Du Bois and Banks. Both Owen and John will later hear in person before the great orator when they stop in Boston. Owen will be more impressed than John by Emerson. John sees Emerson strictly as an orator, not a man who will do much about anything, "What does he know of terror? Ralph Waldo Emerson has neither the wit nor the soul to know terror. And he has no Christian belief in him."[22] Banks's representative man incarnates the practical doer more related to Benjamin Franklin and Lincoln than the rhetorical divines or armchair philosophers of the period, more related to the Epistles of Paul and the Gospel of Mark, than the Gospels of Luke and John. It is as heroic doer and Christian believer that Brown transcends his historical period—he becomes a representative man on the vexed horror of slavery. One might say that Banks employs Emerson in his novel as a coy John the Baptist figure calling for a man to purge the land with blood sacrifice, yet Emerson remains too much of a timid academic to sacrifice himself like John the Baptist—that's what John Brown understood about Emerson, a good poet whose verse Americans tend to forget or despise.[23] Brown saw the split in Emerson's reflection and activism, rejecting it as weakness.[24]

A fascinating tension in the novel remains John's uneasiness with justifying violence in opposing the institution of slavery he so abhors. A kindly and righteous man, he needs to steel himself to be bloodless in the pursuit of justice whose arc the moral universe follows. Such is the counter perspective to Owen's atheism supplied by his father, the "tiny arcs of an enormous curve"[25] that lead to a second cycle of rebirth and regeneration. This metaphor on the eschatological arc of justice, a paraphrased favorite of the Rev. Martin Luther King, Jr., and U.S. President Barack Obama, has its origins in the Unitarian minister

Theodore Parker (1810–60)[26] who supplied John Brown and Kansas state militias with money for guns in the struggle against slavery. As a preacher Parker did not believe in miracles and advocated violating the Fugitive Slave Law of 1850. Parker helped fund and later defended John Brown's stand at Harpers Ferry as morally justified violence in opposition to slavery. Parker's 1853 sermon reads:

> Look at the facts of the world. You see a continual and progressive triumph of the right. I do no not pretend to understand the moral universe; the arc is a long one, my eye reaches but little ways. I cannot calculate the curve and complete the figure by the experience of sight; I can divine it by conscience. But what I see I am sure it bends toward justice. Things refuse to be mismanaged long. Jefferson trembled when he thought of slavery and remembered that God is just. Ere long America will tremble.[27]

Such subtle embedding of the historical abolitionist perspective in Banks's novel indicates the novel to be conscientiously researched, even though the narrative retains a supple spontaneity that often belies such deep background.

Banks serves up some effective and plausible drama around the pursuit of two young runaway house slaves accused of murder. Brown smuggles the two young lovers to Canada and must resist an investigation by a sheriff and marshal, followed by a belligerent bounty hunter. The latter event comes about when Brown severs a distrusted link in the established Underground Railroad, creating his own independent operation. The dropped link, Wilkerson, whose income derives from inhumanely exploiting Irish iron ore miners (only one reason why Brown distrusts him), plots treacherous revenge.

The historical Cyrus, a runaway who lived with the Brown family, finds depiction as the competent Lyman Epps who carries his papers of manumission about him at all times. (The real historical Epps was devoted to John Brown, survived him, and sang at his funeral.) But as much as the reader might admire Brown's dignity and savvy in his defiance of even cunning investigators and betrayers, Banks goes to great lengths to convince the reader of Brown's transcendent tenderness as a shepherd to his literal flock and his family, an aspect that Du Bois emphasizes in chapter four, "The Shepherd of His Sheep," in his biography of John Brown. The two young runaway lovers are eventually nabbed by the law, despite the best efforts of the Brown family and the Quaker ferryman—this provides an example of how the Underground Railroad sometimes failed.

While it is known that Brown sometimes spoke at churches, Banks uses that opportunity for Brown to deliver a long dramatic sermon on the Book of Job, an obsessive theme found in several of Banks's books—Brown becomes an effective and even shocking allegorical speaker like Banks's coffin maker. When Brown compares himself to Job before the congregation that threatens him, any objection to his comparison would appear to risk outright blasphemy rather than reasonable disagreement. This choice of The Book of Job is not mere personal obsession on the part of Banks because The Book of Job, verse 41, contains the long passage on the whale that helped inspire the conception of Melville's *Moby-Dick* (1851). Like Melville, Banks frames and imparts new contexts and meanings to familiar Biblical texts in his own manner, but this sermon also functions as a deconstruction of the 1929 demythologizing biography of John Brown, the same year that Stephen Vincent Benét's epic poem *John Brown's Body* (1928) won a Pulitzer Prize.[28] Robert Penn Warren's biography, "examined the ways Brown constructed himself as a Moses-like figure and Christ-like figure."[29] Warren's biography charged that Brown was a hypocritical Puritan interested in financial gain who dramatized his martyrdom just before his execution, arguing a cynical showmanship on the part of a venial and fickle man. What Warren essentially did was take Emerson's line, "The characteristic of heroism is its persistency,"[30] and attempt to turn the proverb against Brown. By presenting Brown's sense of justice and oratory deeply rooted in the Bible as far back as North Elba (and Brown's letters support this), Banks offers a refutation of Warren's self-serving Southern picaresque perspective on Brown. Warren's biography has been derided by many historians, but it still exerts appeal in the South.[31] Warren staunchly supported desegregation as early as the mid-1950s.[32]

The startling and eloquent sermon on Job may also be interpreted as Banks's homage to the 1909 biography of John Brown by Du Bois who "draped his Old Testament hero in Old Testament prose."[33] While Whitman had invoked Brown as a forceful *weird* figure, "a meteor of war" in his 1859 poem, "The Prophet," Du Bois had acclaimed Brown as "the man who of all Americans has perhaps come nearest to touching the real souls of back folk."[34] Although Du Bois's biography remains firmly rooted in John Brown's letters, Du Bois told Villard that his primary concern was interpretation and not facts as such.[35] While some have criticized the short Du Bois biography as containing too many quotations from letters, it is precisely the fire of Du Bois's interpretation that Banks affirms in his portrait of John Brown. In a Preface to a latter edition of the biography, Du Bois concluded: "Although John Brown's plan failed at the time, it was actually arms and tools in the hands of a half-million Negroes that won the Civil War."[36]

The exciting shoot outs that conclude chapter nine of Banks's novel present a fiction that may be more representative of the Browns in Ohio or Kansas because nothing like that occurred in North Elba or environs, at least that is known. While Stephen Oates's biography of Brown states that Brown, "continued his private war against the fugitive slave law, exhorting his black neighbors—a few of them runaways—to resist the law no matter what authority should invade North Elba and try to enforce it." Brown even encouraged the women to resort to hot water if push came to shove, "no slave catchers or Federal marshals came to North Elba."[37] The wounding of the bounty-hunter Billingsly and the dutiful jailer in Elizabethtown function as small victories under duress, while the murder of the freedman Mr. Fleete during the getaway adds an appropriate pathos to a narrative that works to establish a fearsome reputation for the Browns, even though they and the reader know their victory remains more symbolic than real.

The dynamic of Brown's sermon on Job finds its echo wall not only with the sermon on Jonah in chapter nine of Moby-Dick, but also provides a contrast to Emerson's Sermon in chapter ten. As prelude to the sermon, Banks's wit parallels

Melville's mischievous drollery. In chapter ten of Moby-Dick, "A Bosom Friend," Melville famously employs an outrageous comparison:

> It may seem ridiculous, but it [Queequeg's head] reminded me of General Washington's head, as seen in the popular busts of him. It had the same long regularly graded retreating slope from above the brows, which were likewise very projecting, like two long promontories thickly wooded on top. Queequeg was George Washington cannibalistically developed.[38]

With such casual drollery, Melville creates the gifted universal man. In a similar spirit, yet more inwardly and less obviously, Banks allows Owen in Boston to indulge in one of his constant, disconnected daydreams:

> I loved the city at once and might well have run off from Father then and there and made it my permanent home, like the young Ben Franklin fleeing *his* home to seek his fortune in Philadelphia, had I, like Franklin, a proper trade or some other means of making my living than that of caring for sheep or homesteading northern wildernesses.[39]

Both Founding Father jokes depend upon a second reading because at this point Melville's reader does not yet have a clear idea of Queequeg and his action-virtues, nor does Banks's reader have a good notion of Owen as a monster daydreamer. That such a pathetic demon as Owen would compare himself to Benjamin Franklin, the one Founding Father who actually did something to oppose slavery during his lifetime, comes across as *downer* drollery—as compared to Melville's more insouciant *upper* drollery in comparing Queequeg to U.S. President George Washington. The meta-textual pattern is there, but as so often with such meta-textual patterns, Banks turns it, even when a joke is involved, inside out. As Banks continues Owen's narcissistic monologue, it moves from black humor to solipsism, "But no man of my acquaintance who was my age and was not unhappily married felt as sadly trapped as I. Nor would any one of them have understood it in me. They might well have wished to *be* me." Well, any reader will realize this Mittyesque self-aggrandizement is too much and will begin counting up Owen's marbles.

Owen, who embodies the dark tragic split between mind and act, admires the "ideal poet and sage," as he imagines his father's authority and aura diminished in the bright glow of Boston's city gentry. He's pleased as punch to see his father displaced as the reader's awareness of an unreliable narrator becomes heightened. Owen's account of Emerson's lecture remains fair and accurate, despite the naïve adoration of a student that Owen bestows on Emerson. But while Emerson would like to conjure up a contemporary hero, Brown, the practical hero sitting at Emerson's feet, has no need for those fine airy words Emerson utters. Displaying bottom-line common sense, Brown rejects the speech as the work of an academic *boob*. Emerson, who would have liked to close the gap between intellect and act, appears impotent to Brown. Today, there is still Emerson's incendiary high counsel (treasured by a small coterie of academics), but it was the deeds of John Brown that help bend the arc of history. Owen resembles Homer's Telemachos (Book 16 of the *Odyssey*) who can't recognize his father because of the poor clothing he wears.[40]

Banks more directly imitates Melville's descriptive technique by making a physiological comparison between Emerson and John Brown, "Even physically, the two looked enough alike to have been brothers—although Father would have been the cruder, more muscular version."[41] After the lecture, John skeptically quizzes Owen, finding solace and approval in Owen's opinion that Emerson's talk was prophetic. Like Telemachos and Odysseus, readers witness father and son in a reconciling embrace as John puts his arm over Owen's shoulder—they briskly and happily walk bound to each other that way in a cheerful moment that is nearly as hard to forget as the tearful embrace of father and son in *The Odyssey*. Later, Banks indicates that Brown comes to admire Emerson.[42]

Owen goes to hear abolitionist William Lloyd Garrison speak, but leaves before the event, hinting that he might have been sexually cruising among working-class men, but he's so repressed that he welcomes a serious physical beating when challenged by a gang of teenagers, attacking them first. The beating assuages his guilty conscience and he nearly rejoices in his severe manly punishment as his father plays nurse to his wounds.

Banks's sketch of Brown's failure in England concentrates on his military daydreaming rather than his business venture as an explanation for his defeat. While the military digressions about the Bible and Napoleon remain interesting, they provide such a general air of abstraction that a reader could almost forget Own and John are travelers—after some initial enthusiasm about landing in England, the actual landscape nearly vanishes, except for some comments on smoking factories. The trip to Paris itself where Brown sold some wool is ignored in favor of walking the battlefield of Waterloo, a place that Brown did actually visit. Perhaps an opportunity was missed in not portraying Protestant Brown in Catholic Paris, since Brown was a vigorous admirer of Oliver Cromwell who sought, "to conquer and convert the Irish from paganism and papistry."[43] While Banks pours Brown into the heroic mold, he cites Brown's prejudices and his military daydreams as fundamental character flaws.

At Brown's Springfield church in Massachusetts the subject of black skin color as the mark of Cain, appears in connection to the Fugitive Slave Law and its enforcement, "Well they knew that the color of their skin was now more than ever the mark of Cain."[44] While the Biblical passage in the Cain and Abel story (whose principal point is to oppose the death penalty) clearly indicates that the mark designates an exile and one who is protected from death by a seven-fold vengeance from God,[45] its interpretation in the history of English literature voices a venal prejudice echoing as far back as *Beowulf* (c. eighth or ninth century) and was prominent in the antebellum South.[46] But the role of skin color as the mark of Cain, plays an important role in the dark secret Owen will not admit to the reader.

Banks predates Brown's formation of the League of Gileadites to November 15, 1850, rather than the actual date of January 15, 1851, in order to make Owen present for the event, so that he can send Owen to North Elba before the winter snows. When Lyman returns tired the next day, after three days of driving the wagon on an underground run, Owen enjoys some homoerotic violence against Lyman who has returned dog weary. At first, Owen records his perplexity upon seeing Lyman, "I felt shy as a girl with him, anxious and worried, even worried about my *appearance!*"[47] Twice Lyman's size, Owen picks up the exhausted Lyman and tosses him against a horse stall, something he finds "dark and wonderfully satisfying," admitting to Lyman that he did this because of his skin color. The reader suspects that this is one of the impulsive lies Owen utters in the heat of controversy—as he had previously lied to Frederick Douglass when he said he'd give up his life in the fight against slavery.

It's clear that Owen's impetuous violence stems from some incident withheld from the reader. Owen's stated explanation of compulsive, gratuitous racism is a good example of how the reader must bring some skepticism toward the unreliable narrator whom the reader must rely upon, especially in a narrative that runs counter to what little we know of the historical Owen. This violent incident hangs in the air like a strange mystery, hooking the reader to discover what lies behind it and rethink what has been read. In April, Susan gives birth to a dead boy, "I did not think of Lyman's loss. Only of Susan's, and in some small, illegitimate way, my own."[48] How could the dead baby be *his* loss? Why in his anger at the baby's death does Owen compare himself to "a blinded Sampson"? Was Owen the biological father? Why does Lyman, upon seeing the dead baby, want to leave immediately and set up house elsewhere? Acting like a slave owner, Owen tries to stop Lyman by taking away the horse Lyman rides, so Lyman goes on foot. Why does Owen sadly imagine a tombstone with an inscription of his choice for the unnamed baby? He does not do that for his stepmother's baby. Predictably, Owen feels guilty when he finds out that his father will come for a visit, yet despite his dread of his father finding out what has happened, he says to himself that he had "done nothing wrong," yet the reader knows Owen to be a truth-bender and argumentative self-justifier. Lyman refuses to speak to anyone about his feud with Owen. Why? Embarrassment about a fight can hardly be the answer. No one can make headway in the dispute between Owen and Lyman, no one will say a word.

After the violent confrontation with Lyman, Owen beats himself with a switch and then scourges himself with a leather strap until his blood runs and he passes out. One does not do such things in repentance for a mere tussle, yet performing this penance does not work. Owen probably thinks that the child was born dead to punish his sin, although he refuses to believe in God. Nonetheless, Owen can think only of Susan:

> Her face, her voice, her shape and movement, had constantly been in my mind. No matter what I was doing, no matter whom I was talking to, it was Susan I was thinking of, missing, pining for, longing to speak to. And to touch.[49]

The ostensible reason that Owen's *affair* with Susan remains a secret lay in the fact that Susan is a mulatto and the baby's white skin can be attributed to previous ancestors—except that Lyman at a glance suspects what has happened. Skin color as the mark of Cain—white here—comes to Owen's mind because he will replicate Cain's killing of his brother Lyman. Even in the narration of shame as he calls it, the prefatory remarks to the event of the stillbirth where Owen first identifies himself as a killer arrives as fevered, nearly hallucinatory—and it contains a remarkable statement. Owen speaks of how they slept like Quakers in the attic with a curtain between the sexes "where Ruth and I and the younger children and Lyman Epps and his wife, Ellen, slept on our pallets."[50] Except for a rare and insignificant typo, I had never spotted an error of any sort in Banks's novels or stories. Susan is Lyman's wife not Ellen; at this point in time, Ellen, the wife of Owen's brother Jason, resides in Ohio.[51] Owen has made a Freudian slip. Owen can't even get himself at this moment to admit that Susan is Lyman's wife. This passage functions as the prelude to the narration of the baby's death and violence against Lyman. A sexual narrative lies at the heart of Owen's anguished darkness as well as the narrative that lay at the heart of slavery's darkness—the use and demand of others for sex and the inability to acknowledge in public the issue of offspring, as well as the refusal to accept the sexual independence of African Americans.

Every time Owen catches a glimpse of Susan from a distance, he hears his heart pounding like the guilty narrator of Edgar Allan Poe's story "The Tell-Tale Heart." He's even afflicted with a stammer.[52] While Owen remains capable of analyzing the more public problem of the novel's overtly surface narration—the Abraham and Isaac theme of his relationship with his father—with intelligent and circumspect detail, he cannot plainly confess to the reader his deepest sin, his illegitimate baby—the same dark sin as the Reverend Arthur Dimsdale from Nathaniel Hawthorne's *The Scarlet Letter.*

Susan never loved Owen. She must have woken in the middle of the act one night, afraid to cry out. Afterwards, Owen plays the peeping Tom at their cabin in Timbuctoo, watching them make love. While William Faulkner sensationally employed voyeurism about bestiality (cow love, described as *stock-diddlin'*) in *The Hamlet*[53] to parody Victorian ideals of romance and marriage,[54] Banks parodies contemporary voyeurism concerning white obsession with black-on-black pornography.[55]

Owen briefly meets Susan at a farmer's fair where her conversation sails flatly distant, matter-of-fact, and loyal to her husband Lyman. When Susan suggests that Owen find a white woman to love, he's perplexed, nearly outraged. It's really not Susan whom Owen loves—Susan functions as the homoerotic go-between, the medium of the *sainted* threesome whom American Beat writers extolled in the 1950s. Unlike Carolyn Cassady who had the best of Neal Cassady and Jack Kerouac,[56] Susan has no interest in that kind of relationship. Owen narcissistically projects Lyman as a double:

> Despite our differences, Lyman and I regarded ourselves, except for race, as remarkably similar, the way lovers often do.... My thwarted love for Susan was my love for Lyman gone all wrong.[57]

The double prefigures the murder to follow. The sexual pass and refusal occurs inside an ice cave, a locus of cold frustration not warm fertility. While *Rule of the Bone* featured a sacred cave as in the *Odyssey*, here we have an icicle cave of sin, a place that admits neither light nor warmth. Lyman rejects not only Owen but even the possibility of conversation between them, fearing that his worst suspicions would be confirmed. Owen whines that Lyman "downright shriveled me... struck my manhood away."[58] Hence the impetuous murder of his father's best friend which appears to Owen as absurd.

The killing in secret bears a vague resemblance to Hawthorne's earliest story, the Cain and Abel story, "Alice Doane's Appeal," where Walter Brome falls in love with Alice. Walter tells her brother Leonard he knows of the shame (incest) between brother and sister, and then Leonard murders Walter in secret on a lonely road. Hawthorne also invokes the themes of Narcissus, Oedipus, and Abraham and Isaac in "Roger Malvin's Burial," which David Reynolds cites as an example of "the post-Gothic, Subversive Hawthorne."[59] The story contains a 20-year-long imprisonment in guilt and gloom because Reuben Bourne failed to bring assistance to his wounded father-in-law, a war hero, who treated him as a son, instructing him to marry his daughter. The story ends with the accidental murder of Reuben's son Cyrus while deer hunting at the exact spot where Roger Malvin died, producing a kind of familial suicide, ending the family line. The resemblance to Banks's Owen lies with the long imprisonment in secret family guilt as well as the themes of Narcissus, Oedipus, and Abraham and Isaac in the same narrative.[60] Banks even imitates Hawthorne's circular motif with Owen's return to a granite rock marking the burial of the family patriarch. While Reuben's curse and sin are expiated as he utters his first prayer in years to heaven, Owen's despair culminates in suicide.

Jorge Luis Borges's haunting story "The Circular Ruins" recounts a man's terror at being "the projection of another man's dream—what incomparable humiliation,"[61] the father-son conflict at the heart of Owen's relationship with his father. In Borges's story the sorcerer conceives of his son as a fantastic book; the story is ultimately about homoerotic guilt at not having a real son, "the absent son was nourished by the diminutions of his soul,"[62] which offers a good description of Owen himself. At the end of Borges's ironic story, the sorcerer realizes that he, too, was but the dream of another man—the same problem that Owen wrestles with.

Owen continually asserts that he is not the dream of his father, but his rebellious identity mimics what his father would call the work of Satan. As in Melville's *Pierre: or, The Ambiguities* (1852), Banks makes his narrator Owen an antagonist to his protagonist. Like the character Pierre who murders his cousin, Owen resorts to murder within the extended family commune. Like Pierre, Owen writes a book that not only will no publisher publish, but John Brown's biographer Villard will not even use it in his biography because the memoir is so obviously the infantilized daydream of a deranged and unreliable narrator. Besides being a homoerotic displacement, Owen's love for Susan

Resurrection Dream: *Cloudsplitter*

remains a failed attempt to transfer his admiration for his biological mother's hardworking competence, something he finds lacking in his often sick stepmother. Susan competently picks up the slack at North Elba, acting as a substitute mother for the hardscrabble homestead. Owen's longing for Susan somewhat resembles Melville's Pierre whose daydream for a sister, "expresses the desire of Victorian men to recover the androgynous natural self that had to be repressed in order for men to rise in a fiercely competitive hierarchy."[63] While Owen cannot live up to his father's expectations and refuses martyrdom alongside his father, Pierre cannot live up to his mother's expectations—she throws him out of her house and he eventually ends up in jail. Both Pierre and Owen remain obsessed about their father's stone monument and they both resort to suicide: Pierre's duel and dual suicide with Isabella by employing a poisoned vial mischievously provides a parody of both *Hamlet* and *Romeo and Juliet*; Owen's solitary suicide presents the despairing guilt of a murderer who has left a deluded apology (defense) for his secret crime. Owen convinces himself that he's in purgatory, but the reader easily recognizes the memoir as a non-repentant monologue from hell.

The scene of the murder conjures and counterpoints imagery from book six of the *Odyssey*. In Banks's narrative Owen and Lyman are startled by a mountain lion, an event that directly leads to the murder. As an archetype or icon, the mountain lion has been a traditional symbol of vigorous male heterosexuality. Lyman passes the pistol up to Owen who aims, but the lion suddenly leaps away. Owen then passes the gun back to Lyman and when he realizes the hammer is cocked, then impulsively seizes Lyman's hand, turns the gun to his chest, and pulls the trigger. Owen cuts himself with a penknife, smears his face with blood, rolls in the dirt, and concocts a cover story of accidental death which leads to no investigation. If Lyman had murdered Owen, would there have not been an investigation? The blithe success of Owen's cover-up offers an indictment of a racist society. The imagery of Owen, bloody and filthy, counter echoes the scene of Odysseus with Nausikaa when the hero wakes up in a pile of leaves after his shipwreck:

> He pushed aside the pile of brown leaves, rising up
> from the dense thicket, with a firm grip breaking
> a branch of an olive bush to shield his groin,
> and advanced from the copse like a mountain lion
> that has just weathered a terrible tempest,
> or the determination of a lion tracking doe or gazelle—
> and if famished a lion will even break into a homestead
> to ravage a flock of sheep when the owners are at home—
> thus Odysseus was prepared to face these young girls:
> stark naked and consumed with need in his belly,
> clothed only in a branch he had ripped off a bush,
> seaweed dangling from his hair, shreds of leaves
> matted on his nose and cheeks and chest, eyes burning,
> a rampant, terrifying sight to these innocent girls!

> Clotted with dirt and scabby cuts from the rocks,
> he threw the girls into terror and they fled up the banks,
> finding refuge in the great gleaming wagon,
> yet Nausikaa alone stood firm on the pebbled banks,
> naked and bold with steady heart and sturdy legs,
> for Athena had filled her with a courage unflinching.[64]

Owen appears as a wandering anti-Odysseus, falsely and ironically clothed in his imagery, returning incognito to his home at North Elba, the *ghostly* visage who views the grave of his father and loyal, martyred companions:

> he who was the murderer of the elder Lyman Epps, he who was the secret villain of the massacre at Pottawatomie, the meticulous arranger of the martyrdom of John Brown, and the cause of wasted deaths of all those others whose bodies now lie before me.[65]

Owen destroys his own family instead of restoring its glory like Odysseus who honored his father. While Odysseus tried to save his companions, Owen deliberately destroys them in his version of paradise lost wherein Owen has played the serpent. Because they both betray their leader, Owen compares himself to the famous liar Iago from *Othello*, a confession of duplicity.

The Abraham and Isaac theme provides the principal meta-text of the narrative and fuels Owen's resentment and anger as he perceives himself to be an Isaac-like victim. Banks comments:

> I think the father-son story, in all its various shapes and permutations, has fascinated me since the beginning of my writing life, and since the beginning of my life, for that matter. But it was an approach that I had never quite entertained before. What happens in a relationship between a father and son, for instance, in which the father is a dominating, controlling figure, but also happens to be right? John's an idealistic man, not a brute, not a sadist, not a psychopath, but something more complicated and seductive. To me, it's the Abraham and Isaac story, but told from the point of view of Isaac, the son.[66]

Although both Emerson and Melville's *Moby-Dick* also play a significant role as meta-texts, another important meta-text finds casual reference in the novel—John Brown's favorite poem, John Milton's *Paradise Lost*.[67] *Cloudsplitter* is an American version of Milton's epic without the Puritan mythology—the story of the fall in the Edenic landscape of America, one of America's central myths, the, "New England Puritan dream of God's Protestant utopian City on a Hill, the New Jerusalem."[68] While Milton's Homeric syntax offers a dramatization of early *Genesis* that founders in theological abstraction amid a Manichean, Babylonian angelology written in imitation of Homer's sci-fi theogony in the *Iliad*, Banks's prose epic remains grounded in American history as it offers a dystopian critique of the *peculiar institution* with the violent echo of its legacy in American sociology and psychology as it leverages its focus on the crux of lusty miscegenation. The Cain and Abel motif of two *brothers*, Owen and Lyman,

Resurrection Dream: *Cloudsplitter* 155

working in common cause from within a communal family provides a submerged subplot of guilt that in the end overpowers the more conventional main plot of father-son rivalry.

The novel offers a brilliant meditation and distillation on American history concerning the perils of liberalism gone wrong—how the problem of lust and sex (not in archetypal abstraction) can poison interracial relations in a hyper-racialized society that denies white is a color, then and now. In presenting the story of Owen Brown's unconscious racism, Banks dramatizes the horror that such unconscious racism can inflict not only upon an individual but upon the community and nation when equality of race remains a liberal notion rather than deed.

Owen's point of view infuses a Janus-like perspective rooted in the historical situation of the communal Brown family with its dominating patriarch while Owen's atheism projects a late-twentieth-century postmodern perspective anchored in individual narcissism that surround questions of self-identity, thus rooting Owen as a representative man of our contemporary age. Through Owen, the readers hear, "the voice of the concrete past speaking through and to our imaged present."[69] Owen's diffidence and hesitations, as well as frustrations, stride across both centuries, especially in his liberalism that appropriates blacks for his own fantasies. While the reader may admire the heroic perspective of Emerson and feel uneasy—as well as painfully justified—about the desperate violence Brown and the whole nation was plunged into with the Civil War, Owen remains a representative postmodern anti-hero whose life the reader cannot help but be horrified by.

While Owen's escape from Harpers Ferry becomes the reason he later goes underground in the West, the blaming of Lyman for his own failure to increase and multiply serves up daydream infantilism. Ironically, it is Owen's guilt that marks him with the mark of Cain. In a reversal of antebellum convention, the white man bears the visible mark of Cain and Banks implies a larger symbolism—in creating chattel slavery based upon one color, white society created a system that systematically killed those of black color, while exploiting them in a sexually predatory manner, which was the inset plot of the two runaways in love whom the Browns and the Quaker at Westport could not get to Canada.

Although Owen's account of the infamous Pottawatomie massacre appears nearly delusional in the self-puffing aggrandizement of his role, the account—as well as the victory at Black Jack, the heroic retreat at Osawatomie, and the capture of Harpers Ferry—reads narrowly compatible with Villard's rather extensive documentation,[70] although it was not John Brown but H. H. Williams who drew up the list of those to be executed at the Pottawatomie incident.[71] Owen's agency as a killer at Pottawatomie appears amply documented. Owen's conceit that his confession provides a purgatorial monologue remains strange since he repeatedly affirms his atheism—and besides, Protestants of the nineteenth century did not accept the conceit of purgatory, while they are more apt to accept it today. Owen's *purgatorial* monologue remains more in the tradition of Edgar Allan

Poe who in stories like "The Tell-Tale Heart" and "The Cask of Amontillado," as well as others, built upon the infamous monologues from hell, both short and long, that appear in Dante Alighieri's *Inferno*.

The imagery of Owen clinging and falling from the tree at Harpers Ferry and escaping alone conjures an ironic counterpoint to the imagery of Odysseus clinging to a fig tree from the conclusion of book 12 in the *Odyssey*. While Odysseus conjures patience by thinking of how people abuse the courts of law, Owen wallows in the self-pity of his childhood arm injury and whimpers about his fear of death. Odysseus escapes with courage to fight for his family, while Owen slinks away, abandoning his family.

Owen's betrayal of his father consists in not burning his father's papers, yet if his father really wanted them burned, he would have done it himself. It was pious nineteenth-century convention to ask others to burn one's papers. In a sane world, Owen's omission hardly amounts to betrayal, but his possible suicide at the end effects certain betrayal—of his father's religious ideals and fatherly expectations. While Owen claims to be releasing ghosts from purgatory, we know he speaks from his private hell, so that his concluding daydream of heaven appears as Gothic grotesque:

> Though nothing is forgotten, all is forgiven! Even Susan Epps is here amongst them, and she has beside her, holding tightly to her skirt, a small boy—her son, Lyman's son, emblem of her love for him and his forgiveness of me, for that is how she presents the little boy to me, saying simply, proudly, "I have a son to make your acquaintance, Owen Brown," and that is how I receive him and he me.[72]

Owen declares this son to be Lyman's, but why single out the one stillborn child of Lyman's that obsesses Owen? How is the imagined resurrection of that dead son an emblem of Susan's love for him? Or even of Lyman's forgiveness? To find a character as deluded as Owen Brown one needs to travel back in time to the stories of Poe or the guilty narrator of Melville's "Bartleby, the Scrivener: a Story of Wall Street."

At the conclusion of the novel, there is the image of the box of papers that provides Owen's correspondence with his confidant Miss Mayo. Banks speaks of this framing as a literary convention, citing Hawthorne's *The Scarlet Letter*, a book about undeclared paternity, as an example.[73] But the framing receives a rather astonishing metaphor—the box appears "as if it were a child's coffin,"[74] thus psychologically merging the theme of Owen's stillborn child and his confused Oedipal guilt. It was the death of Owen's child that precipitated his gratuitous violence toward Lyman, his peeping voyeurism, and then his impulsive murder of Lyman and the subsequent his cover-up. Owen even misplaces his guilt on the preservation of his father's box of papers that were to be destroyed! Such displacement appears to be the result of his frustration, denial, and repressed inability to admit the truth amid Victorian decorum—thus his rambling apology and his pathetic disconnected fantasies of a resurrected paradise with Susan, who never loved him.

Resurrection Dream: *Cloudsplitter*

At Harpers Ferry, Owen sat catatonic in the wagon with the box of papers that resembled a coffin. The image of coffin consciously conjures the coming execution of his father and fellow rebels, but the unconscious imagery of the connection to the stillborn son speaks of his rape and sins. Owen eventually migrates west with the entire continent before him, able to escape into anonymity like Wade in *Affliction* (if Wade has indeed escaped) because, as he self-consciously notes to himself, he is white and, "could become an American without a history."[75] That dream of starting over, like Bob Dubois of *Continental Drift*, remains, "essentially the dream of being a child again."[76] That ultimate daydream of collective paternal denial persists in popular culture with all its perfidious corrosiveness today. Do Americans care about John Brown, Douglass, or the great Du Bois whom James Joyce admired as an intellectual giant?[77]

The reception of the French language edition of *Cloudsplitter* found more applause than the American reception. There may have been a number of reasons for this: The strength of the translation; an avid readership for historical novels in the country of Alexander Dumas's historical thrillers; or the popularity of the martyrdom theme in France, something the satirist Michel Houellebecq effectively pokes fun at in *The Elementary Particles* (1998; 2000 English translation). Banks's novel finds itself rooted in the Bible, while Banks's style often exhibits a tendency toward the tightly phrased epigrammatic finesse the French treasure—for example: "What liberates and gives power to one child must often humiliate and weaken another, until it appears that our differences more than our sameness have come to bind us"[78] or "A poor soldier was Jason, he who would be neither private nor general."[79] And finally, the fact that one of the most riveting and famous pen-and-ink sketches by Victor Hugo's depicted the hanging of John Brown as visceral outrage and that sketch was prominently on display in a glass case for decades at the Maison de Victor Hugo museum in Paris. Hugo judged the execution of Brown to be a heinous crime.[80] To Hugo, Brown was an apostle, hero, and martyr. For Brown's epitaph Hugo suggested, "Pro Christo sicut Christus (He followed Christ as if he was Christ)."[81]

Banks puts a special emphasis on the role of conscience and the Protesting dissenting tradition in taking the martyrdom of Jesus seriously and in the case of Brown, literally. In doing so he presents a national epic like Walt Whitman's *Leaves of Grass*. Banks's novel certainly supersedes the award-winning Benét epic on John Brown. While Whitman celebrates himself as the embodiment of the nations' spirit of freedom, Banks communes with the spirit of Brown as if he were still a living light of conscience and model for contemporary Christians, while offering Owen Brown as the conflicted liberal tainted by the insanity of racism.

In a postmodern context, the very idea of a heroic representative man finds itself deconstructed de facto to an anti-heroic level. Amid the Oedipal struggle, this is exactly what happens to Owen, an anti-heroic narrator as obsessed (but not as bitter) in his demented psychology to Fyodor Dostoyevsky's *Notes from Underground* (1864). Owen becomes representative of the unconscious racism paraded by the twentieth century, a century that he alone in the family has survived to see, an "age of Heroism had acceded to an age of Cowardice."[82] Owen is a racist who claims blacks make him uncomfortable, but he denies that he is in any real sense a racist like many late twentieth-century whites who embrace multiculturalism. But when the dynamic secret at the heart of the darkness in racism's epic story rears its head, Owen is as guilty as Cain. He kills his *brother* Lyman in an impulsive fit, then blames the social construction of a racist society as the unjust impediment to fulfilling his daydream of, "a manly love finding itself locked inside a white man's racialist guilt, of Abel's sweet brotherly trust betrayed by Cain's murderous envy."[83] Owen the liberal can only love black people, yet he secretly murders Lyman, blaming Lyman's rejection of his homosexual advance on black racism, not personal inclination. Owen embodies the racist sins of both the nineteenth and twentieth centuries and speaks with, "the voice of the concrete past speaking through and to our imagined present."[84]

As is his habit, Banks's irony digs deep here in its deconstruction of late twentieth-century liberalism. While the portrait of John Brown is defended as a Romantic icon, a heroic representative Christian man who is anti-racist, the portrait of Owen and his like-minded sons of atheistic liberalism remain incapable of divesting themselves of racism as they *lust* after the very soul of racism without being aware of its proprietary nature—no wonder such liberals remain incapable of constructing an anti-racist society. John Brown remains the historic ideal with Owen the contemporary mirror; the former gives his life like Jesus for his brothers; the fictional Owen takes the life of his brother because he cannot be the heroic ideal. Like Oedipus, Owen and liberal whites often become unconscious murderers or betrayers of their own social conscience.

Speaking of the dangers in confusing history with fiction, Banks offers the following distinctions:

> I think that it's wrong to read fiction for history. It's not wrong, however, to read history and hope to get fiction from it. I tend to do that. I tend to read history looking for fiction because I'm looking for universal human truths that transcend historical circumstances but whose germ I'll find lying within historical circumstances—the truth about racism, let's say, is what I'm interested in, not necessarily the truth about racism in 1900 or 1844 or even 1999. I'm interested in racism itself, where the hell in us it comes from and what it means and what my version of it means and so forth. And so I'll use history to get there, but I would never use fiction in order to get history. That's where we make mistakes. You wouldn't read *Gone With the Wind* in order to find out what happened in the South during the Civil War. Or, for that matter, you wouldn't read the *Iliad* in order to learn the truth about the Trojan War, though you might learn about the Trojan war in order to be inspired to write the *Iliad*.[85]

Those readers who have already conjured a fictional portrait of Owen Brown based upon their reading of history might have difficulty accepting Banks's portrait, much like those scholars who have imagined, based upon archeological research, how warfare operated in the twelfth century BC sometimes quibble with how Homer's dramatic narrative operates.

Resurrection Dream: *Cloudsplitter*

William Styron[86] has noted that in fiction, "it has always been a daunting task to make psychopaths credible, much less agreeable—and nearly impossible to make them heroic—so even then I knew that my Nat Turner had to be given rational dimensions."[87] Styron's *The Confessions of Nat Turner* (1967) offers a general precedent for Banks's approach. In Styron's novel, Nat Turner fantasizes about raping a white woman, while in Banks's novel it hazes ambiguous as to whether Owen has raped a black women or whether he has obsessively burdened himself with imagining a marriage with a black woman whose husband he has murdered. In the end, Owen remains a pathetic figure guilty of murder and self-rationalizing daydreams, resembling the unconscious racism of Bob Dubois from *Continental Drift*. Like Bob, Owen pleads that he meant well, but the reality is that neither can cope with their well-earned guilt. Like the childless author of *Gone with the Wind* (1936), Margaret Mitchell, Owen has no children, but more tellingly he romanticizes Susan in an infantile manner, much like Mitchell who explains to her readers that Negroes, "had to be handled gently, as though they were like children."[88] Rarely has a writer written so eloquently on the divide between good intentions and their destructive reality which conjures the psychopathic monologue of a war survivor's guilt, those *walking wounded* about whom Styron wrote so eloquently in his memoir, *Darkness Visible* (1990).

Another aspect of the novel's contemporary relevancy appears in the theme of culture wars. While many journalists wrote about culture wars in the early seventies, that theme still smolders today. Banks employs the leitmotif of the nineteenth-century culture wars surrounding the institution of slavery. Owen's chosen prejudice locates its crosshairs on the urban working class, those "unwashed physiognomies" that are a "subspecies."[89]

Banks gives free reign to Owen's sneering contempt for the class Banks emerged from, depicting lower class racism in such an ignorant, repulsive manner that any reader will be disgusted by Owen's middle-class venom. White middle-class Americans continue to disdain a working class engaged in manual labor that they have escaped from and the resentment of this is often exploited by right-wing pundits. Owen also expresses a debatably justified fear of the mob, yet was it not the angry mob that John Adams, Thomas Paine, and Franklin incited that forged the American Revolution?

As an troubled narrator, Owen activates a return to the techniques employed in *Hamilton Stark* and *The Book of Jamaica*, yet the technique in *Cloudsplitter* raises the problem of American self-delusion to the epic level of subversive pathology, achieving a contemporary relevancy that presents a national tragedy rather the merely personal narratives of the earlier novels. The national tragedy is threefold: a rampant delusional narcissism; an overly self-conscious obsession with sex and its indulgent self-justification no matter the consequences; and an obsession with race that distorts our perception of life. While Banks cheerfully admits that John Brown would be, by any contemporary definition, a terrorist, the novel implies that Americans have not kept faith with the heroic spirit of freedom that Franklin, Emerson, and Brown articulated and acted upon. The novel exposes a culture of narcissism drowning in an unconscious malaise the country may not escape from. Another wry implication remains: We have lost our sense of humor in taking ourselves so seriously, just as we have lost the selfless dedication to the Christian ideals that John Brown embodied. By extension, the dramatization of Owen's guilt and narcissistic self-pity offers the spectacle of a man and a nation deranged by its delusions, schizophrenically cut off from the world and his own ideals, a man whose roots in the problems of the nineteenth century haunt the present in a spectral manner.

Such a dramatic and unhistorical use of a main character with a famous historical setting amid a real-life cast of characters is not unprecedented. One of the most successful examples of such an approach with a forcefully imagined main character on the subject of martyrdom can be found in a novel by Hermann Hesse's friend, Gertrud von Le Fort, whose novella *The Song at the Scaffold* (1932, English, 1933) Georges Bernanos transformed into a 1952 play that became perhaps Francis Poulenc's most successful opera, *Dialogues of the Carmelites* (1957), which then graced the cinema with the 1960 film that featured stirring close-ups of Jeanne Moreau. But such liberties with history remain more common in Continental literature than the more literal, fundamentalist approach to history commonly found in American fiction, although one might cite William Kennedy's light comic touch in *Quinn's Book* (1988) and *The Flaming Corsage* (1996) as more indicative of the European or South American sensibility in historical novels. The fact versus fiction controversy first appeared in Thucydides' Introduction to his fifth-century BC *Peloponnesian Wars*. Thucydides asserted that his meticulous chronicle of war was superior to Homer's poetic account for many reasons, including archeological research—the ensuing debate has never ended, yet one might call writers like Homer, Plato, Thucydides, Hugo, Joyce, Du Bois, and Faulkner cloudsplitters.

13

Radical Irony: *The Darling*

> What she wanted was a love that would seize her whole being, her whole mind and soul, that would give her ideas, an aim in life, and would warm her aging blood.
> —Anton Chekhov, "The Darling," translated by David Magarshack

While Russell Banks had successfully provided the narrative of an anguished and repressed homosexual in *Cloudsplitter*, he now turned toward producing a greater *tour de force* perspective in *The Darling* (2004) by offering the voice of a woman. Ever since Gustave Flaubert's successful depiction of the interior life of a woman in *Madame Bovary* (1857), other authors have been fired to duplicate or surpass that achievement. Leo Tolstoy's imitation of Gustave Flaubert in *Anna Karenina* (1877) remains perhaps the most successful and best known novel written from the point of view of the other sex. Other notable examples include Henry James's *Portrait of a Lady* (1881), Theodore Dreiser's *Sister Carrie* (1900), Willa Cather's *My Ántonia* (1918), and Francois Mauriac's *Thérèse Desqueyroux* (1927). William Styron succeeded with *Sophie's Choice* (1979) and J. M. Coetzee with *Age of Iron* (1980). While novelists like Pierre de Marivaux (1688–1763) and Samuel Richardson (1689–1761) had previously written well, if sensationally, from the other sex's point of view, writers usually remain fixated upon the more detailed achievement of Flaubert that introduced a more documentary realism centered upon ordinary life. Yet, Banks has chosen to portray a not-so-ordinary life—peculiarly American and rooted in the moral idealism of the late sixties.

Banks's title refers to a well-known short story by Anton Chekhov:

> In one sense, Hannah is that darling, privileged, spoiled and entitled. But the word "darling" means many things in English. It's an allusion also to Chekhov's story, "The Darling," which is an affectionate portrait of a narcissist, a very difficult thing to do. But it is one of the things I was trying to do with this novel. I feel personally affectionate toward Hannah, although I'm very aware of her limitations.

I think sometimes we want to either idealize our characters in fiction or to judge them—especially, perhaps, when it comes to female characters. But the only truly believable character—flawed, but not so terribly flawed that we reject them. I wonder how we would feel toward Hannah if Hannah were a man. Because there's nothing that Hannah does except bear children that a man could not do. I suspect if Hannah were a man, the reader would see him as a Hemingway-esque stoical existential hero searching for meaning in a meaningless world and morality in an amoral world.[1]

In "The Darling," Chekhov paints a woman who by all her sentiment and actions would appear destined to be a model mother, but who by an unfortunate quirk of fate remains barren. She marries and mothers two older men only to outlive them, then has an affair with a married veterinarian and ends up unofficially *adopting* his son, yet she lives with the debilitating anxiety that at any moment a telegram might arrive to take away the beloved boy she spoils and dotes on. While she is known by reputation in town as "The Darling," people remain oblivious to the secret suffering and tragedy of her life as everyone presumes upon her charm, cheer, and generosity toward everyone she meets. As a middle-class woman, she has never known poverty. Her intentions are always good, yet people can't take her seriously any more than they can really take Christianity seriously. Everyone pays her lip service with the childishly patronizing epithet, "Oh, the darling!" Olga's reputation in the town operates like a dysfunctional chorus in a Greek tragedy. Olga has no ideas of her own, adopting with complete enthusiasm the ideas of the lovers she mothers. Chekhov's amusing short story deals in character types as does Banks's novel, yet character types are more commonly successful in short stories rather than novels which demand more character development, even in peripheral players.

Banks had successfully written from the vantage point of a woman in a several short stories, most successfully in *Trailerpark*, and in *The Sweet Hereafter*, where Dolores Driscoll exhibits the very motherly qualities Olga possesses in Chekhov's "The Darling." Yet such portrayals were short stints even if they were remarkably effective and diverse. For *The Darling*, Banks adopts that aspect of Olga whereby not having any ideas of her own; Hannah unthinkingly appropriates the ideas of her college peers attracted to rebellion, an aspect of her background that could have undergone more development in the depiction of her college years. After Hannah's one-night stand with the aristocratic Zach from Cincinnati during her freshman year of college, she's sexually attracted to black and Jewish men, but the readers are provided with no further details about her four years at Brandeis University.[2]

As a character, Hannah remains at first an enigma to the reader. She spends three and a half years at Harvard Medical School where she finds the extra time to make pipe bombs and phony IDs. During this time, the only person she appears to meet is her roommate Clara, an ex-stripper, who is romantically idealized and the true love of her life. Clara, so she says, knows nothing of *Dawn's* underground activities—innocent Clara, whose personality does not emerge, does not notice that Hannah makes bombs in her room, which sounds like protective denial. Hannah claims they are not lesbians but lovers off the rebound from men, yet her most satisfying sexual experience in the novel involves Clara in a threesome. Hannah concludes her life by running an all-woman commune managed by a rugged lesbian who can seemingly accomplish the work of two hardy men, including carrying 20 pounds of roof shingles on her shoulder as she climbs up a ladder to smartly roof a house.

Unlike Flaubert's traditional chronology, the novel performs the postmodern time shuffle in memory-slides that computers have popularized. Banks manages his slide show with an associative and accessible clarity within the mind of 60-year-old Hannah Musgrave now located in upstate New York as the novel tells a story about both Africa and America:

> I wasn't so much interested in writing about Africa as I was about writing about Liberia, the reasons being that Liberia is an important chapter in the American story of race, and that's the story I want to write about. I was also interested in Liberia because it is our unacknowledged colony in Africa and has been since its creation in 1820. And I wanted to expose the hypocrisy of our denial of having any colony in Africa and our avoidance of any responsibility for the social and political chaos in that region.[3]

In Banks's most contemporary political novel, he offers a dual study in the politics of both America and Liberia.

Banks wishes to call attention to the historical connections between Liberia and America with the hope that Americans will be aware of their responsibility for the role the American government played in enabling the chaos, destruction, and reign of terror that engulfed what had been a fairly stable society with a Western economy originally engineered by Firestone and other major corporations. Liberia, in effect, had been the only African country free of European domination; it kept its own independence and worked under the umbrella of minimal American patronage. Eager to expand colonial corporatism, America appears to have been acting out the story of race with its imperial ambitions in Liberia, yet such cultural engineering can be, like the surgical war in Iraq, a costly gamble in the loss of life and a story of imperial shame during which the Geneva conventions were trashed.

In *Hamilton Stark*, Banks wrote about a character's journey of self-discovery with ironic ambiguity and in *The Book of Jamaica* about a character deluded by alcoholism and ganga. Owen in *Cloudsplitter* turned his resentment of his father's strong patriarchal aura into criminality, while *The Darling* presents a character who wants to rebel against her father's achievement and her mother's narcissistic incompetence, but like Olga; she has no clear idea of how to accomplish what she wants and so adopts the ideas of those around her. Hannah possesses a frustrated yet idealistic instinct that operates at the liminal borders of her consciousness, much as Owen Brown's racism operates at the border of his consciousness. Also, Hannah's intent dedication to chimpanzees and her mystic dreams about them, parallel Owen's paradisal dreams of his imaginary Susan.

Hannah's rebellion, stemming from Puritan guilt at being born rich and the thrill of being at the center of dangerous upheaval, attracts her to terrorism in the Weather Underground, where she becomes a fugitive. Afterward, she accompanies a fellow fugitive to Accra, Ghana.

Graham Greene departed in 1935 for a trip to an African heart of darkness in order to see firsthand what his most admired novelist, Joseph Conrad, had seen. He chose to walk through Liberia with his cousin Barbara as companion.[4] At that time, there were no roads in Liberia. Halfway through the trip, Greene became ill, nearly dying toward the end. His near-death experience resulted in a resurrection epiphany—he rediscovered his passionate interest in living life, which is how his 1936 travel chronicle about the exploration, *Journey Without Maps*, concludes.[5] Hannah embarks to Africa on a journey without maps to Ghana and Liberia, two countries about which she knows absolutely nothing. She, too, will nearly die (of depression and depersonalization) and will return to America with a renewed sense of life's wonder and vitality that she will eventually transfer back to Liberia when she returns.

In Ghana, a place where Wright in 1953 once spent ten difficult weeks,[6] Hannah haphazardly falls into a job as a clerk in an outfit that has a contract with New York University (which has a branch in Ghana) to supply monkey blood for hepatitis research. This contact with primates will change her life. The choice of Accra, which could use more description in the novel, is eminently plausible. Accra was a place that an international set of counterculture people flocked to in the sixties and seventies. Jamaican Maroons arrived to renew their cultural contacts with the Ashanti. Others came to participate in the then-vital music scene surrounding the palm wine style (the slow mellow beat of which slightly influenced reggae) and the syncretic Highlife Afro-reggae music that peaked in the late sixties, a scene later eclipsed in the early seventies by the popularity of American soul and rock.[7] The cultural aspects of Ghana and Liberia receive only a token nod in the novel through the character of Zach, who deals in art.[8] But unlike Chekhov's Olga, Hannah has no interest in the arts.

Hannah leaves Accra to marry Woodrow Sundiata (surname of a famous thirteenth-century Mali warrior king and first name of the imperial American president), an African state official in Liberia. Yet how much can one trust what Hannah tells us—she who lives her life under several aliases? We get a version of her life:

> I was revealing what I knew of myself to a black African, not a white American, to a Christian, not an atheist, to a conservative government official, a member of the True Whig party, and not to a neo-Marxist fugitive under indictment by her own government for acts of civil disobedience and suspicion of terrorism. I had no choice but to alter, delete, revise and invent whole chapters of my story. Just as, for the same reasons, I am doing here, telling it to you.[9]

As with any of the Weather Underground memoirs,[10] some things are told, some things held back. About Hannah, Banks surmises that concerning "a woman of certain age and character, there is lots of stuff she would never tell and doesn't. Lots of stuff she withholds. A few things she even lies about."[11] Part of the novel's tease consists of trying to figure out how to pin down Hannah's obfuscations or dramatic exaggerations.

Hannah's participation in the wedding reception at Fuama is confined to being invited to taste the special wedding dish—chewing the meat, she gags as she realizes it is bush meat chimpanzee. She dashes to the white limo and sits out the wedding reception with the limo driver. The reception continues with strange customs and a language to which she has no access. Although Hannah has three children with Woodrow, the children are not really hers—they ultimately belong to Woodrow and Liberia, just as Olga's child belongs to another woman.

Like Hannah's pediatrician father, her new husband patronizingly and ominously calls her *darling*. Her husband turns into an alcoholic as she listens to the drunken bed thumping in the maid's room, "It was as if they had been doing this for years, since the first week of our marriage, and I had come to accept it as normal and even necessary. Simply it was how we lived."[12] Nonetheless, she bears three sons in five years, yet bonds more closely to the chimpanzees she works to preserve. She claims all her relationships with people were characterized by a distant detachment—that passion never moved her, whether for parents, lovers, friends, or her children, yet her passion for chimpanzees, the dreamers, provide the ghostly apparitions of her troubled life.

As an American trophy wife who bolstered the credentials and career of a state official who was not a member of the Americo-Liberian elite, Hannah feels trapped without any family or friends in a strange land. Her husband has seen the government files on her terrorist activities (and most probably the promiscuity of her sexual past). A fugitive from America, she has no one she can turn to for support in Liberia. During the Liberian recession of 1979, Samuel Doe launched a successful military coup (April 12, 1980) against the Americo-Liberian elite that had run the Liberian Republic since its creation in 1847.[13] At this critical juncture, Hannah ponders her situation in a fetal position while her husband, a friend of Charles Taylor, cheerfully sets to burning incriminating papers and letters, "I lay there curled on my side like a question mark, listening, unable to shut out the sound of my husband fucking his niece, my sons' nanny, my friend, perhaps the only human friend I had in those days."[14] Having rejected her family, what few friends in America she had, Hannah's only friend in a strange land is the hired wife-mother, her husband's mistress. But the extravagance of this self-pitying portrayal begs cross-examination.

Although Hannah's memoir is addressed to the general reader, it behooves the reader to recall that Hannah quite often tells the reader that the information passed to the reader is what she has disclosed to Anthea, her Adirondack farm manager, who relishes stories about men's insensitive brutality and how they victimize women. Hannah, as she admits, often tells people what they want to hear, and her narcissistic talent for dramatizing herself comes from her mother who performs such narcissistic drama incompetently, which is why Hannah does it so competently. While Hannah rebels against her mother's small-town conventionality, she finds loving inspiration from her father whom she visits in the hospital before he dies. At her father's burial, a trumpet player performs a tune from Charles Ives's masterpiece *The Unanswered Question* and Banks composes a marvelous prose poem fantasy inspired by Ives's unearthly music. The unanswered question in the novel's biography of Hannah remains the important role her father played in her psychology—unanswered by either Hannah or the narrative.

Under U.S. President Jimmy Carter, the 1980 coup in Liberia brought the illiterate but cunning Sergeant Samuel Doe to power as a replacement for the corrupt, despotic, and murderous William Tolbert. U.S. President Ronald Reagan had vigorously backed Doe with much foreign aid, which was dissipated in corruption as Banks's novel indicates. By the middle of the 1980s, Reagan grew disenchanted with Doe after his rigged election and he was dropped when the Cold War with Russia began to crumble. Banks notes, "The United States particularly abandoned Liberia after the end of the Cold War. We just pulled out after showering down [money]. They were the biggest recipient of foreign aid in Africa from the U.S. during the Cold War."[15] The CIA decided on a new course and the American-educated Charles Taylor, whom Hannah finds sexually attractive and whom she aids in his prison escape on September 18, 1985, became *Our Man in Africa* as Sam Clement dubs him,[16] yet ironically the CIA station chief appears not to understand that the spy in Graham Greene's novel *Our Man in Havana* (1958) was an incompetent alcoholic who made a mess of things—in Greene's novel this plays as comedy, but the American backing of Taylor was to result in terrible tragedy.[17]

Prince Johnson has admitted before the Liberian Truth and Reconciliation Commission that he and Taylor were given $10 million to overthrow Doe's government and that about half of that money was spent on guns and ammunition.[18] Taylor has recently confirmed Johnson's previous assertion that the U.S. Government facilitated his escape from an American prison by arranging to leave his prison cell unlocked and providing a prison guard to escort him to a pick-up car occupied by men he did not know, who then took him to a New York City airport. He claims the CIA backed him to overthrow Doe.[19] Although Banks performed prodigious research for the novel, he was not able to enter Liberia during the civil war, yet spent some time in adjacent Sierra Leone where Taylor formed his first army by recruiting soldiers from Sierra Leone's army.[20]

When Hannah is forced out of Liberia in 1983 by Doe, her farewell to her chimpanzees, in its bizarre and poetic transcendent intensity, overshadows her prosaic, trite, and perfunctory goodbye to her three children. The amusing scene of Hannah returning to the JFK airport—she sees so many white people that she freaks out—conjures a similar scene in *Rule of the Bone*.[21] Returning to her New England childhood home, she unconsciously fails to bring her mother any photos of her three children. Her mother has read *The Heart of the Matter* (1948), thinking the novel was set in Liberia. Hannah finds herself exasperated by her mother's error, which allows her to shift the discussion away from her refusal to gratify her mother's wish for photos of her grandchildren, yet had Hannah understood the pitfall parallels between her own life and Greene's novel set in the nearby neighborhood of Sierra Leone, she might have escaped the future fate of her failure.

During World War II, Graham Greene had worked in the MI6 branch of British Intelligence within Sierra Leone, later setting *The Heart of the Matter* in Sierra Leone.[22] The comic kitchen scene of impatient misunderstanding wherein Hannah's mother mistakenly thinks that Greene's novel was set in Liberia[23] offers a joke enhanced by the fact that for literate readers there are both significant similarities and differences between Greene's novel and Banks's novel—the major differences being the sex of the intriguers, Scobie's weakness as compared to Hannah's strength, and Scobie's Catholicism as opposed to Hannah's atheism. Yet some similarities abound: Hannah's mystic devotion to chimpanzees parallels Scobie's deeply haunted feelings toward his religion, the themes of embezzled money and adultery appears in both novels, and the use of a central irony governing the novels. Scobie thinks his infidelity invisible to his wife who has known about it all along and the irony that Hannah's participation in the springing of Taylor from a Massachusetts prison was approved by the CIA, and that Hannah was, according to Clement (the undercover CIA station chief at the American embassy in Liberia), a protected asset. Ultimately, the combative joke in the kitchen rests on Hannah for thinking of her mother as an irrelevant ditz. The apple does not fall far from the tree in terms of genetic personality, although Hannah inherited her father's ambition.

That New England kitchen scene between Hannah and her mother operates with deep psychological complexity. Hannah's mother argues that other Weather operatives have turned themselves in and have not received jail sentences, so why doesn't she turn herself in and her father will pay for a good lawyer. After all, Hannah has not appeared in court for charges of disturbing the peace and conspiracy to riot connected to the 1969 Weatherman Days of Rage.[24] The charges are not serious and would result in a fine (maybe of several thousand dollars because of its political nature). Hannah rejects the proposal with anger and contempt, arguing that it would certainly involve serious jail time in her case, yet the way she presents the argument offers only stubborn assertion and not reasoned argument. Hannah knows she cannot tell her mother that she made bombs. She also knows that in cases like hers, such indictments are merely provisional charges and that more serious charges will be pressed when one enters police custody.

The Weather Underground did successfully bomb several hundred government offices during the seventies, but they did not engage in the kind of terrorism as terrorism has been perceived after 9/11, because they did not kill anyone during those bombings, although several of their own members perished in the process of making bombs. Their policy, modeled on that of the old Irish Republican Army, was to avoid civilian casualties by giving notice of the bomb's timing and maximize publicity through the bombings of Federal buildings in the hope of embarrassing the bumbling incompetence of the government and thus generate public support through their heroic competence. That public support never appeared and with the end of the Vietnam War, which was the Weather Underground's main objective, their organization disbanded and people returned to community work. The contemporary use of the word terrorism evolved from the strategy of Islamic martyrdom that Palestinians adopted as a desperate measure. Because of this difference in the concept and practice of terrorism, Hannah at the end of the novel reflects that her particular autobiography could never again be enacted in America. It could also never be written again because there will probably never be another generation of American women tough enough to fight cops in streets and alleys, courageous enough to sever ties with friends and family in an attempt to preserve the militant independence of the Founding Fathers.

Banks's novel provides a corrective on how Americans might be tempted to distort what the failed idealists of the sixties tried to accomplish. Zach's story, with his millionaire success as an art entrepreneur, parallels the eventual wealth of Jerry Rubin's success as a stock trader—the Rubin who once mockingly tossed bills in the air at the New York Stock Exchange and whose stock-trading company once ran television advertisements featuring smashed windows commemorating the Chicago Days of Rage.

Hannah once more seduces Clara, babysitting her daughter Bettina, like Chekhov's Olga taking care of another man's boy. Hannah is platonically seduced by Taylor and helps him escape from prison. The series of letters Hannah sends to her husband Woodrow and the letters she receives present predictable and polite clichés that stall the novel. Since the marriage between Woodrow and Hannah remains the least convincing aspect of the plot, some humor, even if mischievous, in the letters would have amended this defect and retained a reader's interest.

Once back in Liberia, Hannah institutes responsible regime change in the way the family operates. Several of her chimpanzees have died of neglect and she boldly convinces Doe to fund an institute to preserve chimpanzees. When Taylor begins the civil war, there's a crisis scene at the family compound. When it is clear that Doe will have Woodrow killed because of his past friendship with Taylor, Hannah refuses to flee to Fuama with her family because of her chimpanzees. Woodrow wants her American status as protection for him and the children. When the family driver returns with thugs, Woodrow sits in the car with the boys, waiting for Hannah to get in. She refuses, but shouts for Woodrow to drive when she sees a pistol. Woodrow does not budge because he knows that he will never get away unless Hannah comes with him. The thugs open the car door, drag Woodrow out, and chop his head off with a machete while his sons watch in horror. This stubborn refusal to get in the car, putting her devotion to her primates before her family, constitutes the *secret shame* that Hannah will later lament.

Hannah's boys disappear to join the children's armies of the Liberian civil war. Clement show Hannah the famous video of that Prince Johnson made of the torture and murder of Doe. In the video, her son Dillon cuts off Doe's ear.

Radical Irony: *The Darling* 169

Sam puts Hannah on a plane back to America. If Hannah were a native African, she would have been eventually slaughtered, but the international American privilege of class incarnated in her passport exempts her from that fate, just as the deluded anthropologist of *The Book of Jamaica* finds exemption from justice because of his white skin.

Part of Hannah's dilemma and tragedy lies in the racist background she has had and the difficulties she has in trying to purge that background of racism. Banks says, "she's a white privileged person raised in an oppressive racist society and the higher you get up in the hierarchy of race and class the more difficult it is to scrape away. She's engaged in that struggle. She's attempting to deal with her own racism—and classism. But it ain't simple, you know. Because it reinforces itself when you have the racial privilege and class privilege and she has both."[25] Her determination to expunge her racism appears to have been the unstated reason for her decision to marry Woodrow.

Hannah later rejoices that her children fought with Johnson to revenge their father's death. In the falling out between Johnson and Taylor, America appeared to have switched its support to Johnson, but Taylor's more monstrous violence prevailed.[26] The fate of Hannah's boys, who became famous teenage killing monsters known as Worse-than-Death, Fly, and Demonology, become representative of how America lost control of the explosive situation. Just as America loses control of the civil war against Doe, Hannah loses her children to the nightmare violence. When she secretively returns to Liberia to discover their fate, her children and the chimpanzees have died. Yet at the end, she can rejoice that her sons died fighting to avenge their father and American interests. Hannah imagines consolingly that her sons join their African ancestors. Hannah admits to the missionary Crowns couple (who now fondly regard Taylor because he's converted to evangelical Christianity) that she was Taylor's enemy and because she's white, they help her escape from Liberia by plane. Hannah's realization that the story of her life can have no significance in the world illustrates the renunciation of her ambition and presents the complete opposite of Owen's narcissistic rationalization that he was the most significant player at Harpers Ferry—narcissism deals in absolutes, as does propaganda.

Hannah was a savvy and privileged American darling, not a naïve and provincial Russian darling. Once more, Banks employs a metatext in counterpoint. *The Darling* offers a new departure for Banks—a political thriller in the tradition of Greene, the travel writer and popular novelist who was one of England's top spies. After Hannah retires, she sees no significance in her life amid the larger world. The word darling may be used in many ways, including the ambivalent way she concludes her oblique confession. Banks's novel is not incompetent as some reviewers have hinted, but an ironic puzzle that challenges the reader to unravel the political plot and assemble the truth in the fractured mirror shards of Hannah's life, a technique he employed embryonically in his first apprentice novel *Family Life*.

Hannah does anything a man can do—and more, in bearing children. By the end of the novel, she becomes existential—she would like to find meaning in her life story, but can't. At her husband's grave, Hannah waits for her husband's ghost to rise and punish her because she feels guiltily responsible for his death, since she realizes that her plan to help her husband and America has backfired. At this moment of purgative grief, the reader realizes that Hannah has finally destroyed the narcissistic envelope she has lived within.

She's arrived at the place of an existential hero in an immoral world and continues to be confused emotionally and intellectually on how to deal with it, yet any reader cannot help but notice that on a practical level, Hannah has survived to become a better person despite her delusions and sins. Hannah retreats to a comfortable rural seclusion like a hermit philosopher with her two dogs, arriving at a resigned acceptance of diffident cynicism as she tries to do the best she can, relating with other people in the last days of her life, no longer a political player and nearly self-confident enough to tell the world of her embarrassing and tragic follies—the most embarrassing of which was that her seduction by Taylor destroyed her family, her ideals, and the nation she tried to help.

Banks encourages the reader to grow fond of Hannah, yet some reviewers claim Hannah remains such a distant and dispassionate mystery that she hardly seems real:

> Because Hannah always remains something of a representative figure, she never becomes a completely palpable individual; there remains about her the whiff of the synthetic, a sense that she is more symbol than human being.[27]

It's true that Hannah appears distant, reserved, and reluctant to open her heart to the reader, but she eventually does so, yet this approach demands much patience on the part of any reader. In the concluding fifth section, her emotions explode when Hannah finally arrives at closure, "In the new history of America, mine was merely the story of an American darling, and had been from the beginning."[28] She was everyone's darling: her father's darling, the darling of the Weather Underground, her husband's darling, Charles Taylor's darling, and the darling of the American government as the CIA operative Clement calls her. But by the end of the novel, in a reversal of her making, Hannah arrives at the point where she's nobody's darling, nor does she wish to be anyone's darling.

Hannah copes better with life in her retirement. Like Scobie in Greene's *The Heart of the Matter*, Hannah fails in her goals. But unlike Scobie, who commits suicide, Hannah is a strong character who survives her failure. Banks describes Hannah as, "a person who has lived through tragic events and has been deeply marked by them, a person who has suffered a great deal—but not as a victim. She's simply too powerful to think of as a victim."[29] Because of this, one can eventually warm to her and accept her with all her considerable flaws as an American experiment in good intentions gone wrong, something Banks remains consistently interested in:

> One thing I'm very interested in an on-going way is the unintended consequence of good intentions. And that, you can see that most particularly perhaps in *The Darling*, but also *Cloudsplitter*, but going back even further to *Continental Drift* or *Affliction*.[30]

Just as a reader might eventually warm up to the plight of Jane Austen's heroine in *Emma* (1816) by the end of that novel, a reader might be willing to accept the failures of Hannah. This aspect of Banks's novel is quite accomplished after readers witness the horrors Hannah has endured in the Conrad-like heart of darkness that Liberia becomes amid the carnage, terror, and madness of its civil wars from 1989 to 2003. But that horror and darkness was equally American and the whited sepulcher of Conrad's Belgian government becomes incarnated in the self-confident and ironically named Sam Clement of the CIA.

At the end, readers can feel empathy for the loss of Hannah's children who witnessed their father's execution, though they later became monsters. Readers can feel empathy for the people of Liberia who suffered so immensely when their society unraveled. Readers can feel empathy for the end of Hannah's long New England family line. Perhaps readers can even feel some empathy for the CIA, which could not manage to balance the interests of the American people, the Liberian people, and American corporations. The shame of the tragic disaster that befell Liberia belongs to everyone, because everyone behaved liked know-it-all chimpanzees just released from their cages. Hannah's uninnocent story of ironically benighted narcissism and failure does indeed become representative of American triumphal myopia and America's failed aspirations for a better world, but as a character, she's one of Banks's most memorable, though difficult, singularities. Of Hannah's monologue, one may agree with Greene that no one can speak a monologue for very long and that, "every monologue sooner or later becomes a discussion."[31] If, as the poet Charles Péguy once observed, Christians who follow Christ are not saints,[32] then it could also be said that the would-be revolutionary idealist is hardly a saint.

But if *The Darling* is not an adventure novel but a spy novel, another interpretation emerges. If Hannah was a revolutionary idealist, she could have (it often happens) flipped and become a government spy. Her involvement in the continual manufacture of expert phony IDs (as well as single-handedly producing bombs) while attending Harvard Medical School and working as an intern would have shouldered a heroic insomnia, as well as, an unusual talent in printing, chemistry, and medicine. Hannah stresses the complete secrecy of her work. What better cover for a spy in the Weather Underground could there be, than passing out phony identifications to be tracked? If Zach was her spy companion, their flight to Ghana could have been from a blown cover. Zach's story of his gunshot wound, his need to leave the country, and his extreme panic makes little sense.

Or even later in Ghana, Hannah could have been recruited by the CIA, which might explain the political nature of her marriage because there appears to be little personal basis for the unlikely marriage and the lifestyle the marriage entailed. Or once Zach was nailed for customs fraud, he could have worked out a reduced sentence for befriending Taylor in jail. Taylor thought he was scamming Zach, but it may have been the other way around. The sudden expulsion of Hannah from Liberia might have been an arranged assignment to aid Taylor's escape from prison, which would provide political advancement for her husband, something that didn't work out. Hannah's boasting monologue might be her cover story for a life in the ambiguous political underworld. After all, Greene was a spy who wrote novels and travelogues as a cover. At the end of her career, she retires early to a New England estate, doting on her dogs and the proprietary sensibility of having hired a good farm manager, a lesbian as tough in her own way as Hannah herself. Her singular humiliation and personal disaster is her betrayal by Taylor, a rogue immersed in triple-cross skullduggery, broad comic theater, and a trail of notorious atrocities.

Whatever the case, Hannah offers a reluctant apology (defense) for the intriguing life of one who was never a saint, any more than Greene ever was.

Philip Roth's well-written *American Pastoral* (1997), which won the 1998 Pulitzer Prize, depicted the Weather Underground as a cult of rapists and murderers, blatantly misrepresenting them and offering propaganda, while displaying little understanding of the period's student movements and its psychology. Banks's novel provides an insider's portrait of a representative militant student, complex in her confusion and strength. While the novel might have been buttressed by more extensive college background scenes, it offers more nuances and asks more questions than other comparable treatments.

The ultimate effect of Banks's narrative imbues upon a reader the indelible impression that the best and brightest rebels of the late sixties remain an enduring enigma rooted in the freedom-loving dynamics of American family life. The global setting of Africa calls attention to the impact that radical students (reified and even overshadowed by their associated rock and soul music) had upon the world stage and how their movement and its propaganda celebrated the American Dream as an evolving happening whose heartbeat was informal conscience rooted in the pursuit of freedom rather than repressive government bureaucracy. The recognition of this by third-world populations resulted in a celebration of the American spirit and perhaps ironically did more to promote the perception of America as a beacon of freedom than the designs of official American policy whose Machiavellian machinations delivered much death and destruction, rendering the radicals quixotic.

14

Rural Noir: *The Reserve*

> And I saw it again in a far northern land—
> Not a pansy, not purple and white;
> Yet in beauteous disguise
> Did this poison-plant rise,
> Fair and fatal to my sight.
> And men longed for her kiss and odorous breath
> When no fiend was beside them to tell
> That to kiss was to die,
> That her truth was a lie,
> And her beauty a soul-killing spell.
>
> —John Boyle O'Reilly, "The Poison-Flower"

The character Jordan Groves in *The Reserve* is loosely based on the American artist Rockwell Kent (1992–1971), a painter, printmaker, illustrator, and leftist sympathizer. Banks must have been drawn to Kent for three reasons: Kent lived in Ausable Forks not far from Banks's summer house in Ausable; Kent's illustrations of Herman Melville's *Moby Dick* aided the process of rediscovering the novel as a masterpiece; and Kent's early work, first shown at the Society of American Artists in 1904, featured paintings of Mount Monadnock in New Hampshire. Such proximate factors may have been ignited by the publication of a Canadian novel—*The Big Why* (2004) by Michael Winter who won the 2004 Winterset Award for his novel based upon the life of Kent.[1] While Winter's novel applies a first-person autobiographical narrative of intense immediacy, Banks's novel employs an omniscient narrator with an adjustable camera lens and contemplative perspective. Winter attempts to recreate the inner life of Kent and hews fairly closely to the autobiographical facts in Kent's life while creating a persona half-Kent, half-Winter. Banks merely uses Kent as a model in the way a painter hires a model and uses the model to paint an alternative portrait of a figure rooted in selective particularities of the model. Winter's novel probes deeply into experiential wonder, motivation, and psychology. Banks's novel attempts to paint a larger sociological portrait of the 1930s as it creates structural parallels with contemporary society in order to describe the umbrella of sociological realities that have defined America over the past hundred years.

The structure of the novel mildly recalls the nonlinear slide-approach Banks employed in the long short story "Survivors II" where the funeral meditation shifted forward and back. While occasional italic slides contain a broad and distant encapsulation of a linear plot implicitly linking the two main characters in a bifurcated manner as if the story was a newspaper account from a John Dos Passos novel, the interior story illuminating the main characters recursively retreads plot elements (especially Vanessa Cole's abduction of her mother and the description of Alicia Groves's affair) not previously explained in detail. Italic passages ultimately provide the story of how the two main characters die.

The opening scene of the novel evokes E. L. Doctorow's novel *Loon Lake* (1980),[2] also set in the New York Adirondacks, where a young man sees a naked blonde woman holding up a dress before a mirror in a passing railroad car and becomes determined to succeed in transgressing social class barriers. In Banks's novel, a beautiful young heiress watches a plane circle and land; she becomes secretly determined to transgress class barriers through slumming as she attempts to possess an independent and arrogant artist. Both Doctorow and Banks provide resonant riffs from Theodore Dreiser's *An American Tragedy* (1925), which features a murder, possibly accidental, at a lake in upstate New York. All three novels, set in the middle of the Great Depression, focus on class barriers. While the novels of Dreiser and Doctorow might be considered *bildungsroman*, Banks's novel more closely hews to a novel of early midlife crisis.

At the beginning of the novel, Jordan Groves's wife Alicia, wants to give their homestead a name, suggesting Asgaard and then Valhalla, but Jordan demurs, saying that such placarding smacks of a weekender pretence and that they are not weekenders. Kent's place in Ausable was named Asgaard, a Nordic Troy at the center of the earth where the gods hold daily court and the main city of the people of Asia, the AEsir, according the thirteenth-century *Prose Edda* of Snorri Sturluson. (The cemetery Valhalla,[3] inhabited by the souls who died a glorious death in combat, was within the city.) Toward the end of his life, the house Kent built was destroyed by lightning which ignited a fire, destroying numerous paintings and unpublished manuscripts.[4]

The novel begins in 1936, the year that John Steinbeck's *In Dubious Battle* was published, with the episode of the high-wire artist flying into the Reserve, a communal but exclusive venture of the wealthy to preserve the Adirondack wilderness for themselves and posterity. Groves lands his pontoon plane on the lake to view some paintings of a leading rival. Groves levels criticism on his rival's work as being a worship of nature rather than being a representation of nature (an approach he finds even less laudatory). This reversal of critical perspective on the historical perspectives of Kent and Edward Hopper illustrates Banks's imposition of compulsive irony as it appears to echo Hopper's view of Kent's depiction of nature as a modernist version of New England transcendentalism, although Kent identified with Thoreau rather than dreamy Emerson.[5] The fictional Groves later refers pejoratively to the paintings as *little altars* to nature, although he begrudgingly admits to admiration. Groves has little time to spend on this perfunctory visit to a potentially wealthy patron whose wayward *adopted* daughter, barefoot socialite Vanessa Cole, hops impulsively into the rear plane seat with Groves who allows her a daring beginner's lesson before depositing her after sunset on another lake where she urges him to follow her to the best spot to ogle the Fourth of July fireworks. Yet Groves knows all too well what that would lead to, and summarily departs for his family, leaving her stranded to hoof miles home barefoot in the spangled, gloaming dark.

The style of *The Reserve*, which Banks labels as *wilderness noir*, a hitherto unknown variant of the noir genre, as it blends with a historical setting, offers realism but in a painterly, deftly poetic manner that sometimes finds itself undermined by an overly paratactic employment of *and*, an obvious stylistic homage to Ernest Hemingway, a feat that Algen had performed in his travelogue *Notes from a Sea Diary: Hemingway All the Way* (1965). Banks's voice, like a bass cello, displays a more meditative, wry, and mellow tone appropriate for the subject, an octave that argues for more patience in exploring the explosive nature of class conflict when it becomes embedded in the egos of its dramatic personages. The prose exhibits the quality of a dark mahogany—sculpted, sanded, stained, and burnished with polish. As noir style, its coloration presents the conflicting ambiguity of twilight upon a wooded landscape with deep blue lakes reflecting dimming cumulous clouds and in that painterly sense tries to imitate the more somber twilit colors employed by both Hopper and Kent in their early landscape paintings. Banks often waxes lyrical:, "The only sound was the tick tock of the antique, burled maple clock posted by the door."[6] The opening assonance gives way to the alliteration of segueing into the *b*, *p*, with the closing finality of the *d* consonant as the sentence returns to echo the long open *o* vowels of its opening. While many poetic lines enhance the prose, dialogue passages often sound predictable.

The Tamarack Wilderness Reserve functions as an elite social club. Doctor Carter Cole, its chief member, maintains a genuine, unconventional interest in the arts, raising the question of benevolent patronage within the parameter of class conflict. (The portrayal of Dr. Cole as a philanthropist to art is a tribute nod to the eccentric Virginia millionaire J. J. Ryan who supported Kent.)[7] Many American artists from the period were left-leaning populists like Steinbeck and Dos Passos or Kent and Hopper, both born in 1882 and both students of Robert Henri. Both painted landscapes with similar paints at the leftist communal artist's plantation on Monhegan Island off the coast of Maine.[8]

Like Kent, Jordan Groves donated art to the Soviet people and, like Kent, Groves wrote a book about his excursion to Greenland for which he has yet to do the illustrations. His wife Alicia reads *Gone with the Wind*, a book Groves had declined to illustrate because he could find nothing of interest in the sentimental romance. In 1926 Kent declined to illustrate Richard Henry Dana, Jr.'s, popular *Two Years Before the Mast.* The publisher later agreed to his suggestion for illustrations to a new three-volume edition of *Moby Dick* that appeared in 1930. Kent's now-famous illustrations buttressed the burgeoning revival of Melville's great novel. In Banks's novel, Groves illustrates Mark Twain's *Huck Finn.*

In the second of the numbered chapters, class conflict comes to fisticuffs. Groves drives out to the Reserve when he hears that Dr. Cole, a brain surgeon, had a heart attack, dying the previous night after he flew away. An awkward social scene with Vanessa devolves into her departure for New York City where the funeral will be held. Not a member, Grove is told to get off the property. He looses his two Irish setters on the property for an anarchic and amusing comic romp. Defiant, he bloodies several of his working neighbors who must follow orders to remove him. His two young boys watch wide-eyed in silent terror from the car. Although only a fisticuff tussle,[9] this symbolic scene conjures the era of class warfare that Steinbeck so evocatively captured with *In Dubious Battle*, alluded to by title in the text. Groves leaves as a successfully violent and self-indulgent egotist who has defied the class boundaries, but in the process has hurt his own neighbors. Self-consciousness class conflict appears to be a wellspring of creative tension for the art of Groves and the author.

Vanessa appears with a desperate request to have her father's ashes scattered over a lake in the Reserve, something forbidden by the Reserve, but desired by the unconventional Dr. Cole. Since such a practice is strictly forbidden, Vanessa wants all the more to accomplish this, asking Groves to help with his plane. In a brief nighttime bedroom scene, Banks captures the frail existential condition of his marriage, with its flaws clearly resting on the shoulders of Groves.

Groves had refused Vanessa's request rather rudely after getting Vanessa to apologize for her own former rudeness. The next morning he discovers a beautiful second-century Chinese urn with the ashes in the backseat of his car. He tries to return the ashes, refusing to help her, but the spoiled divorcée manages to manipulate Groves and dumps the ashes, as well as the priceless vase, into the lake. They imbibe some Jamaican rum and Groves declines the pass she makes at him. After Groves soars into the blue and encounters the flight of the swastika-decorated *Hindenburg* with its dangerous hydrogen fuel instead of helium, Vanessa kindly removes the silk scarf gag, untying her mother who had been in the next room. She makes her mother promise "to be good." Vanessa exhibits the riddle of a mentally disturbed and dangerous femme fatale who has been in and out of psychiatric therapy. Most alarmingly, she's been on paregoric for her insomnia, which some think drove the philosopher Friedrich Nietzsche insane.[10] At the moment, she's merely heavily into drink and men, fearing a humiliating return to therapy, which is what her mother desires. She seems to have some talent in the arts, but nothing comes of her many interests because she's haunted by megalomaniac ambition and the spontaneous performance of satiric charades. Groves finds her physically attractive, but he's now trying to be a model father for his children. Ironically, his wife Alicia

Rural Noir: *The Reserve* 177

has never really loved Groves and weary of his constant philandering, begins a genuine love affair with Hubert St. Germain, a local Adirondack laborer who often works as a guide and handyman for the wealthy. Out of deepening religious guilt, she discloses her affair to her potential rival, Vanessa.

One of Vanessa's obsessive fantasies consists of seducing Ernest Hemingway. She elucidates her jealousy by naming that "awful Gellhorn woman."[11] Martha Gellhorn was one of the twentieth century's greatest war correspondents, a noted fiction writer, and the third wife of Ernest Hemingway. Vanessa's contempt and jealousy delineates her ambition to possess the alpha male. Instead of pursuing accomplishment, Vanessa entertains herself with recollections of victimization, even when she discovers that she's the biological daughter of her parents, accusing her dead father of being another Charles Lutwidge Dodgson (the writer Lewis Carroll) by appropriating from Dodgson's biography his obsession with photographing young prepubescent girls in the nude—in this case, she conjectures because of a nearly life-long impotence. The truth of this accusation remains stubbornly unclear, but if it were to be confirmed, it would provide an explanation for Vanessa's compulsive promiscuity, as well as a deep wellspring of anger—having very rich parents who abandon you to an orphanage for one's earliest years remains nearly unforgivable, offering a psychological explanation for Vanessa's rage and hysteria, yet her photographic accusations are probably dramatic delusions. Vanessa has, most likely, contracted a serious mental disorder as a result of her privileged upbringing. There once was a dissolute aristocrat who said that the only difference between those confined to mental institutions and those not incarcerated are their bank accounts. The Cole family dies out in this novel—wealth often so corrupts young people that they are incapable of living a sensible life or fostering the future.

As noir thriller, Banks's contemplative and well-wrought prose runs counter to the immediate, improvisatory suspense the genre demands. The novel's plot pacing sails uneven—at times poetic, tediously self-evident, recursive, yet sometimes suddenly lit with sunlit patches of superb psychological writing and authentic mounting tension. Nothing resembling the genre's panache appears, except a disingenuous reference to its films at a time when Jordan should be intent on plumbing the bottom of Vanessa's disturbed sanity or delusional insanity:

> Jordan Groves had no philosophy for this task, no ethical system with sufficient rigor and discipline to give him a coherent, self-sustaining style. As long as Vanessa kept her cool, however, he could keep his. He tried to hold on to the glittering mixture of warmth and brittleness, of humor and anger, that resisted dissolving in sarcasm or superficial irony. It was sexy to him, and he liked it—two can play at that game—and now he needed it. The last thing he wanted from her was sad sincerity. He thought of those *Thin Man* movies with William Powell and Myrna Loy and *My Man Godfrey* with Powell and Carole Lombard and *The Petrified Forrest* with [Humphrey] Bogart and Bette Davis. He thought of Ernest Hemingway's stories and James M. Cain's *Double Indemnity*. That was the style he needed, and he felt that if he could keep on affecting it, he could become it, and she would become it, too.[12]

Just as Groves fails to achieve the desired and fashionable noir persona, Banks can't quite deliver it in a novel advertised as possessing it, although the novel offers more sophisticated literary charms.

The genre Dashiell Hammett invented[13] demands more concise one-liner wit, both frivolous and caustic, than Banks deliver. The achievement of Banks's novel resides more in its historical symbolism and its deeply etched characters than in its ambition to wear a label. Noir thriller may itself be a misnomer to promote what more closely resembles a historical meditation on class structure. A reader expecting a superficial thriller would be disappointed. The final tragedy presents more of a tragic muddle than the neat wrap-ups the noir genre conventionally provides its readers. The noir genre remains a form of light reading, but Banks retains a compulsion to write with heavy intellectual themes and subtle symbolism.

One of the peculiar portraits in the novel relates to Kent's children, Wolf and Bear, who remain placid characters without taint of mischief in their personalities—they appear as imitation verbal illustrations in the manner of Norman Rockwell's popular magazine covers from *The Saturday Evening Post* from the 1930s. Banks takes the poetic liberty to relocate the Wappingers River (really Creek) from the eastern side of the Hudson River, halfway between New York City and Albany, to the Adirondacks. Why? The chief totem animal of the Wappingers Indians was the wolf[14]—Groves derives the name from the Indian landscape to depict how closely Kent remains connected to landscape and liberal sensibility.

Vanessa seduces the reader into the calculated rational elements of her manic antics, displaying how persuasive a disturbed liar can be. Just when the reader would be willing to grant her a modicum of sanity, she burns down her father's lodge to shield her own self-destructive illusions when she realizes she will not be able to dominate Groves with her wiles. While the femme fatale often conjures up cliché, Banks delivers a memorable etching. The portrait of Vanessa, infatuated with Hemingway in the novel, finds its model in an unstable mistress of Hemingway's who occupied a larger role in the unedited manuscript of *To Have and Have Not* (1937) (the novel "illustrating the virtues of the sturdy poor"[15]), to which Banks had been given access. She appeared also in "The Short Happy Life of Francis Macomber,"[16] one of Hemingway's most famous short stories, published the year before his 1937 novel; in it the hunter's wife Margot pursues a devious, deadly dominance over her husband. Hemingway chronicles the manipulative success of a dangerous femme fatale, while Banks provides a counter narrative wherein she's met her match—in rejected frustration she exerts self-indulgent pique, resorting to gratuitous arson.

The illicit affair between Alicia and Hubert recalls the focus on a similar affair toward the conclusion of Thomas Flanagan's historical novel *The Tenants of Time* (1988), where two illicit lovers defy convention and ethnic background, thereby becoming a political symbol of hope transcending and counterpointing the tragic sectarian divide that destroys Anglo-Irish society. But the class division between Alicia and Hubert cannot be transcended. Banks argues that the romantic union of the upper middle-class with the lower working-class offers no hope for preserving the metaphoric Reserve of independence and love in the pursuit of liberty—unlike the optimism inherent in the personal rebellion of love recorded in Flanagan's novel. The Romantic conception of Hubert as a nature guide marks him as a descendent of James Fenimore Cooper's Natty Bumpo or the rustic hero of Thomas Hardy's rural novel *The Woodlanders* (1887), except by the end of the novel, Banks invokes a more private and deeply earned irony to skewer and even parody that public, patronizing perception of a man from the working class, while the pathetic subservience of Hubert paints him as more of a type barred from the mythic hall of heroes. Hubert's attempt to regain Alicia's love backfires. The denouement destroys the lives of all main characters. Alicia resigns herself to a diminished life without a mate. Vanessa operates like a contagious plague, obliterating all hope or reason, an apocalyptic fire for whom a reader can possess no sympathy when she's finally incinerated in the *Hindenburg* accident.

The tragedy at the novel's center paints an accident in which the main players bear culpability. Vanessa enlists Hubert's aid in the kidnapping of her mother. Hubert complies in the belief he acts as a sensible mediator, but readers know that he should know such a generous fantasy remains naïve when dealing with the upper class. Jordan flies in to visit Vanessa on the lake. Mrs. Cole appears with a shotgun, having finessed a drop on Hubert. They attempt to talk reason but Mrs. Cole attempts to force Jordan at gunpoint—she wants him to fly her out. Jordan tries to acquire the gun through persuasion while Hubert grabs it. In the tug-of-war, the gun flies airborne like a twirling baton and lands on its stock handle, blasting both barrels into Mrs. Cole. The traditional noir novel does not have accidents at the center—it has clear villains who plot and pull the trigger—the climax here presents a parody of the noir novel.

The secret burial of Mrs. Cole in the Reserve might possibly preserve Vanessa from the famous New York State electric chair, yet Jordan doesn't want to have any part of this scene, but with Hubert he buries Mrs. Cole. The affair between Alicia and Hubert is over; Alicia's religious background has predisposed her to prefer guilt over love, but to prove to Alicia that he really loves her in spite of their affair ending, Hubert reports the truth to his sleazy boss Kendall. This effectively destroys the lives of both Vanessa and more indirectly Jordan, who then heads for Spain where he will extinguish his life fighting Francisco Franco. Alicia realizes the class education barrier remains too formidable—she can have satisfying sex with Herbert, but they cannot be true companions because they have nothing to talk about when together.

While Kent sympathized with Spanish Republicans, sending money from awards and fund-raisers, he never accepted the Dos Passos proposition, proposed and accepted in the novel, that they depart together for Spain.[17] Vanessa will eventually get her blissful lobotomy from the elite Nazi doctors in Switzerland with whom her father fraternizes. On the return trip she finds herself on the fateful *Hindenburg*. Alicia will muddle on with the children as the forgotten widow of a great man and Hubert will be stained by the bitter ironies his class branding.

Kendall, the mean and corrupt enforcer for the wealthy, remains the only character untouched by tragedy. The connection between Dr. Cole and the Nazi doctors alludes to the connections of wealthy Americans as financial architects of the Nazis before the Second World War—people like Henry Ford and Prescott Sheldon Bush.[18]

In the end, the woodland Reserve reveals itself as retreat for those who would renew themselves in the transcendental woodland communion of Henry David Thoreau who found in *Nature* the inspiration to defy American tendencies toward authoritarian thought founded on Calvinistic wealth trophies. The Adirondack Park is open to all citizens of New York State able to motor in and pay the increasingly exorbitant park fee, even though the Ausable Club remains closed to the public. Thoreau can still be found in any public library, yet his writings receive more devotional lip service than active emulation.

The Reserve becomes a symbol of the two-tier class structure that crystallized in the 1930s during the Great Depression and endures in American society today. The rich in America have reified a system that disenfranchised those who cannot afford to participate in exclusive clubs (like the Yale University's Skull and Bones club which Dr. Cole belonged to). Such clubs fill the roster of the power players behind the propagandistic *façade* of popular democracy. The struggle for worker's rights that Steinbeck and others chronicled has been lost. While the elite clubs are no longer the secret Masonic organization that brought about the First World War or the elite business clubs that engineered the Great Depression, their legacy continues to operate and govern the American economy, reserving 90 percent of America's wealth for the top 5 percent of the population.

The silvery symbol of the *Hindenburg* dirigible floating through the novel with its unstable hydrogen gas instead of the helium gas, it should have operated on, becomes an icon of social volatility. Only 35 of the 95 passengers died plus one person on the ground. The use of hydrogen-powered autos was much discussed in the press as an alternative fuel solution for carbon emissions, yet most magazine or newspaper articles that discussed or recommended the use of hydrogen ignored its apocalyptic flammable nature. During an interview Banks said:

> about the time I wrote the scene in which Jordan sees the *Hindenburg* above Lake Champlain, I realized that I had stumbled onto a powerful image that signified the rise of European fascism. It drew the international historical context into the narrative. Actually, my research assistant was checking local newspaper accounts of events of the summer of 1936 and came across an article noting that the *Hindenburg* had been sighted flying above the Adirondacks on its way to Lakehurst, New Jersey, from Frankfurt, Germany.[19]

In addition, Banks might have focused on the majestic dirigible in reaction to the happy and innocent fantasy of a time-traveling dirigible as a symbol of blithe optimism for the future of humanity in Thomas Pynchon's whimsical novel *Against the Day* (2006). It similarly flounders in a genre Western where the author's gifts exhibit serious miscasting, despite containing a couple of the most beautifully artistic passages in the history of English poetic prose. For its time, the *Hindenburg* explosion was as sensational in the press as the recent 9/11 event.

The use of the *Hindenburg*, a more public form of transportation (it remains a symbol of elite transportation like the Titanic), contrasts vividly with the use of Groves's private plane, especially when readers encounter them meeting together in the air. Groves feels his significance as an individual dwindle before the immense and stately dirigible. Both dirigible and plane come to disaster; the reader cannot help but sympathize with the *missionary* cause of Groves to bring freedom to Spain through his martyrdom as a volunteer in the Abraham Lincoln Brigade. While every reader remains aware of the undepicted apocalypse of the *Hindenburg* tragedy, our sympathies clearly reside with the anti-hero of the novel who gives up his life for freedom rather than the spoiled elite who travel in such high style above the calamities of mankind that they believe themselves to be immune to life's tragedies. Banks's aerial perspective offers perceptions that vicariously meld with the omniscient narrator. A more contemplative and compassionate view of the difficult problems of class conflict, wealth, the limited options of the lower class, and a portrait of those in the upper class (both responsible and irresponsible) emerges. Banks told Karen Holt, "I was really trying to see this world from above, as if I was hovering over it."[20] The attempt at a larger panorama contrasts with the very narrow windows of deep interiority Banks had provided in earlier fictions. Instead of repeating himself, Banks confounds expectations by attempting a new *flight*. Since events in the novel are telescoped into a single year, they appear to follow a narrower scope of Aristotelian unities to achieve greater dramatic effect.

Banks intends historic parallels. In less than a year after publication, the novel appeared prophetic in its reconsideration of the Great Depression. The economic collapse of autumn 2008 exhibits Banks's basic point that little has changed in America's economic structure over the past 80 years. The wealthy have their pristine land reserves as well as their menacing technological advances and accompanying wars of opportunity, yet in the end, such a template may be a destructive threat to the reserves they wish to perpetuate in their increasingly dysfunctional families. The novel implicitly calls into question the sanity of this arrangement through the tragic deaths of its two main characters who appear driven to resist colonization of their intellects. While the lobotomy of Vanessa recalls Tennessee Williams's great play *Suddenly, Last Summer* (1958), the death of pilot Groves may commemorate the tragic death of Antoine de Saint Exupéry on July 31, 1944, when downed trying to observe German troop movements in the Rhone Valley in anticipation of the Allied Normandy invasion.[21] Exupéry had written, "I will go into combat for Mankind. Against its enemies. But also against me myself."[22] There's a sense in which Groves goes into battle both for and against himself as he flees his domestic problems and responsibilities.

The floating leitmotif of the Dresden doll in the italic passages functions on three levels: It dramatizes a fond parent's love for a child he will never see; as a symbol, it connects to the loss of the great children's writer, Exupéry, the beloved author of *The Little Prince*; and by the time Vanessa boards the *Hindenburg*, she has become a catatonic doll. The fact that the world-famous toy was manufactured in Dresden, the site of a gratuitous fire-bombing holocaust at the end of the Second World War, adds a further poignancy to the narrative thread.

Banks's novel displays a dispiriting Lucretian atheism with a small hymn to erotic love, as well as an abbreviated hymn to the pleasures of domestic love. But unlike the psychological freedom and release promised by Lucretius through his poetic philosophy, Banks offers the reader little hope for Americans who must live under the tyranny of its wealthy scions. The consolation of art and political rebellion fails. As a meditation on art, the book gives voice to Banks's frustration that serious artists with social concerns like Steinbeck, himself, and Kent receive little attention in a society devoted to the success of irrelevant thriller movies which appear to have a love affair with the incendiary properties of gasoline.

At the conclusion of *Continental Drift*, Banks prays that his book will wreck some havoc in a world empire ruled by race consciousness, yet more somber implications about the effectiveness of art to inspire social change find meditative display here. As in Melville's late *Israel Potter: His Fifty Years of Exile* (1855), Banks employs an aesthetic artifact set in the American past to meditate upon the apparently intractable problems in the American social construct. Both *Israel Potter* and *The Reserve* furnish pessimistic endings about the fulfillment of the promise contained in the American Revolution.

While the novel displays a humanitarian sympathy toward the lower classes, it's not the kind of novel like *In Dubious Battle* that a lower-class person might read with identification. The intended audience of *The Reserve* appears to be the class to which Banks has ascended through his well-earned success, although he has courted that success in a limited way by putting his artistic concerns before commercial considerations. The novel argues that any discussion of wealth's responsibility must exhibit sympathy for suffering because suffering and pride are the sources of great art treasured by the wealthy, that the upper classes should exhibit more tolerance for the conflicted tensions that torment artists into greater achievement. Yet the personal flaws or an artist affects only those around him, unlike the massive casualties ambitious politicians like Franco, Benito Mussolini, Adolf Hitler, and Joseph Stalin conjure—or unscrupulous magnates who inflict harm on their countries and our increasingly fragile globe.

15

Postmodern Realism: Audience and the Writer

> A writer's life and work are not a gift to mankind; they are its necessity.
> —Toni Morrison, "Peril"

While Banks began writing as an alienated experimentalist with a penchant for rococo metafiction,[1] he has tempered his experimental inclinations and entered the literary mainstream and larger cultural mainstream through films, yet he continues to be a story-teller willing to take risks with innovation and exploration. He's still willing to gamble artistically, not wanting to fall into formulaic repetition—the path followed by writers more interested in commerce than art. In that respect his work resembles the effort to go further, as in the writings Jack Kerouac, Ken Kesey, Thomas Pynchon, or the many innovative writers who struggle to establish an audience. Although Banks's working-class background resembles Kerouac's, Banks's manner of writing bears a closer resemblance to Nelson Algren and Albert Camus.

One observant critic notes:

> Banks might be described as a dissenting voice in the house of postmodernism. He shares attitudes, themes, and some narrative methods with the work of his most prominent contemporaries, but he consistently shows their limitations by emphasizing the role of inequality, privation, and mundane interest that postmodernist writing, with its emphasis on creative reinterpretation, typically leaves aside.[2]

Banks indicates the limitations of postmodern tools as well as political liberalism by identifying borderlines, especially the intractable role of social inequality, the legacy of racial oppression, and the machinations of cultural deprivation.

Banks has much company in the project of reviving American realism within a postmodern context—a movement that has jettisoned an innovative group of writers to the forefront of American fiction writing. In a general sense, their immediate descent stems from the Zola-inspired Chicago school of realism, which includes Frank Norris, Theodore Dreiser, Upton Sinclair, James T. Farrell,

Algren, Richard Wright, Maxwell Bodenheim, Ben Hecht, and subsequently Saul Bellow, who teleported realism into postmodern methodologies. The most prominent of these contemporary postmodern American writers, who have blended elements of realism into their work include Toni Morrison, William Kennedy, Philip Roth, Tom Wolfe, E. L. Doctorow, Joyce Carol Oates, Don DeLillo, John Edgar Wideman, Paul Auster, Richard Ford, T. C. Boyle, Madison Smartt Bell, Francine Prose, David Guterson, Tim Gautreaux, and Rick Moody. While these writers transmute their private meditations into social critique, the marketing department of publishers often cannot shift gears to the new directions pursued by these authors, yet these authors have managed to attract a significant public audience, domestically and internationally.

The mayhem of switching genres from novel to novel may create difficulty for readers or marketing, and this practice demands a sophisticated understanding of genre. On the other hand, such a swerving challenge may be what attracts Banks's hard-core readership, as well as the readership of novelists mentioned above. This problem of audience becomes magnified if one lists all the good postmodern novelists who don't have a large public—one need only browse the backlist catalogue of the Dalkey Archive Press to get a gist of this dilemma amid a visual culture that has little patience with the time-consuming effort of exploring print.

While following no specific postmodern formula, Banks deconstructs the more facile faces of liberal relativism in many of his novels, especially a liberalism that supports narcissistic daydreaming, a theme critiqued in *Hamilton Stark*, *Continental Drift*, *Cloudsplitter*, and *The Darling*. Unconscious aspects of white racism emerge for critique in *The Book of Jamaica*, *Continental Drift*, *Rule of the Bone*, and *Cloudsplitter*. Banks desires a return to the authenticity of traditional Christian morals that created this country's quest for freedom. From this moral vantage point, Banks's agnosticism dwells not far from the atheistic neoconservatism of Wolfe, except that Wolfe embraces the performance of high art with a revival of excellence amid rugged American individualism, while Banks embraces the haunting revolutionary spirit of those American Romantics rooted in the Bible—Nathaniel Hawthorne, John Brown, and especially Herman Melville with the significant addition of Samuel Clemens. Both Banks and Wolfe look back to the late nineteenth century and early twentieth century for inspiration and models, yet present their own postmodern modifications of the realistic tradition that put American literature on the international map.

The hallmark signatures of Banks's fiction, in reverse order of importance, comprise: the use of Homeric irony as both technique and structure, especially in narrative time-shifts; a quixotic narcissism (tragic or comic) in characters searching for improbable goals; debatable interpretation of events based upon character perception; an exploration of absurd dilemmas in the lives of anti-heroes; and the preponderance of accident in the plot of his novels, which may be categorized as real accidents, questionable accidents, and accidents on purpose. A triumvirate of unconscious (seemingly accidental) brotherly suicides[3] occupies the subplot of *Family Life*. Real accidents constitute the plot of *The Sweet Hereafter* and *Trailerpark* (the lost lottery money), although in both cases circumstances precipitate accident. Questionable accident occurs in *Hamilton Stark* (Ham's disappearance) and *Affliction* (the *accidental* suicide of Twombley and the *accidental* parricide), and the shooting of Vanessa's mother in *The Reserve*. Accidents on purpose appear, unconscious or not admitted, in *The Book of Jamaica* (the amputation), *Continental Drift* (the drowning of immigrants), and *Cloudsplitter* (the murder of Lyman). In *The Darling*, Hannah's radicalism first finds explanation as the accidental circumstance of her liberal peers in school, but readers eventually learn her radicalism stems from her sexual orientation. The tragic importance of accident appeared as early as the short story "The Lie."

That accident should play such a large role in an oeuvre can be no accident. The perception of life as accident has its roots in the poetic philosophy of Lucretius, updated by the relativity of Albert Einstein. For those who confuse the rationalization of intention with accident, there breathes the influence of Sigmund Freud. Banks employs an existential framework, as in the absurd of Camus, for accident: the accident, intentional or not, becomes the project of both his characters and readers who may arrive at different interpretations of climatic accident. Growing up as a New Englander cutting wood and loving poetry, Robert Frost's poem on a wood-cutting accident, "Out, Out," must have imparted an indelible impression upon Banks. Autobiographically, the preoccupation with accident may derive from the accidental damage to one of his eyes during childhood and the accidental death of a brother in a train accident. The theme of a brother's death appears in "Survivor's II," Bob's brother Eddie in *Continental Drift*, Rolfe's brother Wade in *Affliction*, and Owen's brother Frederick in *Cloudsplitter*.

Banks might be labeled a postmodern *absurd perspectivist* due to his reliance on narrators who construct autobiographical apologies within a limited perspective, an angle that admits an element of debatable relativity into narrative. As an American tradition, this approach goes back to the varied narrators of Edgar Allan Poe and Ambrose Bierce, who were inspired by Dante and Giovanni Boccaccio, but preceded by the inset monologues of Homer whose narrators in the *Odyssey* tell their versions of truth with some bias, blindness, or exaggeration. Banks may have been initially influenced by the absurd narrator of Flann O'Brien's *The Third Policeman*, but Banks's existentialism finds its foundation in Camus who emphasizes borders and limits when discussing problems of freedom in the context of the Absurd, which Camus argued engages readers because of its irresolvable tensions,[4] something Banks often dramatizes in his open-ended conclusions. In many ways, Banks has become the novelist that Camus, his life abbreviated by an absurd car accident,[5] wanted to become. Contextualizing the predicaments of Banks's characters within Camus's philosophy and art criticism will reveal a fruitful lane for further discussion of Banks's oeuvre.

One of the pleasures of Banks's fiction consists of contemplating the degree of relativity that admits controversial ambiguity. His extravagant use of the unreliable and partisan narrator in *Hamilton Stark*, gave him the postmodern key to introduce an element of relativity into participant-observers who narrate novels in a revivified strain that admits realistic narration. For subsequent novels, the degree of the narrator's reliability becomes a tantalizing mystery for the reader to interpret. Some narrators offer limitation through dedication and martyr complex, as in *The Relation of My Imprisonment*, Rolfe in *Affliction*, or Merle Ring in *Trailerpark*, while others indulge in dramatic exaggerations like Chappie/Bone in *Rule of the Bone* or Hannah in *The Darling*; yet others may labor under more serious delusions like the narrator in *Family Life* or Owen Brown in *Cloudsplitter*. Dispensing with a relativist narrator in his last novel, *The Reserve*, Banks brought absurdist aerial perspective to omniscient narration.

The influence of The Book of Job runs like a river through *Hamilton Stark, The Relation of My Imprisonment, Trailerpark,* and *Cloudsplitter*. Like Richard Wright who constantly reread the Book of Job and quoted it in four novels (*Native Son, Black Boy, The Outsider,* and *Savage Holiday*),[6] Banks applies the theme of solitary suffering to various characters who attempt to make changes in their lives and in society. These characters present varied studies in rebellion that test the characters' limits of endurance at the borderline of breakdown. Most of these characters become the victim of their egoism and engineer their own destruction. Yet Hannah from *The Darling* endures as a survivor, while Merle Ring embodies Banks's least egotistic antihero. Rebel Chappie/Bone evolves into a character purging egoism. The theme of the rebel as social martyr appears most heroically in John Brown, while the counter portrait of Owen presents a rebel unable to imitate his father's ideal, haunted by guilt like the narrator of Camus's *The Fall* (1956). In *The Reserve* Jordan Groves is unable to overcome the borders that divide the rich from the poor, dying a rebel martyr to his idealism.

The postmodern existential esthetic of investigating elusive dilemmas in identity that Banks employed in *Hamilton Stark* continues its currency on the national and international scene. Most recently, this terrain finds exploration within a larger autobiographical arc in Aleksandar Hemon's collection of interlinked stories, *Love and Obstacles: Stories* (2009), which presents a self-conscious European perspective to many of the perplexing postmodern quandaries about life, psychology, and fiction that Banks had explored in *Hamilton Stark*.

Banks succeeded in resolving the tensions of varied American influences from Hawthorne to Wright and Algren, integrating postmodernism with traditional American realism in the narrative of *Continental Drift*. Banks's postmodern technique reveals an intellectually syncretic writer who achieves dramatic originality through various narrators. In both *Hamilton Stark* and *Affliction*, where the narrator and subject appear akin to the dialectic split of a single consciousness, the disappearance of Stark and Whitehouse function as an enigmatic *figura* of the artist stepping off onto the book's white endpapers into a kind of symbolic death before the next reinvention of a radically different narrative persona. Banks's deep sense of ironic humor resembles Melville's obliquity, while the preoccupation with guilt and anxiety update the Gothic airs of Hawthorne and Poe.

While *Hamilton Stark* contained autobiographical echoes, subsequent novels featured narrators with a thespian otherness.

The dilemma of race plays a significant role in Banks's writing. While some of this consciousness may be autobiographical due to time spent in Florida and the Caribbean, this awareness also connects him to the late work of William Faulkner, especially *Go Down Moses* (1942) where racial themes find more explicit treatment. In "Delta Autumn" Faulkner meditates upon nature and its connection to American Indian stewardship of land as it contrasts with crass commercial development,[7] something Banks does in several novels that mention the Abenaki Indians—*Family Life, Trailerpark, Cloudsplitter,* and *Continental Drift.* That connection between Indian stewardship receives a more explicit ironic echo in the name of the oil company Bob Dubois works for, Abenaki Oil. Commercial exploitation of the landscape activates the sinister malaise lurking beneath the small town in *Affliction* while the opposite dilemma of the wealthy elite appropriating Edenic landscape afflicts the townspeople of *The Reserve.* In general, the unusual use of perspective in Faulkner's "The Bear" may have been the inspiration that led Banks to emphasize perspective in his novels.

Banks locates the spirit of the American Revolution in its historical roots with an emphasis on the vision of Ben Franklin, while a conservative like Wolfe falls back upon the elite skepticism of Alexis de Tocqueville as it combines with an imperial vision of American populism rooted in Manifest Destiny,[8] which Banks calls, "a psychotic dream."[9] Wolfe valorizes a populist revival of French and American realism; Banks courts a postmodern modification of realism from an ironic perspective rooted in the modern antihero afflicted with narcissism, an aspect of American culture sometimes lamented by sociologists.[10] While Wolfe employed the antihero in *The Bonfire of the Vanities* and *A Man in Full,* he reverted to the Romantic hero in *I am Charlotte Simmons,* providing the heroine with an anti-heroic stage of regression. Banks remains more interested in exploring the self-blinding ironies of those who fail in their rebellion, while Wolfe seeks to invigorate the possibility of redeeming antiheroic behavior through satiric social commentary. While both writers work in the great tradition of irony from Homer to Mark Twain, Wolfe presents a more poignantly brash and extroverted surface like the sardonic vibrancy of Jasper Johns's paintings, while Banks offers deeper and darker psychological subtleties with unexpectedly fractured perspectives like the meditative collage paintings of Romare Bearden.

Amid this quandary of audience and representation, Banks has managed to steer a middle ground, connecting to a wider audience, as Camus had urged artists to do. While Camus became the victim of social conditions into which he was born,[11] Banks may have permitted his life to plunge into the social contradictions of America. Like Camus, Banks puts much emphasis on the morality of his characters, leaving his readers to judge them. It might be true that not all readers can undergo the genre shifts Banks offers: From the novel as a collection of stories to the detective novel, to the picaresque novel, to the historical novel (which is not usually treated from an ironic perspective), or the adventure genre. Banks's deep ironic perspective derives primarily from Melville and secondarily from Hawthorne and Twain, that great axial trunk of literature established by Homer and his imitators: Virgil, Dante, Wolfram von Eschenbach, Miguel de Cervantes, William Shakespeare, Alexander Pushkin, Leo Tolstoy, Franz Kafka, and James Joyce. Perhaps Banks does not stand in the very front rank with those writers, but he stands at the head of the second rank with profound ironists like Jane Austen, Edgar Allan Poe, Gustave Flaubert, Thomas Hardy, Nikolai Leskov, Ivan Turgenev, Mark Twain, Joseph Conrad, Edith Wharton, Shen Congwen, Sinclair Lewis, Jorge Luis Borges, Vladimir Nabokov, and Mo Yan. Banks remains a uniquely modest American writer on the international stage, exploring those peculiar social and moral conflicts that will achieve more resonance as time passes. Banks's microscopic character lens focuses on the difficulty of that most elusive goal, individual freedom, that moral goal that made Camus's libertarian politics so atypical.

While not completely surprising, Banks's choice of subject matter and technique for his most recent novel, *The Reserve*, quietly offers mellow ironies and subtle complexities that have baffled reviewers. Rockwell Kent, a great visionary artist in the tradition of William Blake and Winslow Homer, has fallen from public appreciation, most probably because of his leftist political views.[12] There is only one slim biography dating from 1980. Kent's rugged individualism, nearly endemic to the American frontier spirit, now appears in twilit horizon as does much of the work of John Dos Passos,[13] although William T. Vollmann has been reviving Dos Passos's techniques in works like *Imperial* (2009). It might be that Banks's highly developed and introverted ironies have obscured his artistic achievement in terms of public appreciation, just as Wolfe's bellicose talking points have caused intelligent people in academia to dismiss his rightwing populism as ignorant.

Internationalists sometimes claim America cannot produce great writing because of privilege: Americans have forgotten that its great writers like Poe, Bierce, Dreiser, Dos Passos, Steinbeck, Faulkner, and Wright wrote of people burdened with suffering and that most American writing delineates psychological problems emanating from a life of privilege, divorced from the human condition. The tormented afflictions of Banks's narrators connect to the greater empathetic arc of art through Banks's dramatization of the absurd, the contradictory, and seemingly impossible in the lives of ordinary people.

In *Dreaming Up America* (2008), Banks outlines a triad of American Dream myths that motivate the psychology of our New World country.[14] The City of Gold or El Dorado, the search for riches, relates to Northern characters in *Continental Drift* who go south dreaming of wealth and looking for easy jobs; *Affliction* implicates a conspiracy of the few who become rich with the development of a ski resort. The religious dream of the City on the Hill or the New Jerusalem, an idealistic search for justice and freedom, finds treatment in varied ways: *The Relation of My Imprisonment* offers a witty and stubbornly heroic resistance to the established political order; *The Book of Jamaica* invites the reader to meditate on justice through the antiheroic mode of a delusional anthropologist; *The Sweet Hereafter* discovers a young heroine who rejects possible riches in favor of her own dignity; *Cloudsplitter* provides a dual diorama: John Brown as heroic and the anti-heroic betrayal of his worldview through his son Owen. The Fountain of Youth, which Banks considers the strongest temptation of all because it invites people to believe that they can start over, initiates a quest for renewed innocence: The fledgling writer's triumph of originality in *Hamilton Stark* proffers the search for originality as a fountain of youthful renewal; *Rule of the Bone* showcases the youthful outsider, a rebel against hypocrisy who searches for a new map of fate based upon a just sociological critique; *The Reserve* analyzes art as fountain of youthful artistic renewal that challengers (futilely) the two-tiered economic order that has ruled America over the past hundred years.

Meditating upon American history, Banks takes a commonsense approach based to a significant extent upon Camus and the American cultural studies of Sacvan Bercovitch, examining American history through a competing triad of America's spiritual, ethical, and materialistic aspirations as well as achievements. One reviewer claims Banks's analysis of the American Dream to be, "more complicated and interesting than the average academic schemer."[15] In the conclusion to *Dreaming Up America*, Banks argues that American culture is by its history a Creole culture, "It would be very interesting for us and world around us if one day we came around to seeing ourselves in all our component parts, acknowledging the identity that's ours."[16] While Banks began as a writer concerned about individual freedom within limits, as Camus advises,[17] his quest has brought him to ponder, in fiction and talks, the larger questions concerning the ambiguity of freedom in modern life.

Banks's recent essay, "Notes on Literature and Engagement," trenchantly articulates the dilemma that corporate culture poses to artists, warning of declining individual identity in a mass culture and its implication for the social justice artists naturally aspire to, hinting that global political governance remains interested in the few rather than the many. He reviews the history of the protest novel in America, noting limitations, ironies, and unintended consequences. The situation of the artist in society has changed today not only because of technology, depersonalized bureaucracy, tyrannical government, Orwellian public media, and multinational conglomerates that host partisan think tanks to pull the strings of puppet advocates, but also because of the difficulty of the individual under duress when the choir of public artists sings as a powerless voice. Despite his largely dour assessment of the impact of art on politics, Banks— unlike Camus, but the times have changed—perceives artists as ultimately outside public political theater, yet just like Camus,[18] he reaches affirmative hope despite Sisyphean odds:

> No other species needs to be constantly reminded and taught what it is to be itself. And it is our storytellers, our poets, our novelists, and dramatists, who have always performed this task. And sure, in this moment in the history of our species, when there is such a danger of forgetting and so much inducement to forget, we must not waste our limited time here doing anything else.[19]

In presenting his reflections, Banks leavens the weight of his essay with some light humor, reminding the reader that some levity works as a strategic auxiliary in examining the universal nightmare art wishes to awaken from amid its problematic search for freedom. That quest and an awareness of freedom's perilous frailty—something our Founding Fathers knew all too well—lies at the heart of Banks's journey into the psychological depths of varied representative Americans whose engaging lives explore their memorable odysseys.

Notes

Chapter 1

1. Schmidt, Michael, *The First Poets: Lives of the Ancient Greek Poets* (London: Weidenfeld & Nicolson, 2004), 50–77.
2. Niemi, Robert, "Russell Banks," *American Writers* (New York: Charles Scribner's Sons, 2000), vol. 5, 1.
3. Russell Banks in Brown, Wesley, "Who to Blame, Who to Forgive," *New York Times Magazine*, September 10, 1989.
4. Lee, Don, "About Russell Banks," *Ploughshares*, winter, 1993–94, 209.
5. Niemi, Robert, *Russell Banks* (Boston: Twayne, 1997), 2.
6. Ibid.
7. Lee, Ibid., 209.
8. Banks, Russell, "Success Story," *Success Stories* (New York: Harper & Row, 1986), 52.
9. Banks, Russell, "H & I," The 2004 PEN/Hemingway Prize Speech, April 4, 2004 at http://web.bu.edu/agni/essays/print/2004/60-banks.html (accessed 10/01/09).
10. Lee, Ibid., 210.
11. *Howl* contains a few arresting opening lines yet the poem provides a brief but angry same-sex imitation rant from Friedrich Nietzsche's *Thus Spoke Zarasthustra* with a title from the Dadaist Tristan Tzara (Sammy Rosenthal).
12. Banks, "H & I," Ibid.
13. Niemi, Ibid., 6–7.
14. Brown, Ibid., 6–7.
15. Banks, "H & I," Ibid.
16. Niemi, Ibid.
17. Lee, Ibid., 210.
18. Niemi, *American Writers*, Ibid., 3.
19. The headline gossip from the previous year was that the fiction writer Richard Yates had threatened to kill poet and translator John Ciardi who ran the school. Bailey, Blake, *A Tragic Honesty: The Life and Work of Richard Yates* (New York: Picador, 2003), 449.
20. Niemi, Ibid., 9. Childless Algren took other young writers like Terry Southern and Bruce Jay Freidman under his wing.

21. Drew, Bettina, *Nelson Algren: A Life on the Wild Side* (New York: Putnam, 1989), 318–19. Gaiser, a friend of Grace Schulman, translated poetry and novels from Italian and published a short story in *The Paris Review*. The journalist Seymour Krim introduced her to Richard Yates and she became his last lover. Bailey, Ibid., 448–52.

22. Banks's interview with Lewis Burke Frumkes, *The Writer*, August 1998.

23. Lee, Ibid., 211.

24. Niemi, Ibid., 10.

25. Banks, Russell, Foreword to *A Walk on the Wild Side* by Nelson Algren (New York: Farrar, Straus and Giroux, 1998 edition), ix–x.

26. Banks, Russell, "In Response to James McPherson's Reading of *Cloudsplitter*," in *Novel History: Historians and Novelists Confront America's Past (and Each Other)*, ed. Mark C. Carnes (New York: Simon & Schuster, 2001), 71.

27. Klin, Richard, "Interview with Russell Banks," *January Magazine*, June 2003, http://www.januarymagazine.com/profiles/rbanks.html (accessed 10/01/09).

28. Paul Chiasson, an eighth generation architect from Cape Breton, claims in *The Island of Seven Cities* (New York: St. Martin's Press) that archeological excavations, language, and culture of the Mi'kmaq Indians indicate deep cultural ties with China rooted in the thirteenth century.

29. Faggen, Robert, "Russell Banks Interview," *Paris Review*, vol. 40, no. 147, summer 1998.

30. Lee, Ibid., 211–12.

31. Wylie, J. J., "Russell Banks," interview, *Michigan Quarterly Review*, vol. 39, fall 2000.

32. Niemi, Ibid., 19.

33. Freeman, John, "Russell Banks: Class Warrior with a Club Tie," *The Independent*, May 9, 2008.

34. Whitney, Joel, "Telling Details: An Interview with Russell Banks," *Guernica*, Sept. 2005, http://www.guernicamag.com/interviews/81/telling_details (accessed 10/01/09).

35. Kerouac, Jack, "Essentials of Spontaneous Prose" in Parkinson, Thomas, ed., *A Casebook on the BEAT*, ed. Thomas Parkinson (New York: Thomas Y. Crowell, 1961), 65.

36. Wylie, Ibid.

37. Trask, Mike, "Six Questions for Russell Banks," *Las Vegas Sun*, March 8, 2009.

38. A portrait of the poet Gary Snyder.

39. Phillips, Caryl, "The Height of Obsession," *The Guardian*, May 21, 2005.

40. Klin, Ibid.

41. "Russell Banks Bio," *Minneapolis Star Tribune*, Oct. 16, 2004, http://www.startribune.com/lifestyle/11480711.html?elr=KArksUUUoDEy3LGDi07aiU (accessed 10/01/09).

Chapter 2

1. Banks, Russell, *The Angel on the Roof* (New York: Harper Collins, 2000), 503.

2. Niemi, Robert, *Russell Banks* (Boston: Twayne, 1997), 29–46.

3. Banks, Russell, *Searching for Survivors* (New York: Fiction Collective, 1975), 85.

4. The revised version in *The Angel on the Roof* displays more polished style.

5. Niemi, Ibid., 63, provides a more detailed timeline.

Notes

6. Niemi, Ibid., 35–37 and 53–54, traces the Walter Mitty-like theme back to Banks's long ironic poem on Ché Guevara, "Homage," mentioning Julio Cortázar as a possible influence on Banks's use of the jumbled timeline in his first collection of short stories.

7. Niemi, Ibid., 79.

8. Banks, Russell, *The New World* (Urbana: Univ. of Illinois Press, 1978), 54.

9. Banks, Ibid., 79.

10. Banks, Ibid., 103.

11. Ackroyd, Peter, *Poe: A Life Cut Short* (New York: Doubleday, 2009).

12. There are numerous biographies of Edgar Allan Poe. To begin with I recommend Meyers, Jeffrey, *Edgar Allan Poe: His Life and Legacy* (New York: Scribner, 1992) although it is somewhat dated.

13. Lepore, Jill, "The Humbug," *The New Yorker*, April 27, 2009.

14. Banks, Ibid., 111.

15. Russell Banks might have noted the irony of Balbuena's library and manuscripts burnt in his last days by the Puritan Dutch.

16. Banks, Ibid., 130.

Chapter 3

1. The attempted crowning of Shrek in the film by fairy-tale creatures offers homage to Basile as the King of Fairy Tale writers because he invented the literary fairy tale as well as the ogre, who can be either good or bad, depending on the story.

2. Other notable successes in this genre include Angela Carter's *The Bloody Chamber and Other Stories* (1979), as well as Robert Coover's *Pinocchio in Venice* (1991) and *Briar Rose* (1996); also, the fairy tale series created by Terri Windling, which includes Jane Yolen's *Briar Rose* (1992).

3. Banks, Russell, *Family Life* (New York: HarperPerennial, 1996), 8.

4. Ibid., 98.

5. Berlioz, Hector, *Berlioz: Les Troyens*, trans. David Cairns (London: Philips, 1971), 322.

6. Banks, *Family Life*, 105.

7. In Homer's *Iliad* the invading Greeks demand the return of Helen and her treasures. The Trojans say they will not return Helen and do not in any case have her treasures. The invading Greeks do not believe the Trojans don't have the treasures. From book two of Herodotus's *The Histories, readers* learn that the treasures were stowed away in Egypt and from books three and four of Homer's *The Odyssey, readers* learn that Menelaos's great wealth came from his sacking of Egyptian cities. In Virgil's *The Aeneid*, the death of Dido and destruction of Carthage become emblematic of a ruthless will-to-power, establishing a repressive empire based upon patriarchal power.

8. Niemi, 68. The brief anonymous notice in *The New York Times Book Review* proclaimed, "This experiment in satire succeeds at being impenetrable and fails at being funny," "Family Life," April 20, 1975.

9. *The Black Madonna* was published posthumously under the pseudonym H. M Morrow.

10. Niemi, 6–7.

11. Ibid., 75.

12. Bair, Deirdre, "Parable from the Coffin," *New York Times*, April 1, 1984.

13. Arthur Miller's allegory of U.S. Senator Joseph McCarthy's Congressional political inquisition in *The Crucible* (1953) maintains an accurate historical parallel.

14. See Rogin, Michael Paul, *Subversive Genealogy: The Politics and Art of Herman Melville* (New York: Knopf, 1983) and Newman, Lea Bertani Vozar, "Benito Cereno," *A Reader's Guide to the Short Stories of Herman Melville* (Boston: G. K. Hall, 1986).

15. Banks, *The Relation of My Imprisonment* (New York: HarperPerennial, 1996), 9–10.

16. Walton, Isaak, *Lives of John Donne, Sir Henry Wotten, Richard Hooker, George Herbert, and Robert Sanderson*, ed. George Saintsbury (London: Oxford World Classics, 1966), 77.

17. Bald, R. C. *John Donne: A Life* (Oxford: Oxford University Press, 1970), 527–28.

18. Quigley, Christine, *The Corpse: A History* (Jefferson: McFarland, 1996), 14.

19. Ibid., 67.

20. J. M. Coetzee's prideful perspective of the imprisoned magistrate owes its conversion perspective to the influence of Leo Tolstoy's *The Death of Ivan Illych*.

21. Prison statiscs available at http://www.ojp.usdoj.gov/bjs/pub/press/pim07jim07pr.html (accessed 10/01/09).

22. Banks, *Relation*, 84–85.

23. Ibid., 83.

24. Ibid., 97.

25. See Martz, Louis, *The Poetry of Meditation* (New Haven: Yale University Press, 1954) and Collmer, Robert G., "The mediation of death and its appearance in metaphysical poetry," *Neophilologus*, vol. 45, December 1961. In more recent times, Gerard Manley Hopkins was influenced by the Ignatian method of mediating upon death. Also, Mariani, Paul, *Gerard Manley Hopkins* (New York: Viking, 2008), 305.

CHAPTER 4

1. Birstein, Ann, "Metaphors, Metaphors," *New York Times*, July 2, 1978.

2. Callahan, Michael, "Peyton Place's Real Victim," *Vanity Fair*, March 2006.

3. Banks, Russell, *Hamilton Stark* (New York: HarperPerennial, 1996), 123.

4. Herman Melville penned *Bartleby, the Scrivener* as a tribute to Nicolai Gogol, author of "The Overcoat." Melville's story is an original tribute to Gogol whose story inspired his own. Bartleby's life savings are discovered in his office desk by the lawyer he works for; the lawyer steals it and a valuable ring—much of the narrative consists of his self-rationalizations for stealing from a man of lower class and status. Unfortunately, most academics attempt to convert the story into a silly comedy about stubbornness when the story is a trenchant indictment of class entitlement and exploitation. Bartleby ends up in prison starving to death in protest at the injustice, while the opportunistic lawyer remains haunted by guilt at causing his "unreasonable" death.

5. Banks, Ibid., 269.

6. Callahan, Ibid.

7. See Gladfelder, Hal, *Criminality and Narrative in Eighteenth-Century England: Beyond the Law* (Baltimore: Johns Hopkins, 2001).

8. The brilliance of Edward Gibbon's *The Decline and Fall of the Roman Empire* persuaded the English-speaking world Rome harbored something resembling civilization.

9. Banks, Ibid., 129.

10. Banks, Ibid., 112.

11. Banks, Ibid., 199–200.
12. Banks, Ibid., 145.
13. Banks, Ibid., 137.
14. See Toth, Emily, *Inside Peyton Place: The Life of Grace Metalious* (New York: Dell, 1981).
15. Niemi, Robert, *Russell Banks* (Boston: Twayne, 1995), 69.
16. Banks, Ibid., 100.
17. Loudon is an older spelling of London, fort of the Celtic god Lugh, but there was also a novel written by Aldous Huxley entitled *The Devils of Loudon* (1952), a political thriller set in France that depicted fanatical witch hunts. The excellent 1971 film, *The Devils*, has been largely forgotten.
18. Banks, Russell, *The Angel on the Roof* (New York: HarperCollins, 2000), xvi.
19. Niemi, Ibid., 8.
20. Banks, *Angel*, xvi. Had Banks continued to write in the postmodern vein of *Hamilton Stark*, he might have turned into an American Robert Pinget (1919–97).
21. Banks, *Hamilton Stark*, 18.
22. Toth, Ibid., 311.
23. Banks, Ibid., 3–4.
24. Orson Welles's surname itself contains a mirror element.
25. Banks, Ibid., 173.
26. That is why the toilet sometimes finds itself referred to as the John.
27. See http://news.bbc.co.uk/2/hi/americas/8298582.stm (accessed 10/17/09).

CHAPTER 5

1. Nicholson, Geoff, *The Errol Flynn Novel* (1993). Some out-of-print biographies and memoirs about Errol Flynn fetch high prices in the second-hand book market.
2. Banks, Russell, *The Book of Jamaica* (New York: HarperPerennial, 1996), 74.
3. Banks, Ibid., 87.
4. Banks, Ibid., 91.
5. O'Brien, Flann, *The Third Policeman* (New York: Plume, 1967), 139.
6. An old imperial trick. When the Athenian library lent the originals of their major playwrights' texts to the Library of Alexandria for copying, the library sent back the copies, keeping the originals.
7. Banks, Ibid., 167.
8. Banks, Ibid., 192.
9. Banks, Ibid., 193–94.
10. One might argue Camus's late novel *The Fall* (1956), influenced by Dante Alighieri, dramatized an Augustinian guilt for having once encouraged rebellion.
11. The portrait of the criminal mind Algren produced provided significant advance over Jim Tully's more melodramatic *Laughter in Hell* (1932) where an Irishman kills his wife and her lover. Fascination with the criminal mind was popular in early nineteenth-century English novels, Edward Bulwer-Lytton's *Eugene Aram* (1832) being a good example of this.
12. Robertson-Lorant, Laurie, *Melville: A Biography* (New York: Clarkson Potter, 1996), 349–51. See also Sundquist, Eric J., *To Wake the Nations: Race in the Making of American Literature* (Cambridge: Harvard University Press, 1993) and Delbanco, Andrew, *Melville: His World and Work* (New York: Knopf, 2005).

13. Melville, Herman, *The Piazza Tales and Other Prose Pieces* (Evanston: Northwestern Univ. Press, 1987), 109.

14. Banks, Ibid., 194–95.

15. Banks, Ibid., 198.

16. Tom Stoppard's play *Travesties* (1974) parodies Oscar Wilde's *The Importance of Being Earnest* (1895).

17. Banks, Ibid., 296.

18. Niemi, Robert, *Russell Banks*, 105.

19. Boyd, Valerie, *Wrapped in Rainbows: A Biography of Zora Neal Hurston* (New York: Scribner, 2003), 286.

20. Hurston, Zora Neale, *Dust Tracks on a Road: An Autobiography*, ed. Robert Hemenway (Chicago: Univ. of Illinois Press, 1984), 212.

21. See Dutton, Wendy, "The Problem of Invisibility: Voodoo and Zora Neale Hurston," *Frontiers*, 23, no. 2, 1992.

22. Boyd, Ibid., 291.

23. For a brief discussion of these topics see King, Lovalerie, *The Cambridge Introduction to Zora Neale Hurston* (Cambridge: Cambridge University Press, 2008), 61–68.

24. Orme, Mark, *The Development of Albert Camus's Concern for Social and Political Justice* (Madison: Fairleigh Dickinson Press, 2007), 107–08.

CHAPTER 6

1. Interview with Russell Banks in Paris at www.biblioblog.fr/index.php/post/2008/04/16/Interview-of-Russell-Banks (accessed 10/01/09).

2. Elizabeth Strout's "novel in stories" collection of 13 linked short stories, *Olive Kitteridge*, set in hardscrabble Maine, which won the 2009 Pulitzer Prize for fiction, finds its precedent in Banks's 13 linked story collection. While Russell Banks presents excessive empathy as dangerous in Flora and Marcelle, Strout's Olive valorizes excessive empathy as part of the journey of personal discovery.

3. I use the phrase "middle class" in the conventional American sense with all its vagueness and not the more specific European phrase which denotes someone who owns outright at least one house.

4. The meddling priest and the theme of confession appear to have been derived from *Romeo and Juliet*, written by a secular Catholic.

5. Banks, Russell, "Joyce Carol Oates: In a Gothic Manor," *Washington Post*, August 17, 1980.

6. Oates appears to have taken this criticism to heart—her superb Gothic novella *Beasts* (2002) provides a trenchant critique of upper-class education and decadent sexuality.

7. For more on Anderson's grotesques see Lindsay, Clarence, *Such a Rare Thing: The Art of Sherwood Anderson's* Winesburg, Ohio (Kent: Kent Univ. Press, 2009).

8. Anderson, Sherwood, *Winesburg, Ohio*, ed. John H. Ferres (New York: Viking, 1966).

9. Akira Kurosawa's fine 1957 movie adaption remains a classic.

10. Banks, Russell, *Trailerpark* (New York: Houghton Mifflin, 1981), 168.

11. Recounted in David Hadju's gossipy profile of Bob Dylan in *Positively 4th Street* (New York: Vintage, 2002). Richard Farina was the author of the quirky cult novel *Been Down So Long It Looks Like Up to Me* (1966). The detail of the metal plate in the skull reappears in a war vet from the story "Queen for a Day" in *Success Stories*, 7.

12. Banks, Ibid., 184.
13. Metalious, Grace, *Peyton Place* (New York: Julian Messner, Inc., 1956), 176.
14. This story was first published in Eugene Jolas's avant-garde journal *transition*, no 5.
15. Niemi, Robert, *Russell Banks*, (Boston: Twayne, 1997) 125–27.
16. Leckie, Ross, "Plot-resistant narrative and Russell Banks's 'Black Man and White Woman in Dark Green Rowboat,'" *Studies in Short Fiction*, summer 1994.
17. Banks, Ibid., 87.
18. Ibid.
19. *Esquire*, March 17, 2008. Some episodes of Odysseus's life, like his childhood adventures and exploits at Troy, appear narrated by other characters in *The Odyssey*. Since the linear chronology of Odysseus's life appears scrambled in *The Odyssey*, Charles Rowan Beye penned a chronological biography in *Odysseus: A Life* (New York: Hyperion, 2004).
20. Banks, Ibid., 54.
21. Ibid.
22. The story contains a disturbing, obscene, anti-Semitic joke that compares the writings of Franz Kafka to a latrine, perhaps one reason Jorge Luis Borges never won the Nobel Prize for Literature, *Collected Fictions* (New York: Viking, 1998), 104.
23. The name Tessie probably alludes to Thomas Hardy's *Tess of the D'Urbervilles* (1891).
24. Banks, Ibid., 197.
25. Ibid., 241.
26. Omitted from "The Fisherman" in *The Angel on the Roof* collection because there the story floats free of the linked cycle.
27. Banks, Ibid., 242.
28. Niemi, Ibid., 137. In John Huston's 1948 movie masterpiece the despairing look on Humphrey Bogart's face remains memorably haunting.
29. Banks, Ibid., 103.
30. For more on this subject see Douglas, Mary, *Thinking in Circles: An Essay on Ring Composition* (New Haven: Yale Univ. Press, 2007) and Bakker, E. J., *Pointing at the Past: From Formula to Performance in Homeric Poetics* (Boston: Harvard Univ. Press, 2005). An earlier important landmark on the subject was Stanley, Keith, *The Shield of Home: Narrative Structure in* The Iliad (Princeton: Princeton Univ. Press, 1993).
31. Kavanagh, Peter, ed., *The Complete Poems of Patrick Kavanagh with Commentary* (New York: Kavanagh Hand Press, 1996), 244.
32. There's 1948 film musical with the same title directed by Josh Binney that features an array of exuberant African American vaudeville acts.
33. Some of the characters in James Farrell's stories like Ed Lanson and Danny O'Neill (on whom Farrell wrote a pentalogy) link with Farrell's other novels.

Chapter 7

1. Hearing word of Nathaniel Hawthorne's biography in progress, the educator Horace Mann quipped, "If he makes out Pierce to be a great or brave man, it will be the greatest work of fiction he ever wrote." Hawthorne cautiously concurred, saying, "Though the story is true, yet it took a romancer to do it." Miller, Edwin Haviland, *Salem Is My Dwelling Place: A Life of Nathaniel Hawthorne* (Iowa City: University of Iowa Press, 1991), 381.

2. Maslin, Janet, "News Story Inspired Banks's 'Drift,' " *New York Times*, April 29, 1985.

3. For a discussion on this topic see Drew, Bettina, *Nelson Algren: A Life on the Wild Side* (New York: Putnam, 1989), 134–36.

4. Cowley, Malcolm, ed., *Writers at Work: The Paris Review Interviews* (New York: Viking, 1959), 234.

5. Ibid., 235–36.

6. Maslin, Ibid.

7. Wolfe, Tom, "Stalking the Billion-Footed Beast," *Harper's*, November 1989. See the reply by Towers, Robert, "The Flap Over Tom Wolfe: How Real Is the Retreat from Realism?" *New York Times*, Jan. 28, 1990; McEneaney, Kevin T., *Tom Wolfe's America: Heroes, Pranksters, and Fools* (Westport: Praeger, 2009), chapter 10.

8. Banks, Russell, *Continental Drift* (New York: Harper & Row, 1985), 1–2.

9. David Byrne wrote the lyrics for the Talking Heads song "Papa Legba," which appears on their *True Stories* album.

10. Murphy, Joseph M., *Working the Spirit: Ceremonies of the African Diaspora* (Boston: Beacon Press, 1994), 39–41.

11. Davis, Wade, *Passage of Darkness: The Ethnobiology of the Haitian Zombie* (Chapel Hill: University of North Carolina Press, 1985), 291.

12. Boyd, Ibid., 320. For an overview of Voodoo from this perspective see the lively collection of essays edited by Claudine Michel and Patrick Bellegarde-Smith, *Vodou in Haitian Life and Culture: Invisible Powers* (New York: Palgrave Press, 2006).

13. The denigration of Voodoo as ignorant superstition was a Hollywood staple from the thirties through the fifties and might consist of anything from a passing joke to the jury, as in *The Trial* (1955), or an integral part of the plot, as in *Too Hot to Handle* (1938) with Clark Gable and Myrna Loy wherein the primitive barbarism of Brazilian Voodoo is outwitted by the Western magic of film in combination with Western medicine.

14. Banks, Russell, *Continental Drift* (New York: HarperCollins, 1985), 13.

15. Ibid., 41.

16. There appears to be an abundance of characters in Banks's fiction whose name begins with Dor.

17. Banks, Ibid., 87.

18. Métraux, Alfred, *Voodoo in Haiti*, trans. Hugo Charteris (New York: Schocken Books, 1972), Plate XIV, "Passport," issued by a society of sorcerers.

19. Alighieri, Dante, *The Inferno*, Canto III, trans. Ciaran Carson (London: Granta Books, 2002), 15.

20. For a consideration of the zombies in film see Gilmore, Richard A., *Doing Philosophy at the Movies* (Albany: SUNY Press, 2005), 121–22 and Paffenroth, Kim, *Gospel of the Living Dead* (Waco: Baylor University Press, 2006).

21. Davis, Ibid., 57.

22. Banks, Ibid., 179.

23. Ibid., 181–8.

24. Agwé has iconic and healing affinities with Saint Ulrich from Augsburg (c. 890–973), the *first* saint to be canonized by the Vatican in 993. Agwé's depicted as holding a fish (a symbol of Christ), although his biography as a military general and issuer of coins has nothing to do with the sea. Pinn, Anthony B. *Varieties of African American Religious Experience* (Minneapolis: Fortress Press, 1988.), 22.

25. Banks, Ibid., 190.

Notes 199

26. Ogu finds descent from Gu, the Dahomey blacksmith god, but since ironwork was never important in Haiti, Ogu became the warrior god depicted with a saber or machete. Metraux, Ibid., 109.

27. Banks, Ibid., 214–15.

28. Aristotle, *On Poetry and Style*, trans. Grube, G.M.A. (Indianapolis: Bobbs-Merrill, 1958), 36.

29. That all life and the cosmos are ruled by chance.

30. Banks, Ibid., 283.

31. Ibid., 301.

32. Ibid., 363.

33. Ibid., 364.

34. Ibid., 366.

35. Posthumously published but thought to have been written in the early 1580s.

36. "I haven't a thing to kick about, thought Selena, as she walked home one cold December evening after closing the Thrifty Corner. If I had an ounce of gratitude in me, I'd know enough to be grateful for all I have." Metalious, Ibid., 292. This sentiment from a woman facing a murder trial!

37. Jed Esty provides an interesting essay on this subject, "Virginia Woolf's Colony and the Adolescent of Modern Fiction" in *Modernism and Colonialism: British and Irish Literature, 1899–1939*, ed. Begam, Richard and Michael Valdez Moses (Durham: Duke University Press, 2007).

38. Banks, Russell, *Dreaming Up America* (New York: Seven Seas Press, 2008), 48.

39. Ibid., 49.

40. Banks, Russell, Foreword to *A Walk on the Wild Side* by Nelson Algren (New York: Farrar, Straus and Giroux, 1998), x.

41. Banks has a lively essay on the theme of borderlands in his introduction to *Ploughshares*, winter 1993–34. Jay Clayton offers a discussion on the theme of borderlands in *The Pleasures of Babel* (New York: Oxford, 1993), 108–29.

42. Simon, Daniel, Afterword in *Nonconformity* by Nelson Algren (New York: Seven Seas Press, 1998), 81.

Chapter 8

1. Ward, Jerry, Jr. and Robert J. Butler, *The Richard Wright Encyclopedia* (Westport, CT: Greenwood Press, 2008), 125.

2. Drew, Bettina, *Nelson Algren: A Life on the Wild Side* (New York: Putnam, 1989) 179ff.

3. Ward, Ibid., 107–08.

4. Ibid., 17.

5. Ibid., 12–22.

6. Emile Zola did write novels like *La Conquêt de Plassans* (*A Priest in the House*, 1874) and *La Faute de l'Abbè Mouret* (*The Abbè Mouret's Sin*, 1875) with a pastoral setting, but these satiric *religious novels* had little influence on American novels.

7. Sherwood Anderson (1876–1941) followed Zola in emphasizing how environmental elements deforms character and made the transition to Modernism while Maxwell Bodenheim (1892–1954) more closely followed Howells by centering his realism on character in novels like *Replenishing Jessica* (1925) and *Georgie May* (1928) as he added a deterministic element to sexual drive. For overview see Bell,

Michael Davitt, *The Problem of American Realism* (Chicago: University of Chicago Press, 1993) and Pizer, Donald, *Realism and Naturalism in Nineteenth Century American Literature* (Carbondale: Southern Illinois University Press, 1966).

    8. *Cesspool* was Richard Wright's working title for his abandoned first novel begun around 1934 when Wright was about 26; it was eventually published posthumously as *Lawd Today!* (1963). Ward, Ibid., 71–72. K. E. Dohmen used the title *Cesspool* (2004) for his brief postmodern Algren-influenced novel about a sociopath who murders a talk-show host.

    9. Algren, Nelson, *A Walk on the Wild Side* (New York: Farrar, Straus and Giroux, 1998), x.

    10. Walker, Margaret, *Richard Wright: Daemonic Genius* (New York: Warner, 1988), 22–44.

    11. Montague, John, *Selected Poems* (Winston-Salem: Wake Forest University Press, 1982), 26–27. The legend of the Fomorians appears in the medieval *Lebhor gabála érenn* (*Book of Invasions*, c.1000). Banks probably met Montague when he taught in Albany through the novelist William Kennedy. John Montague had sent me a photograph of the Montague family with the children in Halloween make-up to accompany an article the book's author wrote, "Brooklyn's Irish Poet: John Montague," *Irish America*, December 1986.

    12. Banks, Russell, *Affliction* (New York: Harper & Row, 1989), 37.

    13. Niemi, *Russell Banks* (Boston : Twayne Publishers, 1997), notes New Hampshire deer rifle season runs from November 13 to December 8 while shotgun deer hunting season runs from November 2 to November 12, 181.

    14. Banks, Ibid., 79.

    15. Ibid., 86–88.

    16. Ibid., 126–28.

    17. The circle included Maxim Gorky, Viktor Shklovsky, and Mikhail Zoshchenko among others. The name refers to a four-volume collection of stories by E. T. A. Hoffmann, which is presented as the work of a group of authors.

    18. Banks, Ibid., 176.

    19. Niemi, Ibid., 181.

    20. Banks, Ibid., 245.

    21. Pfeil, Fred, "Beating the Odds: The Brechtian Aesthetic of Russell Banks," *Another Tale to Tell: Politics and Narrative in Postmodern Culture* (New York: Verso, 1990), 80.

    22. See Douglass, James W., *JFK and the Unspeakable: Why He Died and Why It Matters* (Maryknoll: Orbis Books, 2008).

    23. Pfeil, Ibid., 81.

    24. Banks, Ibid., 351.

    25. Ibid., 354.

    26. Ibid., 355.

    27. DeLillo, Don, "The Fictional Man." In *Novel History: Historians and Novelists Confront America's Past (And Each Other)* by Mark C. Carnes (New York: Simon & Schuster, 2001), 91.

    28. Ham points a rifle at his sister Jody's husband Chub in *Hamilton Stark*, 135.

    29. Banks, Ibid., 247.

    30. Douglass, Ibid.

    31. Banks, Ibid., 255.

    32. Williamson, Joel, *William Faulkner and Southern History* (New York: Oxford University Press, 1993), 369.

Notes

33. Williamson, Ibid., 182–85. Banks acknowledges Faulkner as an early influence in "H & I," The 2004 PEN/Hemingway Prize Speech, April 4, 2004, http://web.bu.edu/agni/essays/print/2004/60-banks.html (accessed 10/01/09).

34. Mirsky, D. S., *A History of Russian Literature: From Its Beginnings to 1900*, ed. Francis J. Whitfield (Evanston: Northwestern University Press, 1999), 284–87.

35. Booth, Wayne C., *The Company We Keep: An Ethics of Fiction* (Berkeley: University of California Press, 1988), 152.

CHAPTER 9

1. That same year Banks's friend Caryl Phillips published *Cambridge* (1991), a historical novel about slavery that employs narrative crossing, and Rick Moody's *The Ice Storm* (1991) also features four narrators.

2. Banks, Russell, *The Sweet Hereafter* (New York: HarperCollins, 1991), 15.

3. Ibid., 10.

4. Fried, Margaret J. and Lawrence A. Frolik, "The Limits of Law: Litigation, Lawyers and the Search for Justice in Russell Banks's *The Sweet Hereafter*," *Cardozo Studies in Law and Literature*, vol. 7, no. 1, Apr 1995, 5.

5. Banks, Ibid., 254.

6. Nashe, Thomas, "The Praise of the Red Herring," subsection to "Lenten Stuff" In *The Unfortunate Traveller and Other Works* (New York: Penguin, 1972), 377ff.

7. In *The Republic* Plato jokingly exiles cynics to the border of his ideal state because their austere absurdity will discourage barbarians from entering the state.

8. Freud, Sigmund, "The Uncanny," *The Standard Edition of the Complete Psychological Writings of Sigmund Freud*, trans. and ed. by James Strachey, vol. 17, 235.

9. "Russell Banks," interview with J. J. Wylie, *Michigan Quarterly Review*, vol. 39, fall 2000.

10. Banks, Ibid., 73.

11. Ibid., 81.

12. Fried, Ibid., 10–11.

13. Banks, Ibid., 99.

14. Banks, Russell, *Dreaming Up America* (New York: Seven Seas Press, 2008), 110.

15. The duplicitous Jacques Chambrun, Ben Hecht's agent, invented Marilyn's apocryphal prophecy of her death from drug overdose back in 1974 when he sold a doctored version of Ben Hecht's ghostwritten autobiography "My Story" to Stein and Day. See http://benhechtbooks.net/ben_hecht__marilyn_monroe (accessed 9/01/09). This popular cover story provided the plausible explanation for her eventual *suicide*. There exist many theories about who ordered the fatal injection the night before her tell-all press conference. A recent FBI document has come to light at http://www.smh.com.au/news/world/kennedy-link-to death/2007/03/16/1173722744304.html (accessed 10/01/09).

16. Wylie, Ibid.

17. Those writings of Paul that demean women are considered by scholars to be later second-century forgeries.

18. Landwehr, Margarete Johanna, "Egoyan's Film Adaptation of Banks's *The Sweet Hereafter*: 'The Pied Piper' as Trauma Narrative and Mise-en-abyme," *Literature/Film Quarterly*, vol. 36, no. 3, 2008.

19. Banks, *The Sweet Hereafter*, 72–73.

20. Landwehr, Ibid.
21. Ibid.
22. Banks, Russell, in Klin, Richard, "Interview with Russell Banks," *January Magazine*, June, 2003 at http://januarymagazine.com/profiles/rbanks.htm (accessed 10/01/09).
23. Published in the first and last issue of *Fire!* magazine which Zora Neale Hurston co-edited with Langston Hughes. Reprinted in *Spunk: The Selected Short Stories of Zora Neale Hurston* (Berkeley: Turtle Island Press, 1985).
24. Dillon, Steven, "Lyricism and Accident in *The Sweet Hereafter*," *Literature/Film Quarterly*, vol. 31, no. 3, 2003, 227ff.

Chapter 10

1. Louis Menand includes Sylvia Plath's novel *The Bell Jar* (1963) in his meditation on the influence of Salinger in his essay "Holden at Fifty," *The New Yorker*, Oct. 1, 2001.
2. Salinger, J. D., *The Catcher in the Rye* (Boston: Little Brown, 1951), 156.
3. Neider, Charles, ed., *The Autobiography of Mark Twain* (New York: HarperPerennial, 1990), 40. The tramp was Denis McDermid. At the time Clemens was 18. See Rachels, David, ed., *Mark Twain's Civil War* (Lexington: University Press of Kentucky, 2007), 10. *Madame Bovary's Ovaries: A Darwinian Look at Literature* by David and Nanelle Barash (New York: Delacorte, 2005) offers a lively discussion of Huck and Holden with regard to parental conflict, 192–201.
4. Twain, Mark, *Adventures of Huckleberry Finn* (New York: Oxford University Press, 1996), 57–58.
5. Banks, Russell, *Rule of the Bone* (New York: HarperCollins, 1996), 94–95. The book was first published in Canada the year before by Canadian Knopf.
6. Kesey, Ken, *Demon Box* (New York: Viking, 1986), 56–90.
7. Banks, Ibid., 107.
8. Banks, Ibid., 130–31.
9. Campbell, Joseph, *The Hero with a Thousand Faces* (Princeton: Princeton University Press, 1949), 72.
10. Banks, Ibid., 206–07.
11. Banks, Ibid., 156. An obvious reference to Hunter S. Thompson.
12. *Odyssey*, Book 10: 51–53. My translation.
13. Ibid., Book 12: 426–46. My translation.
14. Banks, Ibid., 230–31.
15. See Papalos, Demitri F. and Janice Papalos, *The Bipolar Child* (New York: Broadway Books, 2002) and Geller, Barbara and Melissa P. DelBello, *Bipolar Disorder in Children and Early Adolescence* (New York: Guilford Press, 2003).
16. Edwards, Jonathan, *Sermons and Discourses, 1739–1742 (WJE Online Vol. 22)*, Ed. Harry S. Stout, http://edwards.yale.edu/archive (accessed 10/01/09).
17. Melville, Herman, *Redburn: His First Voyage* (Evanston: Northwestern University Press, 1969), 10.
18. Ibid., 87.
19. Banks, Ibid., 360.
20. Fiedler, Leslie, *Love and Death in the American Novel* (New York: Stein and Day, 1966), 285.
21. O'Loughlin, Jim, "The Whiteness of Bone: Russell Banks's 'Rule of the Bone' and the Contradictory Legacy of 'Huck Finn,'" *Modern Language Studies*, vol. 32, spring 2002, 37.

22. In his essay on Mark Twain, "Out at the Edges," Russell Banks comments, "Hemingway was right, perhaps more right than even he thought. It all goes back, not only to one writer, but to one book, *Huckleberry Finn*. I think that Huckleberry Finn is our Homeric epic, or the basis for one. It stands in relation to our literature as *The Iliad* and *The Odyssey* stand to Greek and European literature." Ward, Geoffrey C., ed., *Mark Twain* (New York: Knopf, 2001), 224.

23. Doctorow, E. L., "Sam Clemens's Two Boys," in *Creationists* (New York: Random House, 2006), 104–05.

24. Morrison, Toni, "Introduction," in *Adventures of Huckleberry Finn* by Mark Twain (New York: Oxford, 1996), xli.

25. Joyce, Cynthia, "The Salon Interview: Russell Banks," http://www.salon.com/books/int/1998/01/cov_si_05int.html (accessed 10/01/09).

26. Klin, Richard, "Interview with Russell Banks," *January Magazine*, June 2003, http://januarymagazine.com/profiles/rbanks.html (accessed 10/01/09).

27. Whitman, Walt, *Leaves of Grass and Selected Prose*, ed. John Kouwenhoven (New York: Modern Library, 1950), 118.

28. Recounted by Linda Hutcheon, *Narcissistic Narrative: The Metafictional Paradox* (New York: Methuen, 1984), 155.

Chapter 11

1. See Niemi, Robert, *Russell Banks* (Boston: Twayne Publishers, 1997), 138–48 and Hennessy, Denis M., *Dictionary of Literary Biography* (New York: Gale, 1993), vol. 130, 22–27. The influence of Jorge Luis Borges on Banks's parables might be further explored.

2. Dr. Seuss has a character by that name not unlike the sensibility of this Knox.

3. In his novel of the fantastic, *Salamander* (New York: Washington Square Press, 2001), the Canadian writer Thomas Wharton features a typesetter with extra digits by the name of Djinn who comes to a mysterious, bookish end. Parts of Wharton's novel appeared in 1999; Banks's story appeared in *Esquire*, June 2000. Other than the name and the encounter with the fantastic, there's no correlation, yet Banks remains one of the few American writers who regularly reads Canadian literature. He has selected and penned an introduction to Mavis Gallant's *Varieties of Exile: Stories* (New York: New York Review Books, 2003).

4. Banks, Russell, *The Angel on the Roof: The Stories of Russell Banks* (New York: HarperCollins, 2000), 229. Thomas Wolfe's original title for his first novel was *Look Homeward, Angel* with its reference to a line in John Milton's "Lycidas," but while writing the novel he changed it to "The Angel on the Porch," yet when a Scribner's editor frowned and asked what the original title was, it was changed back to *Look Homeward, Angel*. The angel on the porch referred to an angel of white Carrara marble that once stood on the porch of the Wolfe marble shop. See Johnston, Carol, *The Thomas Wolfe Review*, vol. 13, fall 1989, 53–62. Reprinted in *Short Story Criticism* (New York: Gale), vol. 33, 1999.

5. Banks, Ibid., 177.

6. Ibid., 192.

7. Ibid., 118.

8. Banks's daughter Caerthan, wrote the screenplay, directed, and co-produced a 20-minute film of *The Moor* (2005). The film can be viewed at the IMDb Web site, http://www.imdb.com/video/wab/vi1205600537 (accessed 10/01/09).

9. Banks, Ibid., 348.
10. Ibid.
11. See the entry *geis*, *The Oxford Companion to Irish Literature*, ed. Robert Welch (New York: Oxford, 1996), 212–13. The earliest text of the Deirdre story employs it.
12. Noonan is the surname of an Irish musician who performs for a middle-class Irish American audience.
13. Banks, Ibid., 501.
14. Banks, Russell, "Transplant," *The Yale Review*, 97, no. 2, 2009, 90–97.

Chapter 12

1. "Russell Banks: The Salon Interview," with Cynthia Joyce, http://www.salon.com/books/int/1998/01/cov_si_05int.html (accessed 10/01/09).
2. U.S. President Abraham Lincoln said John Brown's actions were wrong for two reasons, "It was a violation of law and it was, as all such attacks must be, futile as far as any effect it might have on the extinction of a great evil," Donald, David Herbert, *Lincoln* (Simon & Schuster, 1995). 239.
3. Quarles, Benjamin, ed., Introduction, in *Allies for Freedom: Blacks on John Brown* (Chicago: University of Illinois Press, 1972).
4. Ibid., 116–18.
5. A general overview can be found in Trodd, Zoe and John Stauffer, eds., *Meteor of War: The John Brown Story* (Maplecrest: Brandywine Press, 2004).
6. For further elaboration see the short video clip of the New Yorker Writers Institute at http://www.youtube.com/watch?v=M-SbzC-jqJI&feature=PlayList&p=81B77FC5252F8DA7&playnext=1&playnext_from=PL&index=17 (accessed 10/01/09).
7. Villard, Oswald Garrison, *John Brown 1800–1859: A Biography Fifty Years After* (Boston: Houghton Mifflin Company, 1911), 11.
8. Ibid., 111ff.
9. Ibid., 25.
10. Banks, Interview by Richard Klin, *January Magazine*, June 2003, http://januarymagazine.com/profiles/rbanks.html (accessed 10/01/09).
11. Banks, Russell, *Cloudsplitter* (New York: HarperCollins, 1998), 24.
12. Ibid., 18.
13. Ibid., 218.
14. Ibid., 217–18.
15. Ibid., 251.
16. Villard, Ibid., 10–11.
17. For an astute assessment of Henry Adams's bleak views on the Civil War see Poole, W. Scott, "Henry Adams's Civil War" in *Memory and Myth: The Civil War in Fiction and Film from* Uncle Tom's Cabin *to* Cold Mountain, ed. Sachsman, David B., Rushing, and Morris (West Lafayette: Purdue University Press, 2007), 105–113.
18. Emerson, Ralph Waldo, *The Selected Writings of Ralph Waldo Emerson* (New York: Modern Library, 1950), 881.
19. Ibid., 880.
20. Other noted abolitionists compared Brown to John the Baptist, Jesus, or saints. See Tripp, Bernell E., "The Many Faces of John Brown" in Poole, Ibid., 49–58. While Tripp does not discuss Banks's novel, he quotes Frederick Douglass noting Brown had

Notes

struck a significant blow for freedom. Douglass presented the sale of his manuscript speech to fund a John Brown Professorship.

21. Hutchison, Anthony, "Representative Man: John Brown and the Politics of Redemption in Russell Banks's *Cloudsplitter*," *Journal of American Studies*, 41, 2006, 69. The expansion of Hutchison's essay in *Writing the Republic* (New York: Columbia University Press, 2007) provides perceptive comments on Abraham Lincoln and Herman Melville's *Moby-Dick* with regard to Banks's novel.

22. Banks, Ibid., 314.

23. Fiedler, Leslie A., "The Unbroken Tradition," in *Waiting for the End* (New York: Stein and Day, 1964), 209.

24. For a brief discussion of W. E. B. Du Bois's awareness of this split in consciousness see Henry Lewis Gates, Jr., "The Black Letters on the Sign: W. E. B. Du Bois and the Canon" in *John Brown* by W. E. Burghardt Du Bois (New York: Oxford University Press, 2007), xiii–xiv.

25. Banks, Ibid., 202.

26. Mentioned in passing, Banks, Ibid., 318.

27. Parker, Theodore, *Ten Sermons of Religion* (Boston: Crosby, Nichols & Company, 1853), 84–85. In 1850 Parker also made popular the phrase "of the people, by all the people, for all the people" first used by John Wycliffe in the prologue to his English vernacular translation of the Bible (1382).

28. Stephen Vincent Benét's book is little read today because of its strict and overly formulaic prosody and perhaps to a certain degree because Benét's strength as a poet lay in his ability to wax eloquent about the varied states of weather—the tempo of rain, the variegations of clouds, the quality of snow, a meditative lyric quality which often disrupts and distracts from the narrative drive of his epic—such Wordsworthian contemplation appears at odds with a narrative drive about martyrdom.

29. Blum, Edward J. and Sarah Hardin Blum, "The Search for Community and Justice: Robert Penn Warren, Race Relations, and the Civil War," in Sachsman, Ibid., 75. This article vociferously defends Warren's approach by asserting his methodologies were innovative and sound while he always advocated communal justice.

30. Emerson, "Heroism," Ibid., 258.

31. For example, Gilpin, Robert Blakeslee, "The Fugitive Imagination: Robert Penn Warren's *John Brown*" in Sachsman, Ibid., 59–70 and Blum, Ibid., 71–80. Also, Gilpen's review of Andrew Taylor's *The Afterlife of John Brown* (2005) in *Biography*, vol. 30, Winter 2007, 114–18.

32. Warren, Robert Penn, "Segregation: The Inner Conflict in the South," *A Robert Penn Warren Reader* (New York: Random House, 1987), 268–69.

33. Lewis, David Levering, *W. E. B. Du Bois: Biography of a Race, 1868–1919* (New York: Henry Holt and Company, 1993), 358.

34. Du Bois, W. E. Burghardt, Preface, Ibid.

35. Lewis, Ibid.

36. Du Bois, W. E. Burghardt, Ibid.

37. Oates, Stephen B., *To Purge This Land With Blood: A Biography of John Brown* (New York: 1970), 75.

38. Melville, Herman, *Moby-Dick* (New York: Norton Critical Edition, 1967), 52. This passage was the likely origin for Diane Wakowski's many humorous George Washington poems.

39. Banks, Ibid., 308.

40. *Odyssey*, Book 16, 186–219.

41. Banks, Ibid., 315.
42. Ibid., 472.
43. Ibid., 357.
44. Ibid., 425.
45. *Genesis*, 4:15.
46. *Beowulf*, line 1266, where the mark of Cain indicates a monster to be slain—Grendel, a native occupant of Britain (presumably Welsh?), is identified by the Anglo invaders as being descended from Cain, but in the epic it appears to me that the mark of Cain is the foreign language of Grendel. For an overview of the mark of Cain in the antebellum South see Goldenberg, David M., *The Curse of Ham* (Princeton: Princeton University Press, 2004), 178ff.
47. Banks, Ibid., 464.
48. Ibid., 480.
49. Ibid., 487.
50. Ibid., 443.
51. Ibid., 297.
52. Ibid., 505.
53. Faulkner, William, *The Hamlet* (New York: Vintage, 1991), 186–204.
54. Williamson, Joel, *William Faulkner and Southern History* (New York: Oxford University Press, 1993), 374.
55. The great Japanese novelist Shusaku Endo comically employed the peephole motif to satirize contemporary pornography in *Scandal* (1986; 1988, English).
56. "I had the best of all worlds—two men I really liked," Carolyn at a symposium, Charters, Ann, ed., *Beat Down to Your Soul* (New York: Penguin, 2001), 630.
57. Banks, Ibid., 519.
58. Ibid., 515.
59. Reynolds, David S., *Beneath the American Renaissance: The Subversive Imagination in the Age of Emerson and Melville* (New York: Knopf, 1988), 114.
60. Miller, Edwin Haviland, *Salem Is My Dwelling Place: A Life of Nathaniel Hawthorne* (Iowa City: University of Iowa Press, 1991), 110–15.
61. Borges, Jorge Luis, *Collected Fictions*, trans. Andrew Hurley (New York: Viking, 1998), 100.
62. Ibid.
63. Robertson-Lorant, Laurie, *Melville: A Biography* (New York: Clarkson Potter, 1996), 307.
64. *Odyssey*, Book Six, lines 127–41. My translation. In the past some translators have omitted this passage because of the implication that *lion* advances—Odysseus awakes with an erection that the olive branch attempts to conceal—the obvious reason for not grabbing Nausikaa's knees in traditional supplication. Nausikaa finds amusement in the awkward situation.
65. Banks, Ibid., 532.
66. Banks's interview with Lewis Burke Frumkes, *The Writer*, August 1998.
67. Mentioned in Banks, Ibid., 326, 345, 739.
68. Banks, Russell, *Dreaming Up America* (New York: Seven Stories Press, 2008), 6. See Bercovitch, Sacvan, *The Puritan Origins of the American Self* (New Haven: Yale University Press, 1977).
69. Banks, Russell, "In Response to James McPherson's Reading of *Cloudsplitter*," in *Novel History: Historians and Novelists Confront America's Past (and Each Other)*, ed. Mark C. Carnes (New York: Simon & Schuster, 2001), 75.

Notes   **207**

70. James McPherson's positive book review provides a partial list of historical errors, the more egregious of which are deliberate on the part of Banks as he notes in his fairly extensive and fascinating reply. Both pieces are conveniently available in Mark Carnes, Ibid., 61–76. Banks says that McPherson has seriously misread the novel by not looking closely enough at Owen's voice, the central vehicle of the novel. In his review, McPherson fails to comprehend the novel concerns the fictional Owen and not the historical John Brown.

71. Villard, Ibid., 148–88.

72. Banks, *Cloudsplitter*, 694.

73. Wylie, J. J., "Russell Banks," interview, *Michigan Quarterly Review*, vol.39, fall 2000.

74. Banks, Ibid., 757.

75. Ibid.

76. Banks, Russell, *Dreaming Up America* (New York: Seven Seas Press, 2008), 7.

77. James Joyce admired W. E. B. Du Bois's *The Souls of Black Folk* (1903) for its cultural analysis of music. Joyce saw parallels in pathos and sentimentality between Irish and African American music, especially when it reached public performance on the stage—for example the sentimental airs of Thomas Moore's melodies and a sentimental song like "Ol' Man River." In "Soullfreide" at http://fadograph.wordpress.com/finnegans-wake-african-world-fulani-west-indies-dubois-garvey/soullfriede-dubois-and-marcus-mosiah-garvey/, Karl Reisman elucidates some passages in *Finnegans Wake* on how Du Bois and Marcus Garvey informed Joyce's thinking.

78. Banks, *Cloudsplitter*, 282.

79. Ibid., 283.

80. See Zoe and Stauffer, Ibid., 169.

81. Villard, Ibid., 569.

82. Banks, *Cloudsplitter*, 740.

83. Banks, Ibid., 519.

84. Banks in Carnes, Ibid., 75.

85. "Russell Banks," interview with J. J. Wylie, *Michigan Quarterly Review*, vol. 39, fall 2000.

86. Like William Styron, who lived not far from the location of Nat Turner's rebellion, Russell Banks lived near the John Brown family homestead in New York. Both Styron and Banks married poets.

87. Styron, William, "More Confessions," Carnes, Ibid., 220. For a good example of that rational voice attending to final preparations see Styron, William, *The Confessions of Nat Turner* (New York: Random House, 1967), 356–57.

88. Fiedler, Leslie A., quoted in "*Gone With the Wind*: The Feminization of the Anti-Tom Novel," in *What Was Literature?* (New York: Simon & Schuster, 1982), 200.

89. Ibid., 320–21.

Chapter 13

1. Burns, Carol, "Off the Page: Russell Banks," *Washington Post*, Dec 16, 2004.

2. Two Brandeis University students, Katherine Ann Power and Susan Edith Saxe, were, like the fictional Hannah Musgrave, on the FBI most wanted list in 1970 for participating in a Boston bank heist where a third accomplice, an ex-convict, shot and killed a police officer, http://www.menstuff.org/issues/byissue/reallybadwomen.html (accessed 10/01/09).

3. Burns, Ibid.

4. Barbara Greene published her account of the trip in *Land Benighted* (1938), subsequently reprinted in 1981 as *Too Late to Turn Back*, introduction by Paul Theroux. Banks employs the phrase "benighted land" on page 390 in the mouth of Christian missionaries who occupy Hannah's former Liberian home during her 2001 visit. The use of the phrase illustrates the continuity of racism and how Western governments encourage missionaries to perform colonization within foreign countries as a first step in the process of political indoctrination.

5. Graham and Barbara Greene averaged about 12 miles a day. Diseases like smallpox and yaws were widespread. Graham liked the Liberian natives whom he found to be honest and peaceful. Sherry, Norman, *The Life of Graham Greene*, vol. 1 (New York: Penguin, 1989), 522–24.

6. Wright suffered severe cultural shock and remained appalled at the prevalence of disease. Walker, Margaret, *Richard Wright: Daemonic Genius* (New York: Warner Books), 240–43. Wright wrote about the visit in *Black Power* (New York: Harper, 1954).

7. Collins, John, *West African Pop Roots* (Philadelphia: Temple University Press, 1992). Collins later played with Fela Kuti after he fled Nigeria. A new biography of Kuti by Collins will be out shortly.

8. A survey of Liberian culture can be found in Sankawulo, Wilton, *Sundown at Dawn: A Liberian Odyssey* (Houston: Dusty Spark, 2004) and Olukoju, Ayodeji, *Culture and Customs of Liberia* (Westport: Greenwood Press, 2006).

9. Banks, Russell, *The Darling* (New York: HarperCollins, 2004), 100–01.

10. Weather Underground memoirs are a genre unto themselves. Susan Stern's *With the Weathermen: The Personal Journal of a Revolutionary Woman* (1974) is recommended for its emotional intensity and Cathy Wilkerson's *Flying Close to the Sun: My Life and Times as a Weatherman* (2007) for the political dynamics of the Weather Underground and its historical evolution. While the radicals of the late sixties lost the battle in the streets, they continue to provide a powerful cultural critique of American history, a perspective also continued by Banks.

11. Birnbaum, Robert, "Russell Banks: Author of *The Darling*," identitytheory.com, http://www.identitytheory.com/interviews/birnbaum156.php (accessed 10/01/09).

12. Banks, Ibid., 208. As someone who nearly completed her medical degree to become a doctor, Hannah muses, "I wondered if the symptoms of alcoholism were different for Africans than for Americans, for blacks than for whites."

13. For the coup and general background see Pham, John-Peter, *Liberia: Portrait of a Failed State* (New York: Reed Press, 2004); Levitt, Jeremy, *The Evolution of Deadly Conflict in Liberia* (Durham: Carolina Academic Press, 2005); Williams, Gabriel, *Liberia: The Heart of Darkness* (Manchester: Trafford Press, 2006).

14. Banks, Ibid., 207.

15. Birnbaum, Ibid.

16. Banks, Ibid., 376.

17. See Huband, Mark, *The Liberian Civil War* (London: Cass, 1998).

18. *The Informer* (Monrovia), July 21, 2009.

19. Gurd, Tracy, "Taylor dismisses charges as 'lies'; alleges CIA involvement in his jailbreak," July 17, 2009, http://www.charlestaylortrial.org/2009/07/17/taylor-dismisses-charges-as-lies-alleges-cia-involvement-in-his-jailbreak (accessed 10/01/09).

20. "The Trial of Charles Taylor," July, 23, 2009, http://www.charlestaylortrial.org/2009/07/23/taylor-says-liberian-fighters-in-sierra-leone-were-recruited-by-the-sierra-leone-army (accessed 10/01/09).

Notes

21. Banks, *Rule of the Bone*, 266–67.

22. Unlike Graham Greene, Russell Banks does not provide the overly exaggerated Poe-like atmospherics of African weather, insects, and rats, as he seeks to concentrate ironically on the theme of a woman's fanatical fascination with our chimpanzee cousins, thus providing an allegorical analogue for the domestic and political behavior of our contemporary arrogant species.

23. Banks, *The Darling*, 265.

24. There were two reasons the 1969 Weathermen *Days of Rage* in Chicago failed: The very low turnout of student protestors, most of whom realized that the event had the potential of becoming a second Harpers Ferry incident, and the pervasive presence of informers amid the SDS (Students for a Democratic Society) leadership, although that problem was solved by 1970 when the Weather Underground became a closed shop.

25. Whitney, Joel, "Telling Details: An Interview with Russell Banks," *Guernica*, Sept. 2005 at http://www.guernicamag.com/interviews/81/telling_details (accessed 10/01/09).

26. For a recent engaging memoir from an Americo-Liberian perspective by a former Iraq War journalist see Cooper, Helene, *The House at Sugar Beach* (New York: Simon & Schuster, 2008).

27. Kakutani, Michiko, "A Radical Uninnocent Abroad," *The New York Times*, Oct. 12, 2004.

28. Banks, Ibid., 391.

29. Mudge, Alden, "Free Radical," http://www.bookpage.com/0410bp/russell_banks.html (accessed 10/01/09).

30. Banks, Russell, "Off the Page," interview with Carol Burns at http://www.washingtonpost.com/wp-dyn/articles/A52016-2004Dec9.html (accessed 10/01/09).

31. Greene, Graham, *The Heart of the Matter* (New York: Viking, 1948), 289. For substantive commentary on Greene's novel see Baldridge, Cates, *Graham Greene's Fictions: The Virtues of Extremity* (Columbia: University of Missouri Press, 2000).

32. Epigraph to Graham Greene's *The Heart of the Matter*: "Le pécheur est au coeur meme de chrétienté.... Nul n'est aussi compétent que le pécheur en matière de chrétienté. Nul, si ce n'est le saint."

Chapter 14

1. While winsome and entertaining, Winter's novel about Rockwell Kent in Newfoundland (1914–15) exhibits a slapdash improvisatory style more immersed in impish anecdote and comic high jinks than any literary sensibility as it scatter-shots wit and obscenity through conversation and falling snow.

2. Faggen, Robert, *The Paris Review* Interview, vol. 40, Issue 147, Summer 1998: Banks says, "Ed Doctorow is one of those writers I most look up to. Of that generation, he and Grace Paley are the two who stand out for me as models. They are exemplary figures, really, both in their lives and in their work."

3. Valhalla achieves more prominence and description in the thirteenth-century *Poetic Edda*.

4. Martin, Constance, *Distant Shores: The Odyssey of Rockwell Kent* (Berkeley: University of California Press, 2000), 120.

5. Traxel, David, *An American Saga: The Life and Times of Rockwell Kent* (New York: Harper & Row, 1980), 46.

6. Banks, Russell, *The Reserve* (New York: HarperCollins, 2008), 84.

7. Martin, Ibid., 119.

8. While Edward Hopper's landscapes convey an easy and humanized intimacy, Rockwell Kent's landscapes depict the transcendental otherness of Nature, even when inhabited by humankind.

9. A similar tussle appears in Michael Winter's novel (pages 245–47) played for genial effect. In the local court scene that results from it, Winter filches some humorous lines from Rockwell Kent's hearings before U.S. Senator Joe McCarthy. See Martin, Ibid., 118–19.

10. Kriwacyek, Paul, *In Search of Zarathustra* (New York: Vintage, 2004), 51. For choral, heroin, and other poisons see Köhler, Joachim, *Zarathustra's Secret* (New Haven: Yale, 2003), trans. Ronald Taylor, 219–222, 226.

11. Banks, Ibid., 96.

12. Banks, Ibid., 227–28. Most of the Thin Man franchise flicks were made after 1936, the year of the novel's setting; the second Thin Man film was released in 1936, the same year that *My Man Godfrey* and *The Petrified Forest* (a version of Euripides's *Electra*) were released, while *Double Indemnity* was not released until 1944. Groves is portrayed as an outdoor artist type like Rockwell Kent who would rather live with Eskimos than enter a movie theater. While the only moment in the novel Kent falls out of character, this pedantic non-sequitur lecture on films arrives at a moment of high emotional crisis. It strains credulity to think the outdoor man of action meditates on the history of American cinema, both present and future, at such a crucial juncture in a love affair.

13. See Collins, Max Allan, "The Hard-Boiled Detective" in *Encyclopedia Mysteriosa* ed. William L. DeAndrea (New York: Prentice Hall, 1994), 153–54.

14. Ruttenber, Edward Manning, *History of the Indian Tribes of Hudson's River* (Albany: J. Mansell, 1872), 84. Banks displaces Tunbridge in Vermont to New York. Tunbridge was the site of the last British Raid of the American Revolution in Vermont when British troops with Indian allies came down from Canada and burned the village, kidnapping many people.

15. Fiedler, Leslie, *Love and Death in the American Novel* (New York: Stein and Day, 1966), 316.

16. Birnbaum, Robert, http://www.identitytheory.com/interviews/birnbaum156.php (accessed 10/01/09).

17. Traxel, Ibid., 145.

18. Phillips, Kevin, *American Dynasty: Aristocracy, Fortune, and the Politics of Deceit in the House of Bush* (New York: Penguin, 2004), 19–20. For an extended portrait of the Bush family's contribution to America see Baker, Russ, *Family of Secrets* (New York: Bloomsbury Press, 2009).

19. Anonymous publisher's promotional interview, http://www.harpercollins.com/author/authorExtra.aspx?authorID=479 (accessed 10/01/09).

20. Holt, Karen, "Class Rules," *Publishers Weekly*, vol. 254, no. 50, Dec. 17, 2007.

21. More details about Exupéry's death were recently revealed. See Tagliabue, John, "Clues to the Mystery of a Writer Pilot Who Disappeared," *The New York Times*, April 11, 2008.

22. Saint-Exupéry, Antoine de, *Pilote de Guerre* in *Oeuvres* (Paris: Gallimard, Pléiade, 1959), 384. Translated by Kevin T. McEneaney.

Chapter 15

1. Lee, Don, "About Russell Banks," *Ploughshares*, winter, 1993–94, 212.

2. McCann, Sean, "Training and Vision: Roth, DeLillo, Banks, Peck, and the Postmodern Aesthetics of Vocation," *Twentieth Century Literature*, vol. 53, no. 3, fall 2007, 298.

3. The suicide of Tom Smith (trailer number nine) in *Trailerpark* appears to be deliberate while the suicide of Owen Brown appears probable. Albert Camus rejects suicide in his famous essay "The Myth of Sisyphus."

4. Carroll, David, "Rethinking the Absurd: *Le Myth of Sisyphe*" in *The Cambridge Companion to Camus* by Edward J. Hughes (Cambridge: Cambridge University Press, 2007), 61.

5. Olivier, Todd, *Albert Camus: A Life* (New York: Knopf, 1998), 413.

6. Walker, Margaret, *Richard Wright: Daemonic Genius* (New York: Warner, 1988), 175, 313.

7. Karl, Frederick R., *William Faulkner: American Writer* (New York: Weidenfeld & Nicolson, 1989), 649–51.

8. Wolfe, Tom, "One Giant Leap to Nowhere," *The New York Times*, July 18, 2009. This elevates Manifest Destiny to a cosmic level, an idea that Stephen Hawking supports. See http://www.dailygalaxy.com/my_weblog/2009/07/how-the-right-stuff-went-wrong-tom-wolfe-stephen-hawking-on-the-apollo-moon-landing.html (accessed 10/01/09). The concept of such a heavenly destiny is nothing knew—Genghis Khan espoused it long before it became an American ideology.

9. Banks, Russell, *Dreaming Up America* (New York: Seven Seas Press, 2008), 45.

10. See Lasch, Christopher, *The Culture of Narcissism* (New York: Norton, 1978) and most recently Twenge, Jean M. and W. Keith Campbell, *The Narcissism Epidemic: Living in the Age of Entitlement* (New York: Free Press, 2009).

11. Todd, Ibid., 420.

12. Martin, Constance, *Distant Shores: The Odyssey of Rockwell Kent* (Berkeley: University of California Press, 2000), 117–20.

13. Doctorow, E. L., *Creationists* (New York: Random House, 2006), 105. Doctorow remarks that after nearly a century a reader "cannot help remarking how current characters are" in John Dos Passos's *U.S.A.* trilogy.

14. Banks, Ibid., 6–7.

15. Welsh, Jim, "Dreaming Up America," *Journal of American Culture*, vol. 32, no.2, 2009, 169–70.

16. Banks, Ibid., 127.

17. Camus, Albert, *The Rebel: An Essay on Man in Revolt*, trans. Anthony Bower (New York: Vintage, 1992), 13.

18. Carroll, Ibid., 60.

19. Banks, Russell, "Notes on Literature and Engagement," in *Burn This Book* ed. Toni Morrison (New York: HarperCollins, 2009), 65.

Select Bibliography

Russell Banks's Fiction and Essays (in chronological order)

Banks, Russell. *Searching for Survivors*. New York: Fiction Collective, 1975.
———. *Family Life*. New York: Avon, 1975; rev. ed., Sun & Moon Press, 1983; HarperPerennial, 1996.
———. *The New World*. Urbana: Univ. of Illinois Press, 1978; 1996.
———. *Hamilton Stark*. Boston: Houghton Mifflin, 1978; New York: HarperPerennial, 1996.
———. *Trailerpark*. Boston: Houghton Mifflin, 1981.
———. *The Relation of My Imprisonment*. Washington, D.C.: Sun & Moon Press, 1983; New York: HarperPerennial, 1996.
———. *Continental Drift*. New York: Harper & Row, 1985.
———. *Success Stories*. New York: Harper & Row, 1986.
———. *Affliction*. New York: Harper & Row, 1989.
———. *The Sweet Hereafter*. New York: HarperCollins, 1991.
———. *Rule of the Bone*. New York: HarperCollins, 1995.
———. *Cloudsplitter*. New York: HarperCollins, 1998.
———. *The Angel on the Roof*. New York: HarperCollins, 2000.
———. *The Darling*. New York: HarperCollins, 2004.
———. *The Reserve*. New York: HarperCollins, 2008.
———. *Dreaming Up America*. New York: Seven Seas Press, 2008.

Books

Algren, Nelson. *A Walk on the Wild Side: A Novel*. New York: Farrar, Straus and Giroux, 1998.
———. *Nonconformity*. New York: Seven Seas Press, 1998.
Anderson, Sherwood. *Winesburg, Ohio*. Ed. John H. Ferres. New York: Viking, 1966.
Bald, R. C. *John Donne: A Life*. Oxford: Oxford University Press, 1970.
Bell, Michael Davitt. *The Problem of American Realism*. Chicago: University of Chicago Press, 1993.
Bercovitch, Sacvan. *The Puritan Origins of the American Self*. New Haven: Yale University Press, 1977.

Borges, Jorge Luis. *Collected Fictions.* Trans. Andrew Hurley. New York: Viking, 1998.
Boyd, Valerie. *Wrapped in Rainbows: A Life of Zora Neal Hurston.* New York: Scribner, 2003.
Camus, Albert. *The Rebel: An Essay on Man in Revolt.* Trans. Anthony Bower. New York: Vintage, 1992.
Carnes, Mark C. *Novel History: Historians and Novelists Confront America's Past (and Each Other).* New York: Simon & Schuster, 2001.
Cooper, Helene. *The House at Sugar Beach.* New York: Simon & Schuster, 2008.
Davis, Wade. *Passage of Darkness: The Ethnobiology of the Haitian Zombie.* Chapel Hill: University of North Carolina Press, 1985.
Delbanco, Andrew. *Melville: His World and Work.* New York: Knopf, 2005.
Doctorow, E. L. *Creationists: Selected Essays, 1993–2006.* New York: Random House, 2006.
Donald, David Herbert. *Lincoln.* New York: Simon & Schuster, 1995.
Drew, Bettina. *Nelson Algren: A Life on the Wild Side.* New York: Putnam, 1989.
Du Bois, W. E. Burghardt. *John Brown.* New York: Oxford University Press, 2007.
Emerson, Ralph Waldo. *Selected Writings of Ralph Waldo Emerson.* New York: Modern Library, 1950.
Faulkner, William. *The Hamlet.* New York: Vintage, 1991.
Fiedler, Leslie A. *Love and Death in the American Novel.* New York: Stein and Day, 1966.
———. *Waiting for the End.* New York: Stein and Day, 1964.
———. *What Was Literature?: Class Culture and Society.* New York: Simon & Schuster, 1982.
Greene, Graham. *The Heart of the Matter.* New York: Viking, 1948.
Huband, Mark. *The Liberian Civil War.* London: Cass, 1998.
Hughes, Edward J. *The Cambridge Companion to Camus.* Cambridge: Cambridge University Press, 2007.
Hurston, Zora Neale. *Dust Tracks on a Road: An Autobiography.* Ed. Robert Hemenway. Chicago: Univ. of Illinois Press, 1984.
Hutchison, Anthony. *Writing the Republic: Liberalism and Morality in American Political Fiction.* New York: Columbia University Press, 2007.
Karl, Frederick R. *William Faulkner: American Writer.* New York: Weidenfeld & Nicolson, 1989.
King, Lovalerie. *The Cambridge Introduction to Zora Neale Hurston.* Cambridge: Cambridge University Press, 2008.
Lasch, Christopher. *The Culture of Narcissism: American Life in an Age of Diminishing Expectation.* New York: Norton, 1978.
Lewis, David Levering. *W. E. B. Du Bois, 1868–1919: Biography of a Race.* New York: Henry Holt and Company, 1993.
Martin, Constance. *Distant Shores: The Odyssey of Rockwell Kent.* Berkeley: University of California Press, 2000.
Martz, Louis. *The Poetry of Meditation.* New Haven: Yale University Press, 1954.
Metalious, Grace. *Peyton Place.* New York: Julian Messner, Inc., 1956.
Metraux, Alfred. *Voodoo in Haiti.* Trans. Hugo Charteris. New York: Schocken Books, 1972.
Melville, Herman. *The Piazza Tales and Other Prose Pieces.* Evanston: Northwestern Univ. Press, 1987.
———. *Moby-Dick.* New York: Norton Critical Edition, 1967.
———. *Redburn: His First Voyage.* Evanston: Northwestern University Press, 1969.

Select Bibliography

Miller, Edwin Haviland. *Salem Is My Dwelling Place: A Life of Nathaniel Hawthorne.* Iowa City: University of Iowa Press, 1991.

Mirsky, D. S. *A History of Russian Literature: From Its Beginnings to 1900.* Ed. Francis J. Whitfield. Evanston: Northwestern University Press, 1999.

Niemi, Robert. *Russell Banks.* Boston: Twayne, 1997.

Oates, Stephen B. *To Purge This Land With Blood: A Biography of John Brown.* New York: 1970.

O'Brien, Flann. *The Third Policeman.* New York: Plume, 1967.

Olivier, Todd. *Albert Camus: A Life.* New York: Knopf, 1998.

Orme, Mark. *The Development of Albert Camus's Concern for Social and Political Justice.* Madison: Fairleigh Dickinson Press, 2007.

Parker, Theodore. *Ten Sermons of Religion.* Boston: Crosby, Nichols & Company, 1853.

Pfeil, Fred. *Another Tale to Tell: Politics and Narrative in Postmodern Culture.* New York: Verso, 1990.

Pizer, Donald. *Realism and Naturalism in Nineteenth-Century American Literature.* Carbondale: Southern Illinois University Press, 1966.

Quarles, Benjamin, ed. "Introduction," In *Blacks on John Brown.* Chicago: University of Illinois Press, 1972.

Reynolds, David S. *Beneath the American Renaissance: The Subversive Imagination in the Age of Emerson and Melville.* New York: Knopf, 1988.

Robertson-Lorant, Laurie. *Melville: A Biography.* New York: Clarkson Potter, 1996.

Rogin, Michael Paul. *Subversive Genealogy: The Politics and Art of Herman Melville.* New York: Knopf, 1983.

Sachsman, David B. Rushing, and Morris, eds. *Memory and Myth: The Civil War in Fiction and Film from Uncle Tom's Cabin to Cold Mountain.* West Lafayette: Purdue University Press, 2007.

Salinger, J. D. *The Catcher in the Rye.* Boston: Little Brown, 1951.

Sherry, Norman. *The Life of Graham Greene*, vol. 1: 1904–1939. New York: Penguin, 1989.

Stern, Susan. *With the Weathermen: The Personal Journal of a Revolutionary Woman.* New York: Doubleday, 1975.

Styron, William. *The Confessions of Nat Turner.* New York: Random House, 1967.

Sundquist, Eric J. *To Wake the Nations: Race in the Making of American Literature.* Cambridge: Harvard University Press, 1993.

Toth, Emily. *Inside Peyton Place: The Life of Grace Metalious.* New York: Dell, 1981.

Traxel, David. *An American Saga: The Life and Times of Rockwell Kent.* New York: Harper & Row, 1980.

Trodd, Zoe and John Stauffer, eds. *Meteor of War: The John Brown Story.* Maplecrest: Brandywine Press, 2004.

Twain, Mark. *The Adventures of Huckleberry Finn.* New York: Oxford University Press, 1996.

Twain, Mark. *The Autobiography of Mark Twain.* Ed. Charles Neider. New York: HarperPerennial, 1990.

Twenge, Jean M. and W. Keith Campbell. *The Narcissism Epidemic: Living in the Age of Entitlement.* New York: Free Press, 2009.

Villard, Oswald Garrison. *John Brown 1800–1859: A Biography Fifty Years After.* Boston: Houghton Mifflin Company, 1911.

Ward, Jerry, Jr. and Robert J. Butler. *The Richard Wright Encyclopedia.* Westport, CT: Greenwood Press, 2008.

Walker, Margaret. *Richard Wright: Daemonic Genius*. New York: Warner Books.
Warren, Robert Penn. *A Robert Penn Warren Reader*. New York: Random House, 1987.
Whitman, Walt. *Leaves of Grass and Selected Prose*. Ed. John Kouwenhoven. New York: Modern Library.
Wilkerson, Cathy. *Flying Close to the Sun: My Life and Times as a Weatherman*. New York: Seven Stories Press, 2007.
Williamson, Joel. *William Faulkner and Southern History*. New York: Oxford University Press, 1993.

ARTICLES

Bair, Deirdre. "Parable from the Coffin." *The New York Times*, April 1, 1984.
Banks, Russell. "Joyce Carol Oates: In a Gothic Manor." *The Washington Post*, August 17, 1980.
———. "Notes on Literature and Engagement." in Morrison, Toni, ed., *Burn This Book*. New York: HarperCollins, 2009.
Callahan, Michael. "Peyton Place's Real Victim." *Vanity Fair*, March 2006.
Dillon, Steven. "Lyricism and Accident in *The Sweet Hereafter*." *Literature/Film Quarterly*, vol. 31, no. 3, 2003.
Dutton, Wendy. "The Problem of Invisibility: Voodoo and Zora Neale Hurston." *Frontiers*, 23, no. 2, 1992.
Faggen, Robert. "Russell Banks Interview." *Paris Review*, vol. 40, no. 147, summer 1998.
Freeman, John. "Russell Banks: Class Warrior with a Club Tie." *The Independent*, May 9, 2008.
Fried, Margaret J. and Lawrence A. Frolik. "The Limits of Law: Litigation, Lawyers and the Search for Justice in Russell Banks's *The Sweet Hereafter*." *Cardozo Studies in Law and Literature*, vol. 7, no. 1, April, 1995.
Frumkes, Lewis Burke. "Russell Banks." *The Writer*, August 1998.
Hennessey, Denis M. "Russell Banks." In *Dictionary of Literary Biography*. New York: Gale, 1993.
Holt, Karen. "Class Rules." *Publishers Weekly*, vol. 254, no. 50, Dec. 17, 2007.
Kakutani, Michiko. "A Radical Uninnocent Abroad." *New York Times*, Oct 12, 2004.
Klin, Richard. "Interview with Russell Banks." *January Magazine*, June 2003 at http://www.januarymagazine.com/profiles/rbanks.html (accessed 10/01/09).
Landwehr, Margarete Johanna "Egoyan's Film Adaptation of Banks's *The Sweet Hereafter*: 'The Pied Piper' as Trauma Narrative and Mise-en-abyme." *Literature/Film Quarterly*, vol. 36, no. 3, 2008.
Leckie, Ross. "Plot-resistant narrative and Russell Banks's 'Black Man and White Woman in Dark Green Rowboat.'" *Studies in Short Fiction*, summer 1994.
Lee, Don. "About Russell Banks." *Ploughshares*, winter 1993–1994.
Lepore, Jill. "The Humbug." *The New Yorker*, April 27, 2009.
Maslin, Janet. "News Story Inspired Banks's 'Drift.'" *The New York Times*, April 29, 1985.
Newman, Lea Bertani Vozar. "Benito Cereno." In *A Reader's Guide to the Short Stories of Herman Melville*. Boston: G. K. Hall, 1986.
Tagliabue, John. "Clues to the Mystery of a Writer Pilot Who Disappeared." *The New York Times*, April 11, 2008.

Select Bibliography

Niemi, Robert. "Russell Banks." In *American Writers*. New York: Charles Scribner's Sons, 2000, vol. 5.

O'Loughlin, Jim. "The Whiteness of Bone: Russell Banks's 'Rule of the Bone' and the Contradictory Legacy of 'Huck Finn'" *Modern Language Studies*, vol. 32, spring 2002.

Phillips, Caryl, "The Height of Obsession," *The Guardian*, May 21, 2005.

Welsh, Jim. "Dreaming Up America." *Journal of American Culture*, vol. 32, no. 2, 2009.

Wolfe, Tom. "Stalking the Billion-Footed Beast: A Literary Manifesto for the New Social Novel." *Harper's*, Nov. 1989.

Wylie, J. J. "Russell Banks." interview, *Michigan Quarterly Review*, vol. 39, fall 2000.

INDEX

Abenaki Indians, 23, 40, 74, 187
absurdity, 16, 24–27, 38, 48, 50–55, 89, 92, 98, 103–18, 132, 144, 152, 184–88, 201
Alger, Horatio, 74, 77, 81, 83
Algren, Nelson, 3, 4, 50–51, 55, 68–69, 71–72, 74, 84, 87, 175, 183, 186
Alighieri, Dante, 47–48, 78, 156, 188
Anderson, Sherwood, 58–61, 72, 199
Ariosto, Ludovico, 19–20, 44, 58
Aristotle, 13, 79–80, 109
Austen, Jane, 171

Balbuena, Bernardo de, 19–20, 193
Banks, Russell, 1–8; *Affliction*, 6, 87–99, 141, 157, 170, 185–88; *The Angel on the Roof*, 6, 14, 41, 131–40; *The Book of Jamaica*, 5, 7, 45–55, 57, 68, 70, 73, 74, 79, 90, 124, 159, 163, 169, 184–88; *Cloudsplitter*, 7, 8, 141–61, 163, 170, 184–89; *Continental Drift*, 6, 7, 71–85, 88–89, 127, 141, 157, 159, 170, 182, 184–88; *The Darling*, 7, 133, 161–72, 184–86; *Dreaming Up America*, 7, 83, 104, 188–89; *Family Life*, 5, 9, 13–14, 21–26, 33, 36, 40, 74, 116, 169, 184, 186–87; *Hamilton Stark*, 5, 10, 12–16, 19–20, 26, 31, 33–45, 47–48, 52, 55, 57, 75, 88–92, 96, 105, 141, 159, 163, 184–87, 189; *The New World*, 14–20, 45; *The Relation of My Imprisonment*, 5, 14, 26–31, 65, 75, 186, 188; *The Reserve*, 7, 173–82, 185–89; *Rule of the Bone*, 6–8, 107, 111–29, 141, 152, 166, 184, 186, 189; *Searching for Survivors*, 5, 9, 10, 14; *Success Stories*, 6, 131; *The Sweet Hereafter*, 6, 90, 101–10, 114, 162, 185, 188; *Trailerpark*, 6, 7, 57–70, 72–74, 90, 106, 131, 138, 185–87
Barthelme, Donald, 22, 25
Basile, Giambattista, 21, 193
Beauvoir, Simone de, 87
Beckett, Samuel, 21, 25, 43
Bell, Madison Smartt, 8, 184
Bellow, Saul, 112, 184
Benét, Stephen Vincent, 147, 205
Benjamin, Walter, 47
Bierce, Ambrose, 11, 43, 185, 187
Boccaccio, Giovanni, 43, 185
Bodenheim, Maxwell, 184, 199
Book of Job, 31, 146, 186
Borges, Jorge Luis, 6, 13, 16, 65, 98, 125, 152, 188, 203
Boyle, T. C., 76, 83, 184
Brown, John, 7, 134, 141–60, 207
Browning, Robert, 108
Bunyan, John, 26, 48

Cain and Abel, 50, 149–58, 206
Calvino, Italo, 37
Camus, Albert, x, 45, 50–55, 98, 183–89

Carroll, Lewis, 57, 177
Castro, Fidel, 2, 44
Cather, Willa, 111, 124–25, 161, 167
Cervantes, 19–20, 188
Chekhov, Anton, 59, 137, 140, 161–64, 168
Christmas, 21, 30, 41, 66, 74, 131–33
Coetzee, J. M., 8, 29, 161
Conrad, Joseph, 164, 171, 188
Cooper, James Fenimore, 111, 118, 179

Dana, Richard Henry, 176
de Tocqueville, Alexis, 187
DeLillo, Don, 8, 94
Dickens, Charles, 18, 21, 60, 72
Doctorow, E. L., 128, 174, 184
Donne, John, 28–29
Dos Passos, John, 98, 174–75, 179, 188
Dostoevsky, Fyodor, 17, 43, 95–98, 157
Dreiser, Theodore, 32, 72, 88, 161, 174, 183
Du Bois, W. E. B., 74, 145–47, 157, 159–60, 205, 207

Edwards, Jonathan, 122
Egoyan, Atom, 6, 107
Einstein, Albert, 106–9, 185
Emerson, Ralph Waldo, 145, 147–49, 154, 159, 175
Euripides, 83, 210

Farina, Richard, 62, 196
Farrell, James T., 69, 84, 87–88, 183, 197
Faulkner, William, 36, 58–59, 87, 93, 96–98, 151, 160, 187–88, 201
Fiedler, Leslie, 126
Fielding, Henry, 112
Fitzgerald, F. Scott, 111, 124
Flanagan, Thomas, 178–79
Flaubert, Gustave, 15, 88, 161, 163, 188
Flynn, Errol, 44–48, 195
Fowles, John, 42
Freud, Sigmund, 102, 151, 185
Frost, Robert, 3, 4, 12, 14, 19, 22, 185

Gellhorn, Martha, 177
Giroux, Jr., Leo, 3, 21, 26

Gorky, Maxim, 60, 200
Gothic, 14, 17, 19, 57–70, 97–98, 139, 152, 156, 186
Grateful Dead, 27–28, 128
Greene, Graham, 19, 164–72, 209–10

Haiti, 71–85
Hammett, Dashiell, 178
Hardy, Thomas, 163, 179, 188, 197
Harington, Sir John, 44
Hawthorne, Nathaniel, 12, 15, 66, 71, 151–52, 156, 184–86, 197
Hecht, Ben, 184, 201
Hemingway, Ernest, 2, 3, 8, 62, 127–28, 162, 175–78, 203
Hemon, Aleksandar, 186
Homer, 1, 68, 70, 111, 119–21, 125, 154, 203; *Iliad*, 1, 25, 54, 68, 154, 158, 193; *Odyssey*, 1, 58, 68, 75, 83, 98, 149, 152–56, 185, 193, 206
Hopper, Edward, 174–75
Hugo, Victor, 157, 160
Hurston, Zora Neale, 53–55, 72–74, 110

Ives, Charles, 8, 125–26, 166

Jackson, Shirley, 30, 65, 69
Jamaica, 5–7, 14, 16, 19, 26, 28, 45–55, 70, 78, 79, 81, 82, 112, 116–29, 164
Joyce, James, 41, 53, 57–58, 75, 160, 207

Kavanagh, Patrick, 68
Kennedy, John F., 91–96, 98, 118
Kennedy, William, 8, 139, 160, 184
Kent, Rockwell, 136, 173–82, 188, 209, 210
Kerouac, Jack, 1–2, 7, 8, 151, 183

Lawrence, D. H., 8, 19
Liberia, 163–72
Lindsay, Vachel, 125–26, 141
Lowry, Malcolm, 3
Lucretius, 83, 143, 182, 185

Maroons, 48–55
McMurtry, Larry, 85

Index

Melville, Herman, 14, 27, 33, 35, 51, 65, 115, 148–56, 161, 176, 182, 184, 194
Metalious, Grace, 9, 33–44, 81, 83, 96, 106, 131, 141
Milton, John, 21, 154, 203
Mitty, Walter, 10–11, 74, 81, 137, 148, 193
Monroe, Marilyn, 105, 201
Montague, John, 89, 200
Morrison, Toni, 8, 128, 184

Nabokov, Vladimir, 22, 132, 188
narcissism, 11–13, 23–24, 37, 42–43, 52, 55, 59, 70, 85, 102, 114–21, 126, 133, 154, 140, 151, 148, 152, 155, 159–71, 184, 187, 203
Nashe, Thomas, 102
New Hampshire, 1–3, 5, 10–14, 33–36, 39–45, 49, 53, 57, 60–69, 73–74, 76, 80, 88–90, 115, 132–36, 173, 200
Nietzsche, Friedrich, 37, 42–43, 176, 191

Oates, Joyce Carol, 58–59, 69, 147, 184, 196
O'Brien, Flann, 34, 37–40, 49, 185
Othello, 137, 154

Paz, Octavio, 47
Petrarch, 22
Phillips, Caryl, 8, 201
Plato, 36, 83, 201
Poe, Edgar Allan, 17–18, 53–54, 71–72, 98, 151, 155–56, 185–86
Pound, Ezra, 129
Pulitzer Prize, 7, 85, 147, 172, 196
Pynchon, Thomas, 8, 128, 180, 183

Rockwell, Norman, 178

Roth, Philip, 172, 184

Saint Exupéry, Antoine de, 181–82, 210
Salinger, J. D., 111–13
Sartre, Jean-Paul, 51, 87–88
Schrader, Paul, 6, 96–99
Shelley, Mary, 58, 105
Shusaku Endo, 206
Sidney, Sir Philip, 83
Smith, Adam, 124
Sophocles, 106
Steinbeck, John, 81, 174, 176, 182
Sterne, Laurence, 19, 21, 37
Styron, William, 159, 161, 207
Swift, Jonathan, 27

Taylor, Charles, 165–72
Terkel, Studs, 84
Thoreau, Henry David, 18, 175, 180
Thurber, James, 10–11, 81
Turgenev, Ivan, 17, 74, 88, 188
Twain, Mark, 7, 76, 88, 111–14, 126–29, 176, 184, 187–88, 202

Virgil, 21, 25, 34, 37, 38, 41, 122, 188, 193
Vollmann, William, 188
Voodoo, 71–85, 198

Warren, Robert Penn, 147, 205
Weather Underground, 133, 164, 167–72, 208–9
Welles, Orson, 42, 46, 195
Whitman, Walt, 19, 129, 145, 147, 157
Wilde, Oscar, 37
Winter, Michael, 173–74, 209
Wolfe, Tom, 72, 76, 184, 187, 188, 211
Woolf, Virginia, 8, 83
Wright, Richard, 71, 87–88, 91, 93, 98–99, 164, 184, 186, 200

Zola, Emile, 88, 183, 199

About the Author

KEVIN T. McENEANEY is the author of the poetry collections *The Enclosed Garden* and *Longing*, which was translated into French, Japanese, and Croatian. His book *Tom Wolfe's America: Heroes, Pranksters, and Fools* (Praeger, 2009) won an Outstanding Academic Title award from the American Library Association's *Choice* magazine. He has taught at Marist College, St. Thomas Aquinas College, State University of New York Purchase College, Quinnipiac University, and University of Hartford. He has been working on a new poetic text of Homer's *Odyssey* for many years.